EMANCIPATION

WITHOUT

EQUALITY

THOMAS E. SMITH

EMANCIPATION

WITHOUT

EQUALITY

PAN-AFRICAN ACTIVISM AND
THE GLOBAL COLOR LINE

University of Massachusetts Press
Amherst and Boston

Copyright © 2018 by University of Massachusetts Press
Printed in the United States of America

ISBN 978-1-62534-395-6 (paper); 394-9 (hardcover)

Designed by Sally Nichols
Set in Monotype Dante and Univers
Printed and bound by Maple Press, Inc.

Cover design by Thomas Eykemans.

Library of Congress Cataloging-in-Publication Data

A catalog record for this book is available from the
Library of Congress.

British Library Cataloguing-in-Publication Data

A catalog record for this book is available from the
British Library.

CONTENTS

PREFACE

During the late nineteenth and early twentieth centuries Pan-Africanists fought for equality and rights for people of African descent. Their activism was, of course, subject to the construction of the global color line and pervading ideas of racialized thinking. Yet despite these obstacles, they continued to question the narrative of progress and rights that transcended nation-state boundaries.

In this book, I have worked to recover this significant moment in history, which has been largely ignored in mainstream scholarship. My interest in the project arose from both my lived experiences and my academic training. During the 1990s, I watched with interest the path of Nelson Mandela and the anti-apartheid struggle. I, like so many, was struck by the magnanimity of his calls for a post-apartheid Rainbow Nation. Later, in my graduate training, I read classic scholarly works on race relations and noted that many scholars were contending that intellectuals of African descent had progressive conceptions of cultural pluralism at the turn of the twentieth century. Since then, I have spent considerable time trying to understand the promise of such ideas and their failure in practice. *Emancipation without Equality* is the result of such explorations.

EMANCIPATION
WITHOUT
EQUALITY

PAN-AFRICANISM, THE SAVAGE SOUTH AFRICA EXHIBIT, AND THE STANDARD OF CIVILIZATION

In the summer of 1900, the reformer Henry Sylvester Williams—born in Trinidad but a resident of London—organized the first Pan-African Conference, an international gathering to consider the conditions facing people of African descent. In a keynote address at the London-based conference, the African American intellectual W. E. B. Du Bois spoke directly "To the Nations of the World" when he prophesied that the problem of the twentieth century would be the global color line: that is, the elevation of whiteness that was creating a racially divided world.[1] Williams's staging of the first Pan-African conference and Du Bois's warning about the color line are examples of how the quickening of globalization offered opportunities for reformers to consider international issues.

Globalization shrinks the world, creating connections outside each individual's immediate locale and providing opportunities for an expanded understanding of the world and of human experience. In varying degrees of intensity, it promotes an awareness that is directly associated with modernity.[2] Powered by industrialization and fueled by imperialism, global interconnectivity increased profoundly in the late nineteenth and early twentieth centuries. While European nation-states had long been at the forefront of modern imperialism, the United States took part in this global imperial push, despite its long-standing exceptionalist claims to the contrary.[3]

In an era marked by technological improvements in transportation and communication, the world witnessed increased connections among multiple sites around the globe, links that stretched beyond nation-to-nation or regional interactions. The pace of Euro-American imperialism increased political, economic, and ideational connections, which were framed as evidence of modernity and progress. Williams and Du Bois understood that this connectivity gave them a chance to reflect on the past and predict the future of a modern global world. Yet even as both men sought international forums, they were forced to reckon with the motivating force of imperialism as it emanated largely from specific nation-state interests.

The construction and authority of the nation-state also connect to understandings of modernity in the Euro-American context, which involved the transfer of authority from traditional sources, such as church and crown, to the individual. This shift emphasized the human capacity for awareness and agency and, in turn, promoted new ideas about political life and governing order. In some parts of Europe and the Americas, it helped to initiate the social contracts of the liberal republican revolution whereby individuals agreed to form representative bodies and invest them with authority and the power of governance in exchange for protections and rights.[4] By the late nineteenth century, the nation-state—a locus of authority and power with specific sets of practices and interests—was a defining institution of modernity, both the arbiter of imperialism and the main conduit for the realization of political rights.

Race relations overlapped with both Euro-American imperialism and nation-state practices concerning political rights.[5] The pace of imperialism only intensified these questions, and race relations informed Du Bois's description of the problem of the global color line. His characterization remains prophetic as well as an oft-referenced starting point for scholarship.[6] Less emphasized, however, is the fact that it occurred at an international gathering of people of African descent. Moreover, "To the Nations of the World" was not a statement of acquiescence but a call to "crown" the work of abolitionism by opening to all individuals, regardless of skin color, the "opportunities and privileges of modern civilization."[7] The 1900 Pan-African Conference and the wider Pan-African network posited the struggle for post-emancipated rights as a global issue transcending borders. Crucially, both the conference and Du Bois's speech contested the construction of racialized hierarchies and were part of a Pan-African challenge to the global color line.

This book analyzes the Pan-African challenge to the construction of the global color line during a period roughly framed by two international forums: the 1884–85 Berlin Conference and the 1911 Universal Races Congress. At the Berlin Conference, Euro-American powers constructed a normative "standard of civilization" to guide the course of imperialism. It not only called for the fair treatment of colonized peoples but also articulated a language of social equality and political rights. Of course, imperialism was rife with practices that violated these normative standards and Pan-Africanists consistently challenged these transgressions. The Pan-Africanists I study also recognized that post-emancipated people of African descent had legal standing as subjects and citizens of the British Empire and the United States, and they connected their protest of imperial practice to their ongoing claims to their rights.

This protest, however, had difficulty navigating a related Euro-American standard of civilization, one that constructed a template of progress that measured preparedness for equality and citizenship. While this standard presented itself as merit-based and open to all, it was, in fact, connected to the practice of exclusionary racial classification. In a period abounding in quasi-scientific Darwinian language, the belief in biological essentialism informed widespread practices that linked observable characteristics such as skin color to preparedness. This consistently blocked meaningful consideration that people of African descent could meet the level of preparedness established by the standard. Members of this group recognized that biological essentialism and racial categorization continued to shackle their aspirations to rights and equality. As my book documents, while they continued to give evidence of their progress and achievements and asserted concepts of racial destiny, Pan-Africanists denounced the notion that skin color should be the basis for the denial of equality and rights. By the time of the 1911 Universal Races Congress, Pan-Africanism had become more critical of the practices of imperialism and was beginning to question the standard of civilization that these practices violated. Against the background of continued challenges to biological essentialism (as summarized by Franz Boas in an address to the Universal Races Congress), Pan-Africanists were also reinterpreting African history and understanding African cultures in ways that did not demonstrate adherence to Euro-American standards of civilization. These shifts in Pan-African thought prefigured a turn toward anticolonialism as the answer to the problem of the global color line.

World's Fairs and the Savage South Africa Exhibit

When planning the first Pan-African Conference, Henry Sylvester Williams certainly considered the symbolic power of the first year of the twentieth century, and he explicitly looked to stage it to coincide with the popular international platform of world's fairs—specifically, the 1900 Exposition Universelle, held in Paris. World's fairs were pinnacle statements in the late nineteenth century's explosion of Euro-American international gatherings fashioned as expressions of a connected, fast-modernizing world.[8] Inaugurated by the 1851 Great Exhibition at the Crystal Palace in London, world's fairs, by century's end, had become very popular, and the 1900 Exposition Universelle in Paris was a culminating turn-of-the-century international event. It was the highest-attended world's fair to date, received substantial international coverage, and was an archetypal representation of modern experience.

This modern experience represented at world's fairs was directly linked to Euro-American imperialism.[9] The fairs evoked confidence that such knowledge was central to the mastery of nature and the advancement of science. The exhibitions featured products from the colonies and showcased technological advances in resource extraction, transportation networks, and communication links that informed the Euro-American shrinking of the world. This display of globalizing expertise strengthened a deeper ideological commitment to the measuring of progress according to western norms, which endorsed Europe and America as leaders of the modern world. Further, world's fairs, while constructing the backdrop of this superiority, also allowed the individual host nations (primarily through the hosting itself) to claim that they were leaders in modernity and progress.

World's fairs often confirmed confidence in Euro-American leadership and superiority through the notion of the ethnographic other, a dichotomous conception of racial difference with strong connotations of inferiority. In the popular entertainment areas of the fairs (known as the midway), this dichotomy was often displayed in stark depictions of savages and civilized people. Such perpetuation of the ethnographic other was part of the projection and maintenance of difference that, as Frederick Cooper and Ann Stoler argue, "justified different intensities of violence" in an imperial world.[10] A rich literature demonstrates how world's fairs contributed profoundly to the Euro-American control of others during periods of imperialism.[11]

Constructing racial difference as savage versus civilized sought to cement Euro-American superiority. Of course, this perpetuation of racial difference has a long history. However, quasi-scientific references incorporating language found in Charles Darwin's 1859 *On the Origin of Species* significantly empowered the legitimacy of difference based on race. There were two important variants of these social theories, and both placed biological considerations at the forefront. The first, labeled *social Darwinism*, argued that race was a permanent biological characteristic intimately connected to behavior. The second, labeled *scientific racism*, argued that, while biology still dictated racial difference, there was capacity for behavioral change resulting from interaction with the environment. This perspective borrowed Lamarckian ideas of adaptive, heritable acquisition of traits to imply that racial groups could advance (or degenerate) along the racialized continuum. The first theory often resulted in "survival of the fittest" discourse, which generated strategies of control and domination, while the second was at the core of uplift strategies. These classifications were constructed partly to help further understanding, and in practice they did not exist in isolation. Indeed, social theorists argued that a host of different permutations concerning race could exist, as long as they were verified by Darwinian sounding terms or logic. Of course, both of these biologically based theories are wrong. Not only do phenotype distinctions have limited, if any, connection to behavior or natural selection, but the idea of Lamarckian inheritance was discredited near the turn of the twentieth century. Nevertheless, racialized pseudo-science intimately linked biology to constructions of so-called savage peoples and lent credibility to the ethnographic other, whether in stark depictions at world's fairs or in the folds of the temporally open-ended periods of uplift and tutelage. Thus, a fundamental challenge facing people of African descent was debunking biologically based theories that were used to justify the promotion of the global color line.[12]

The construction of the ethnographic other was evident to the British anti-imperial critic J. A. Hobson, who argued that the flood of imperial propaganda aroused ever-growing fascination with the colonial "wild." According to him, creating this interest through imperial tropes accomplished two objectives. First, it contributed to the adoption of imperialism's civilizing mission by the metropole's cultured and semi-cultured population. Second, it made a sensationalist appeal to the "primitive lusts," which, for Hobson, referred to the vicarious desire of the popular masses for bloodshed associated with imperialism. That these lusts were framed within the modernity of consumption not only reminded viewers of their own evolutionary path from the primitive but also provided a safe distance to support the imperial project of domination. The phenomenon was at the core of jingoism, which was "merely the lust of the spectator, unpurged [sic] by any personal effort, risk, or sacrifice." To Hobson, this support from a detached yet superior perspective prepared the way for imperial capitalists to pursue a "policy fraught with material gain to a minority of co-operative vested interests which usurp the title of the commonwealth."[13]

While Hobson throughout his career concentrated on denouncing the capitalist exploitation associated with imperialism, he also provided insights on race relations; and in these commentaries, he certainly retained racialized paternalism.[14] His insights on forums like world's fairs captured how spectacle viewing endorsed the superiority of Europe and America and provided an integral backdrop for modern imperialism. The midways' depiction of the ethnographic other presented modern-day spectators with a journey through the stages of humankind that reified Euro-American imperialism vis-à-vis racialized difference. Historically, African peoples were seen as a readily accessible canvas on which to paint racial difference and had long been subjected to intense Euro-American imperial control and violence.

Only a few miles away from London's Westminster Town Hall, where the 1900 Pan-African Conference took place, a host of exhibitions and performances catering to imperial sentiment were staged regularly at the Empress Theatre at Earl's Court Arena during the 1890s.[15] In July 1899, a year before the Pan-African Conference, the Greater Britain Exhibition opened. The gathering followed the world's fair template, offering evidence of material progress in the empire and presenting visual spectacles for fairgoers that pandered to patriotic imperial sentiment. With an emphasis on "loyalty to Mother Country," the exhibition sought to legitimize claims of empire by creating a sense of unity among people in the colonies and the metropolis.[16]

This unity was not one of equality. The 1899 Greater Britain Exhibition elevated a standard of whiteness that sought to order the imperial moment by contributing to what Du Bois labeled "a global color line" at the Pan-African Conference. Charles Dilke's 1868 book *Greater Britain*, the establishment of the dominion of Canada in 1873, and William Gladstone's Home Rule Bill for Ireland in 1886 together promoted calls for autonomy from the empire's settler colonies and stimulated the dominion movement of the late nineteenth century. Accompanying this dominion push was the perception of a rising threat from the "lower races" in the international racial struggle.[17] Those sympathetic to dominion argued that colonies with sufficient British settlers deserved latitude regarding local rule as well as distinction from other non-Anglo imperial possessions.[18] The dominion movement argued that unity in empire should be in line with racialized worldviews and that whiteness not only linked the colonies to the metropole but also prefigured self-rule in the colonies. While the 1899 Greater Britain Exhibition did not articulate an official position on the dominion movement, it contained disproportionate testaments to advances in Australia, the most recent area to lobby for a realignment of the colonial relationship.[19]

As the Greater Britain Exhibition lauded the progress of Australia, it also affirmed Anglo loyalty and racial hierarchies using the depiction of the ethnographic other. Indeed, the main attraction at the Empress Theatre, Savage South Africa, was performed twice daily before well-attended audiences at a prime location of the exhibition.[20] These performances, the only display at the exhibition that was acted out as a show, presented Africans as a violent threat, accentuated the lines between savage and civilized, and catered to the crude lust of the white metropolitan public. Central to the show was the reenactment of the 1896 Matabele War in Rhodesia. This segment included a scene depicting the Matabele

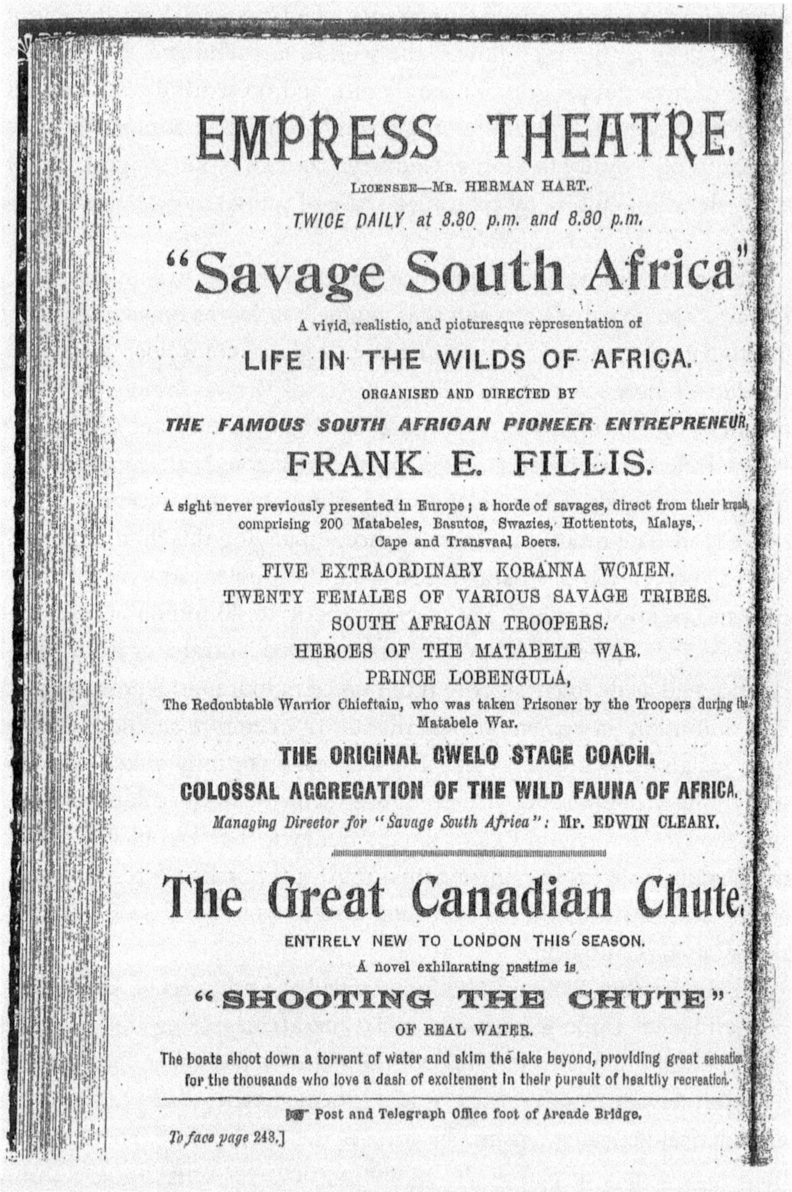

EMPRESS THEATRE.

TWICE DAILY at 8.30 p.m. and 8.30 p.m.

"Savage South Africa"

A vivid, realistic, and picturesque representation of

LIFE IN THE WILDS OF AFRICA.

ORGANISED AND DIRECTED BY

THE FAMOUS SOUTH AFRICAN PIONEER ENTREPRENEUR,

FRANK E. FILLIS.

A sight never previously presented in Europe ; a horde of savages, direct from their kraal, comprising 200 Matabeles, Basutos, Swazies, Hottentots, Malays, Cape and Transvaal Boers.

FIVE EXTRAORDINARY KORANNA WOMEN.
TWENTY FEMALES OF VARIOUS SAVAGE TRIBES.
SOUTH AFRICAN TROOPERS.
HEROES OF THE MATABELE WAR.
PRINCE LOBENGULA,

The Redoubtable Warrior Chieftain, who was taken Prisoner by the Troopers during the Matabele War.

THE ORIGINAL GWELO STAGE COACH.

COLOSSAL AGGREGATION OF THE WILD FAUNA OF AFRICA.

Managing Director for "Savage South Africa": Mr. EDWIN CLEARY.

The Great Canadian Chute,

ENTIRELY NEW TO LONDON THIS SEASON.

A novel exhilarating pastime is

"SHOOTING THE CHUTE"

OF REAL WATER.

The boats shoot down a torrent of water and skim the lake beyond, providing great sensation for the thousands who love a dash of excitement in their pursuit of healthy recreation.

Post and Telegraph Office foot of Arcade Bridge.

To face page 243.]

Figure 1. Handbill, Savage South Africa exhibit, *Official Catalogue of the Greater Britain Exhibition* (London: Spottiswoode, 1899), 5.

massacre of white homesteaders and Chief Lobengula (reportedly played by the real chief's son) calling for the annihilation of the white man. The performance ended with the famous Rhodesian settler column defeating the Matabele and restoring white order.[21]

This trumpeting of racial difference vis-à-vis replications of war and violence took on a charged jingoistic tint because Great Britain was in the midst of the Boer War. In connection with this conflict, the exhibition took another liberty with constructions of the ethnographic other. The Savage South Africa exhibit included Boer peoples within the visual display of essentialized difference; and as the show's handbill promised, it was "a sight never previously presented in Europe; a horde of savages, direct from the kraals, comprising 200 Matabeles, Basutos, Swazies, Hottentots, Malays, Cape and Transvaal Boers."[22] The Greater Britain Exhibition not only sought to affirm the dichotomy of savage and civilized through the common trope of Africa and its peoples but also used this platform to specifically drum up support for British efforts against the Boers in the South African War.

The Standard of Civilization

Although the Savage South Africa exhibit was wildly popular, it was also subject to a host of criticism, including protests from the organizer of the 1900 Pan-African Conference. Williams was offended by crass depictions of the ethnographic other represented by the exhibit and immediately denounced the production in a letter to the colonial secretary, Joseph Chamberlain, stating that the exhibition was counter to "your policy" and "demoralizing to the race." Further, Williams echoed Hobson's arguments when he condemned the sensationalist depiction of African peoples and protested that Savage South Africa was a "spectacle of constant ridicule and caricature." He argued that the native Africans taken from their "primitive homes" should be introduced to the benefits of civilization during their stay in England. Touting potential British imperial rule as a dramatic improvement for African peoples in comparison to Boer authority, he declared that an introduction to "Christian civilization," would not only help the African participants in Savage South Africa but also benefit "their people" upon their return to Africa.[23]

While influenced by racialized hierarchies, Williams implied in these calls that all people of African descent had the capacity to participate in the pursuits of the modern world and potentially meet the accompanying measures of progress. Indeed, a continuum of difference always accompanied stark dichotomies of savage and civilized, especially during imperialism, when the most notable complement to racialized hierarchies was the progressive zeal for uplift.[24] The mission of uplift relied on positioning non-Anglos as inferior and sharing the message that their inferior status could be improved. Hence, while world's fairs invariably depicted non-Anglos in subordinate positions, the very nature of a progressive scale implied that racial difference was not inherent or stable. This language of progressive uplift was in wide use at the meetings and resolutions of the Berlin Conference of 1884–85 and the 1890 Brussels Anti-Slavery Conference, the two international gatherings that officially sanctioned a new era of imperialism known as the Scramble for Africa.

The Berlin and Brussels conferences never wavered from their confidence in Euro-American superiority, promoting self-interest and security as prominent objectives for imperial powers, especially as they related to the continent of Africa. This blueprint sought to extend the marketplace, guarantee access to resources, and weigh balance-of-power objectives. As Gallagher and Robinson argue, this ordering used an array of informal and formal mechanisms, including economic agreements on trading rights and the imposition of political systems ranging from indirect rule to formal annexation.[25] Whatever mechanisms and political systems were used, their results fundamentally marginalized colonial peoples through dispossession, exploitation, and violence. Yet the discourse of the conferences did not rely on racial difference as justification for this Euro-American imperial rule or even mention widely available theories of racialized competition and race extinction. Instead, the conferences consistently articulated theories of progress and uplift as part of the standard of civilization that had been constructed to order the international world.[26] This standard of civilization did not ignore race or dismiss racial hierarchies, but it made the uplift of non-Anglo peoples a powerful stabilizer of the imperial project. Generally, humanitarian concern for the welfare of colonized people was its main emphasis. However, the conferences circumscribed earlier Christianity-based uplift as the core of the civilizing mission and indeed made allowances for religious toleration in the course of imperialism. This shift was accompanied by clear references to the state's responsibility to its subjects, including a right-based script that referenced political representation.

The debates and resolutions of the Berlin and Brussels conferences and of the Lausanne Institute of International Law in 1888 did not emphasize Christianity as the bedrock of the civilizing mission. While the redemptive qualities of Christianity retained significant resonance in the late nineteenth and early twentieth centuries, all three conferences introduced watered-down support for its civilizing mission. Though the Berlin gathering protected missionaries operating in Africa and the proceedings of all three grounded their language in references to God and Christian morality, article 6 of the General Act of the Conference of Berlin limited the Christian uplift model by guaranteeing religious toleration and freedom of conscience to all "natives."[27] That article is representative of the conferences' collective withdrawal from the primacy of religion. Moreover, while this shift may not have lessened the missionary impulse in practice, it did contribute to the questioning of long-standing confidence in the Christian imperial mission.

With this official retreat from religious confidences and prescriptions, the imperial conferences augmented the older message of Christian uplift with the articulation of political progress as a crucial aspect of the civilizing mission. Of course, the standard of civilization erected steep paternalist hurdles before colonized people could become full political subjects. However, without question, the language of political rights and agency for colonized peoples crept into the conferences. The committee commentary on the final clause of the Berlin Act, which explicitly guaranteed the "preservation of the native tribes," also included the requirement that colonial powers had a duty to assist natives to "attain a higher political and social status." Further, the representative from the United States to the Berlin Conference, John Kasson, argued that the "discoveries" in Africa "should be utilized for the civilization of the native races" and that "modern international law . . . leads to the recognition of the rights of native tribes to dispose freely of themselves and of their hereditary territory."[28] While Kasson's notion was not included in the final clause of the Berlin Act, it contained a rights-based discourse that is emblematic of the shift away from the religious and toward the political.[29]

In its 1888 session at Lausanne, the Institute of International Law further defined the conditions under which so-called civilized states could claim sovereignty over a region. Lausanne continued Berlin's move toward protecting freedom of conscience and religious faith. It also declared that authority over a territory demanded that colonial powers demonstrate respect for all rights—both individual and communal—of indigenous people as well as foreigners. By the time of the 1890 Brussels Anti-Slavery Conference, this discussion of rights intertwined with conditions necessary for European sovereignty had led to a more direct interrogation of colonialism: "The object of the congress is the study of the moral and social questions growing out of colonization." Further, the conference recognized that the predicament of colonized peoples was a transnational issue: "Certainly, if there be one problem which can be said to be international, it is that of the condition of aboriginal peoples."[30] The participants at Brussels recognized the inextricable links between imperialism and race and understood that the relationship was in flux and subject to interrogation.

The answers to this examination were measures to promote antislavery, an agreement not to introduce alcohol to indigenous people, and the commitment to reduce the entry of firearms into Africa. The Brussels Conference, however, also considered the political conditions of colonized peoples. Pertaining to the retention of native cultural traditions and institutions, it stated, "As respects the organization of their family life, and the use of their property, it is desirable to leave the aborigines the benefit of their own customs." The conference also argued that "aboriginal subjects" should have the means to defend their rights and seek redress of their grievances from colonial authorities and that "representative institutions" were the surest means of "putting aboriginal populations in a position to defend their rights." Moreover, the conference's language implied that colonial subjects should have a direct relationship with the state and that the state could intervene to secure rights. The Brussels conference not only contributed to the process of underwriting the imperial fervor launched by the Berlin gathering but also continued to contemplate its political implications.[31]

This pronounced shift in the international discourse was rarely reflected in practice and did not result in immediate change for colonized peoples. In terms of agency, the comment of Sir Edward Malet, Great Britain's representative at the Berlin Conference, seems to have been especially understated: "I cannot forget that the natives are not represented among us, and that the discussions of the Conference will, nevertheless, have an extreme importance for them."[32] Regardless of how these supposedly international conferences considered rights, there was no direct voice for those who were most exploited by the imperialism that the meetings promoted. Moreover, while the language of Christian uplift became less prominent toward the end of the nineteenth century, a paternalist ethos restricted political rights with a distinct language of preparedness that tempered the reference to representative institutions. In the same sentence of the resolution at Brussels that hearkened to rights and representation, the conference added, "[We] consider that the regime of representative institutions is one that presupposes the concurrence of moral, intellectual, and political conditions which can be conceived of as realizable by aboriginal peoples only in a future more or less distant."[33]

This statement reflects how the paternalist attachment of temporally open-ended "conditions" circumscribed the promise of political rights contained in the standard of civilization. Furthermore, it illustrates the gap between normative standards of liberal inclusion and exclusionary practice in the late nineteenth century.[34] Indeed, the ability of both Europe and America to define the political standard of civilization while using measures of progress to defer sharing its benefits underwrote the projection of difference and the exertion of control and dominance. But Pan-Africanists recognized that the contradiction between promise and practice was where the imperial project was most vulnerable.[35] Moreover, because the realization of rights inevitably involved an appeal to the nation-state, people of African descent had unique claims, given that emancipation in the British Empire and the United States had directly contributed to the formal definitions of *subject* and *citizen*.

Post-Emancipation and Citizenship

Rights for peoples of African descent in the British Empire and the United States originated in emancipation. In Great Britain, the 1833 Act for the Abolition of Slavery freed slaves throughout the empire, making all people in Britain and the colonies equal subjects of the crown.[36] In the United States, the Thirteenth Amendment (1865) abolished slavery, and the Fourteenth Amendment (1868) granted citizenship and equal protection under the law to all people born or naturalized in the United States. These acts transformed the struggle over slavery into a discussion of what freedom meant in the British Empire and the United States. As such, debate over how ex-slaves might fit into the political body of a nation emerged on both sides of the Atlantic. Yet the attachment of voting rights—perhaps the most important symbol of modern political agency to these categories of citizenship—was contested throughout the nineteenth century. The British reform acts of 1832, 1867 and 1884, while progressively expanding the electorate, also retained property requirements and were applicable only to males. The Fourteenth Amendment in the United States prescribed penalties for the denial of voting rights to adult males, and the Fifteenth Amendment clarified that voting was a right of citizenship. While neither amendment mandated property requirements, both excluded women.[37] The expansion of franchise in the British reform acts applied only to the people of England, Scotland, Wales, and Ireland. In addition, reflecting the hesitancy regarding the expansion of the franchise to colonized peoples, voting rights in the colonies largely devolved to the control of the Colonial Office or the legislatures of the self-governing colonies.[38] In 1877, the withdrawal of federal enforcement severely compromised the intended effect of the Fifteenth Amendment on voting rights and political participation for male ex-slaves in the former Confederate states. These conditions demonstrate that both Great Britain and the United States articulated some expansive but not wholly inclusive meanings regarding the rights connected to citizenship. And as this book emphasizes, the effects were conditioned by local contexts.

While *subject* and *citizen* had some basic formal definitions, what they meant and symbolized remained largely open-ended, which encouraged expansive understandings of rights. Crucially, these understandings were most readily seen in the discourse of those who were excluded from the privileges.[39] After emancipation, the meaning of citizenship coalesced around the symbolic power of the ballot, which implied an entire host of rights: protections of corporal integrity; rights to freedom of speech, assembly, and contract; participation in the public sphere of civil society; and recognition of political equality. Thus, citizenship, in the modern sense, and especially for those outside its pale, meant valid and active participation in society.⁴⁰ The scripts of Berlin and Brussels largely reflected the normative scripts of Anglo-American liberalism. And while the realization of the scripts was a process that was subject to the interests of the nation-state and refracted through both the global color line and local lenses, the notion of subject and citizen was a powerful symbol in post-emancipated reform.⁴¹

Although highly contested, subject to local conditions, and not uniformly enjoyed, there were real gains in the expansion of political rights in the British Empire after emancipation. In the British Cape Colony in southern Africa, for example, African males were given the vote—with relatively minimal qualification standards—in the Cape Constitution of 1853. The most notable experiment in citizenship for people of African descent in the British Empire occurred in Jamaica. By the 1840s, men of African descent had limited voting rights and small representation in the colony's House of Assembly. Whatever inclusive promise these rights achieved and portended soon slipped amid the specific fears prompted by the violence of the 1865 Morant Bay Rebellion and its subsequent reprisals and the 1857 Indian Mutiny. For much of British society, Morant Bay and the Indian Mutiny reaffirmed the argument that colonized peoples were unprepared for political participation, and the events intensified sentiments of inherent, permanent difference. In March 1866, Parliament declared Jamaica a crown colony and excluded all of the island's African-descended population from selecting its governing legislative council.⁴²

In the United States the experiment with African American citizenship began shortly after the Morant Bay Rebellion. With the passage of the Fourteenth Amendment, the search for citizenship rights became a major focus of Reconstruction policies following the Civil War. There were initially some dramatic gains for people of African descent. Full possibilities of citizenship, however, remained elusive, and the end of activist Reconstruction in 1877 was a severe setback for post-emancipated rights. The perceived failings of post-emancipated experiments in both the United States and the British Empire highlight the Anglo-American retreat from expanded notions of citizenship for people of African descent.⁴³ Crucially, however, despite the supposedly experimental nature of rights and their eventual reduction, they did accumulate some rights in the post-emancipated period.

These events in Jamaica and after Reconstruction illustrated that it would be an uphill struggle to permanently crown abolitionism with political rights. In some ways mainstream abolitionism contributed to this post-emancipated struggle. While voices within the movement clamored for post-emancipated political rights, a deep religious message was the primary building block of abolitionism. Relying heavily upon the ubiquitous mantra "am I not a man and a brother?" the movement fundamentally appealed to equality before God. Abolitionists also argued that slavery violated a basic conception of liberty—the freedom to dispose of one's labor. The calls for free labor hearkened to a Lockean tradition, which argued that society and government had a responsibility to protect the inalienable rights of life, liberty, and property.[44] To many abolitionists, emancipation fulfilled the providential claim of equality before God and freed the chains of bondage labor. As abolitionists took solace in the fact that emancipation had achieved the goals of free labor and equality before God, post-emancipated urgency waned, especially as experimental rights were curtailed. While references to abolitionism never left the language of reform, a decidedly muted version of its application to people of African descent was the post-emancipated legacy of what was arguably the most successful reform movement of the modern era.[45]

The quickening of Euro-American imperialism, however, only increased contact among regions and peoples of the world and intensified the discourse on race relations. Evoking the transatlantic abolitionist focus on emancipation in the United States, post-emancipated conditions in the American South became a popular case study as the global racial encounter ensued. Just as the South was a central target of abolitionism, post-emancipated conditions in the United States comprised the main comparative context for the consideration of race relations in Great Britain and its empire.[46]

As Great Britain's imperial encounter with Africans intensified in the late nineteenth century, the language of progress and citizenship—lost in the tumult of Morant Bay and the Indian Mutiny—slipped back into the discourse. As the empire negotiated race relations within its colonies, many in Great Britain (the self-proclaimed moral leader of the nineteenth century) were especially concerned with the progress of African Americans. In a 1882 article, the *Pall Mall Gazette* reprinted parts of a report from the American South that celebrated their advancement. Aligning with the imperial mission's endorsement of the civilizing aspects of labor, the article stressed that "there is no better labourer than the negro to be found among any race of the world. . . . They are particularly suited for labour in semi-tropical climates." The article also opined that African Americans were "fast-learning" and, "as they acquire education, they will become better citizens."[47] In 1889, the British *Anti-Slavery Reporter* reprinted an article from the London *Times*, which commented that "chiefs like Khama and Sechele and their people have shown themselves so capable of progress, and of assimilating civilised ideas and habits, that there is every good reason to hope that, under good guidance, they may become creditable British citizens."[48] Clearly a paternalist uplift agenda informed the "good guidance" of the *Anti-Slavery Reporter,* and the *Pall Mall* article reflects another popular strand in imperialist conversation—the distinctions made regarding the suitability of different races to the temperate and tropical zones—and overtly conflates uplift with labor efficiency. However, these statements indicate that the logical end of the civilizing mission—citizenship—was part of the era's discursive debate about Euro-American imperial encounters with people of African descent, and the American South was often a comparative case.

Others did not search for evidence of progress but linked conditions in the South to the transgressions of late-nineteenth-century imperialism. The positivist movement, as I will discuss, offered a distinct critique of race relations. A representative passage in the *Positivist Review* lumped together lynching in the United States with a host of other affronts suffered by colonized peoples: "The sufferings of the natives of India, the practical slavery of thousands in South Africa, the lynchings in America, the horrors of the Congo, must make the most convinced optimist hesitate and qualify his statements."[49] Theoretical understandings of colonialism emphasize the metropolitan-colonial distance but also allow for concepts of internal colonialism.[50] The conditions facing people of color in the British Empire and the United States, while subject to local variation, had similar characteristics of marginalization. These conditions not only suggest that the South qualified as a colonial space but also reiterate that the color line was global in nature.[51] This helps explain why Pan-Africanists directed their protest across nation-state boundaries.

Pan-Africanism

Pan-African activists who challenged the global color line were transnational actors.[52] Beyond critiquing similar conditions across nation-state boundaries, they also used the historical legacy of slavery, the common post-emancipated position of people of African descent in modernity, and new understandings of Africa as a platform of connectivity. Further, they crafted their protest in an international fashion. This global activism was not only expressed in a vibrant Atlantic-based print culture but was also pitched toward a changing Anglo-American progressivism that was navigating the dislocations of modernity.[53] This progressivism distanced itself from the classic liberal concentration on individual freedom and instead conceptualized society as a social organism. The shift did not completely jettison individualism, and many social theorists were suspicious of ideologies that suggested a social path toward realizing individual rights. Yet the emphasis on organic holism created an ethical commitment to mutual responsibility. This progressivism also encouraged immediate statist intervention into the workings of society and pushed the consideration of the state's responsibility to its citizens. The belief in the interconnectivity of society, the commitment to ethical responsibility, a sense of immediacy, and an understanding of the interventionist role of the state combined with the implications of the standard of civilization to reinvigorate discussions of reform and rights.

Nonetheless, the use of the term *organism* in the language of progressivism was a reminder of the continuing relevance of Darwinian language. Transatlantic progressive ideology suggested a discussion of reform and rights and did not support overt platforms of competition and control. Aspects of obdurate racialized essentialism reflected in strategies of imperial control and represented in displays of the ethnographic other were readily available. The ubiquity of, at the minimum, racialized hierarchies prevented mainstream reformer efforts from fully considering what was obvious to Pan-Africanists: the pressing need for post-emancipated equality and rights. Thus, the Pan-African activists whom I focus on in this book had a difficult relationship with mainstream progressivism, usually feeling in but not of the conventional reform movement. Reflective of this tension was the inclusion of Du Bois's American Negro exhibit in a turn-of-the-century statement of transatlantic reform—the Musée Social at the 1900 Exposition Universelle—that took place against the backdrop of the display of the ethnographic other on the midway of the world's fair.

The American Negro exhibit coincided time-wise with the first Pan-African Conference in London. Both were important markers for people of African descent who were conversant with the standard of civilization and used transnational networks and forums to critique the processes of rights accumulation within particular nation-state frameworks. Historians today study such networks to consider the specific discursive content and policy successes of the actors and to investigate the cultural context of the participants.[54] Network studies often take a transnational focus, and an understanding of Pan-African activism contributes to this investigation.

Indeed, historiography has long reflected the transnational nature of Pan-Africanism. One of the most formative contributions to the field, George Shepperson's 1962 article "Pan-Africanism and 'Pan-Africanism': Some Historical Notes," made the distinction between *Pan-Africanism* and *pan-Africanism*.[55] He characterized the former as a formal movement with institutional strength and a political agenda and the latter as a broad and vibrant understanding of the struggles of African people that did not coalesce into a significant, politically targeted movement. Using this test as an evaluative tool, Shepperson centered his analysis of the beginnings of twentieth-century Pan-Africanism on the struggle between two important historical figures: W. E. B. Du Bois and Marcus Garvey. He argued that the Du Bois–led Pan-African congresses between 1919 and 1945 achieved Pan-Africanism partially by minimizing Garveyism to pan-Africanism. It was not until Du Bois's influence waned that post-1945 African leadership rehabilitated Garvey into an important building block of Pan-Africanism. Regardless of the differing emphasis on leadership, Shepperson and most other scholars concentrate primarily on post–World War I Pan-African political manifestations, especially those connected to growing anticolonialism, decolonization, and the resulting questions facing African nation-states. The Pan-African scion George Padmore reiterates this post-1919 emphasis with his contention that Pan-Africanism lay dormant until revived by Du Bois after the war.[56]

While neither Padmore nor Shepperson accord the 1900 Pan-African Conference large-*P* status, both acknowledge the gathering as an important moment in the history of Pan-Africanism. The German historian Imanuel Geiss agrees and has credited the assembly with sparking a narrower political Pan-African movement. He also overtly uses *pan-Africanism* as an umbrella term for "cultural and intellectual movements" and locates the concept in the history of the modern slave trade and the abolitionist campaign. Further, he notes that the continued emphasis on religious arguments in the immediate post-emancipated period was partially indebted to the cultural traditions of abolitionism.[57] Shepperson, Padmore, and Geiss have provided invaluable and lasting insights on the study of Pan-Africanism yet they have also contributed to familiar political-cultural divisions that characterize historical inquiry. Political history focuses on behaviors of actors in the formal political realm, while cultural history concentrates on the more quotidian expressions of human activity. This division deeply affects the historiography of Pan-Africanism. Moreover, it elucidates another difficulty in the larger scholarship. Historians traditionally concentrate on the great moral campaign of the nineteenth century—abolitionism—and post-1919 political Pan-Africanism and the associated history of the civil rights movement (especially in the U.S. context). These concentrations skip over the late nineteenth and early twentieth centuries, deeming the era as relatively insignificant in the history of Pan-Africanism.

Although Geiss argues that the 1900 Pan-African Conference established a political narrowness, Pan-African reform at the turn of the century remains understudied, sitting uneasily amid this historiographical framing. The immediate post-emancipated period is not included in the study of abolitionism but is also not seen as fully political and hence not included in large-*P* studies.[58] Yet while the dichotomy between the political and the cultural helps our understanding, Shepperson warns that, in practice, the boundaries between the two domains are often blurred.[59] Of course, the overlap between the political and the cultural is a fundamental feature of cultural studies. Paul Gilroy's seminal work, *The Black Atlantic*, argues that the metaphoric Atlantic operates as an analytical field in which to consider the unique modern experience and resulting worldview of people of African descent, neither of which fall into clean categories of *political* or *cultural*. Gilroy makes a distinction between the "politics of fulfillment" (the practice of articulating claims on modern society) and the "politics of transfiguration" (the more organic and opaque expressions that transcend modernity). For him, the profound experience of slavery and the transition to citizenship have enabled people of African descent who have been exposed to western norms to deny the separation of "ethics and aesthetics, culture and politics" in ways that provide space for a countercultural sensibility.[60]

The Black Atlantic provocatively suggests that the experience of slavery and oppression along with the modern struggle for post-emancipated agency provide a rich terrain for an invigorated study of Pan-Africanism. Moreover, when combined with cultural studies scholars' flattening of the boundaries between politics and culture, the academic contest between small-*p* and large-*P* is mitigated considerably. This study concentrates on how the politics of fulfillment animated Pan-African calls for political rights and argues that these calls emanated from a shared cultural space that expressed Pan-African unity.

Holistic understandings of Pan-Africanism temper the dichotomy between the cultural and the political. Such approaches view it as a broad cultural unity based on both common African roots and the dislocations caused by western-driven modernity. This shared worldview produces particularized expressions dependent on historical context that seek to improve the position of African peoples. Thus, holistic Pan-Africanism provides the malleability necessary to link initial lamentations about the oppression of the slave trade to contemporary political manifestos about postcolonial conditions in twenty-first-century Africa.[61] The holistic investigation of Pan-Africanism combines with explorations of the Black Atlantic, post-emancipated studies, diaspora studies, postcolonial studies, and the history of human rights.

In this book, I use a holistic approach to analyze Pan-Africanism during a period roughly bookended by two international forums: the 1884–85 Berlin Conference and the 1911 Universal Races Congress. At this time, Pan-Africanism mixed the moral ethos of abolitionism with appeals for secular participation in society for post-emancipated subjects and citizens. These claims on citizenship were empowered by imperialism's normative standard of civilization and its constant violation of this standard. Pan-Africanism saw the marginalized position of people of African descent as a phenomenon transcending nation-state boundaries and consistently sought international forums to air grievances. In doing so, the movement collapsed the distinctions between domestic and international politics, a division that worked to obviate full recognition of the global nature of the color line. While nation-states promoted the standard of civilization at world's fairs and other global conferences, they consistently sought to minimize international censure of practices, either domestic or international, that violated the standard. Pan-Africanism always recognized that nation-states consistently transgressed the standard of civilization, both in practices that violated fair treatment of colonized people and in their refusal to recognize progress and grant full rights.

Over time, however, Pan-Africanists began to realize that the nation-states were also largely ignoring censure of such practices. By the 1911 Universal Races Congress, they were beginning to argue that white-led societies were using the standard of civilization as a tool of oppression. In response, they moved some of their discourse away from criticism of practices to a protest that denounced the broader imperial project and prefigured later expressions of anticolonialism. This critique unfolded against ongoing questioning of biological essentialism, most notably articulated by Franz Boas at the Universal Races Congress, where his address suggested a worldview of cultural pluralism. Pan-Africanism used this shift to reinterpret African history and understand African cultures in ways that were unhindered by the need to demonstrate adherence to Euro-American standards of civilization. Nonetheless, this reinterpretation did not reduce the Pan-Africanists' belief in the empowerment conferred by citizenship. They continued to argue that modern political participation was central to both decolonization and the civil rights movement. This Pan-Africanist reform, caught in the contradictions that constructed the global color line, often had difficulty providing tidy answers to complex problems. Its ideologies remained powerful especially in a period often described as "the nadir" for people of African descent. Thus, these actors kept alive a voice of human rights.[62]

Chapter 1 of this book looks at the building blocks of Pan-Africanism in the 1890s through the lens of the people of African descent who participated in the 1893 World's Columbian Exposition in Chicago and the 1895 Cotton States and International Exposition in Atlanta. African American women at the Chicago event used the forum of the World's

Congress of Representative Women to appeal for inclusion in the broader women's movement and to critique race relations in the United States. At the Congresses on Africa, held in both Chicago and Atlanta, people of African descent began to express dissatisfaction with the prescriptions of the 1884–85 Berlin Conference concerning the imperial mission in Africa. Instead, these reformers argued that control of the Christianizing mission should belong to people of African descent.

Chapter 2 demonstrates that the summer of 1900 was a propitious occasion for Pan-African protest. The American Negro exhibit at the 1900 Exposition Universelle in Paris was part of the official U.S. contribution to the halls of the Musée Social, which was a crowning statement of transatlantic reform. The first Pan-African Conference in London not only included Du Bois's discussion of the global color line but also offered several Pan-African ideas and platforms to battle that line's construction. The chapter contextualizes these events against the backdrop of a changing transatlantic progressivism movement, which included challenges to the widespread acceptance of the link between biology and progress.

Chapter 3 revisits the critique of Euro-American Christianity through an analysis of the writings of Pan-Africanist reformers connected to the African American journalist John Bruce. These testimonies reiterated the power of Ethiopia as a unifying concept of Pan-African identity and continued to encourage the rescue of African history and the continent's people in a way that transcended pervasive Dark Continent stereotypes. The chapter also analyzes the protests against imperial practices in the Congo by both traditional reform societies and people of African descent, including the direct observations of George Washington Williams.

Chapter 4 argues that both turn-of-the-century imperial conflicts— the Spanish-American War and the South African (Boer) War—provided an opportunity for people of African descent to make claims on equality and political rights by participating in the so-called legitimate violence of nation-state warfare. In the South African War, people of African descent derided Boer injustices and saw British imperial rule as a dramatic improvement. These claims were constructed around the notion of manliness, which was a core component of Pan-African protest. However, Clause 8 of the Treaty of Vereeniging that ended the war expressly delayed the question of African enfranchisement in the annexed colonies until after the achievement of responsible government, dashing hopes for full citizenship. Participation in the Spanish American War also failed to change domestic conditions for African Americans.

Chapter 5 considers the voices of female reformers through their analysis of the "Negro problem," which was perhaps the most debated aspect of race relations in the late nineteenth and early twentieth centuries. The protests of Ida B. Wells, Catherine Impey, Anna J. Cooper, Mary Church Terrell, and Pauline Hopkins emphasized rights and equality for all people of African descent, including women.

The conclusion analyzes the 1911 Universal Races Congress, the last major international conference dedicated to race relations before the outbreak of World War I. This congress was the culmination of many of the intellectual currents of Pan-Africanism analyzed in this study and included a summative statement from Franz Boas questioning biological essentialism. The conclusion also details Dusé Mohamed Ali's *African Times and Orient Review*, which shifted from criticism of imperial practice to more radical anticolonial claims in its writings. This shift indicated a new era of Pan-Africanism that began to embrace distinctly anticolonial platforms, most clearly represented in the figure of Marcus Garvey. The conclusion also summarizes how this book contributes to Pan-African studies and the history of human rights

CHAPTER 1

PAN-AFRICAN THOUGHT

Chicago (1893) and Atlanta (1895)

By the 1890s, the urgency of the abolitionist movement must have appeared, to many, to be a distant memory. This was especially true in the United States, which was often the main comparative template for those considering race relations.[1] As a result of the ascendance of local discriminatory legal codes and the assertion of racist social norms reaffirmed by a perceived lack of progress in discussions of the so-called Negro problem, African Americans found themselves at the "nadir" of race relations.[2] In the United States, two prominent world's fairs—the 1893 World's Columbian Exposition in Chicago and the 1895 Cotton States and International Exposition in Atlanta—demonstrated how far African Americans were from the post-emancipated abolitionist promise of political rights and social equality. At both of these fairs, African Americans were denied inclusive participation in the trumpeting of national progress. Exposition organizers in Chicago denied them a place in the official exhibitions of the United States, and they were given only a segregated exhibition space in Atlanta. Nonetheless, their presence at both fairs gave them an international platform for their participation and argumentation. In Chicago, women of African descent argued for inclusion in the women's movement and simultaneously criticized race relations in the United States. In both Chicago and Atlanta, the Congresses on Africa considered the meaning of Africa outside the stereotyped boundaries of the dark continent, established a sense of unity, and critiqued the Euro-American direction of the civilizing mission as a violation of the standard of civilization.[3]

While the United States participated in numerous international exhibitions in the late nineteenth century, it made particular use of the 1893 Columbian Exposition in Chicago to display itself as a force in the international world of imperialism and progress.[4] Yet even though the fair's official narrative celebrated American advances, it pushed aside the issue of race relations, and African Americans were denied the opportunity to organize and present an official exhibit. Despite this formal ostracizing, people of African descent had a distinct presence in Chicago.[5] It created a "counterpublic sphere" for their expressions, which included insight on the domestic and international facets of race relations.[6]

Indeed, the world's fair in Chicago was an important moment for African American leadership as it allowed the prominent abolitionist, Frederick Douglass, to share one of his last statements on post-emancipated race relations. At the time, he represented an aging generation that had made significant contributions to abolitionism and continued to agitate for post-emancipated rights and equality. Douglass, along with other reformers I discuss later in this book (notably, Ida B. Wells and Frederic Loudin), produced a pamphlet entitled *The Reason Why the Colored American Is Not in the World's Columbian Exposition*.[7] The 136-page tract lambasted the fair for not including African Americans in its formal proceedings. Douglass's introduction to the pamphlet critiqued post-emancipated conditions in the United States and argued that, because of the clear documentation of the progress of African Americans available at world's fairs, such gatherings were obligated to address their marginalization. Wells, encouraged by Loudin, who had funded the document's publication, contributed a trenchant essay, "Lynch Law," that not only denounced lynching but also demonstrated her commitment to airing such grievances in an international forum.

As a former U.S. ambassador to Haiti, Frederick Douglass was that nation's official representative in Chicago, and he played a major role in the Haitian exhibition. He was also part of the controversial event known as Jubilee Day, which was offered to African Americans as recompense for their lack of official participation in the exposition. While Wells and others denounced the forum, Douglass thought that he could use it to draw attention to the African American cause. At Jubilee Day, he delivered a speech titled "The Race Problem in America" that argued there was "no Negro problem" and ridiculed the failure of white society to live up to the mandates of the U.S. Constitution. To strengthen his argument, Douglass relied on the ubiquitous notion of the scales of progress, noting that the progress of African Americans since the end of slavery had been substantial. He argued, however, that this progress should not be compared to the "splendid civilization of the Caucasian" but to the depths of "Dahomey." It is telling that Douglass invoked the ethnographic other. On the one hand, like Henry Sylvester Williams in his critique of the Savage South Africa exhibit, he countered the stereotypes of people of African descent that were being plied to large crowds on the midway. On the other hand, he demonstrated how deeply ingrained the racialized measurement of humankind was in the late nineteenth century and showed the many difficulties that activists faced when dealing with the paternalist illogic of this measurement.[8]

Douglass's harsh criticism demonstrates how important the consideration of race relations in the United States was to the larger question of the global color line. At the 1893 World's Columbian Exposition—which took place almost thirty years after emancipation—Douglass gave one of his last comments on race relations in the United States, lamenting the failure to crown abolitionism with the realization of full political rights for African Americans. His activism spanned crucial decades of the struggle, originating in his enslavement and continuing for more than sixty years. He sought, first, to end slavery and then agitated for post-emancipated recognition of African Americans as citizens. The attachment of measures of progress complicated this pursuit for people of African descent, who were seen as falling short of the standard of civilization; yet the notion of crowning the abolition of slavery with full political equality was fundamental to his intellectual leadership. Douglass, Wells, Loudin, and others made sure that, despite the exclusionary overtones of the Columbian Exposition, people of African descent used the international platform to critique post-emancipated conditions.

The 1893 World's Congress of Representative Women

Wells was not the only female activist present at the Chicago world's fair. Several other African American women also attended the event as part of the 1893 World's Congress of Representative Women, which was held within the World's Columbian Exposition and sponsored by the International Congress of Women (ICW). Just as Douglass used his Haitian connections to gain a platform, female reformers used international bodies to help them navigate the exclusionary nature of the fair. More importantly, their reform efforts continued to move between the domestic and international arenas long after the exposition closed.[9]

Formed in 1888, the ICW's goals, as described in its constitution, framed the organization as one fundamentally dedicated to "communication" among women's groups around the world but did not explicitly endorse a suffragist platform.[10] Although the group's 1893 meeting was originally slated for London, it was changed to Chicago to coordinate with the world's fair. The weeklong congress featured 209 official delegates from sixteen countries, and its seventy-six sessions drew more than six hundred participants. Most delegates were from Europe, the United States, and the British Empire; there was no representative from Africa. Organized along a model of country-by-country reporting, the event sought female commentary on "every issue affecting humanity—upon the Home, the Church, the State and her own function in these institutions." Like other marginalized groups protesting exclusion from contemporary society, the ICW felt the need to document progress; in fact, one of the first passages in its official record of the event notes that the congress was "intended to afford a proper and convenient opportunity for presenting the progress of women."[11] Again, the ubiquitous standard of civilization required reformers to present such documentation—in this case, nearly 1,000 pages of published text. Much of the record relates to roles and activities traditionally associated with women—their contributions to teaching youth, to church and missionary work, to social purity and ethics of dress, to anti-prostitution and temperance movements—but it also documents the achievements of women in education and their contributions to literature and science.

The ICW's constitution did not overtly call for political rights, and the World's Congress of Representative Women concentrated on progress in areas that were traditionally associated with women. Nonetheless, many leading suffragists, including Susan B. Anthony, Lucy Stone, and Elizabeth Cady Stanton of the United States and Florence Balgarnie, Ursula Mellor Bright, and Florence Fenwick Miller of Great Britain, either attended or submitted ancillary correspondence.[12] In addition, thirty-four different organizations commented on the "Civil and Political Reform" plank of the ICW's platform, more than the number that commented on any of the nine "purposes or objects" discussed at the gathering. These discussions shifted the terrain from traditional concerns and laborious documentations of progress toward a questioning of the belief in biological essentialism that had long claimed that women had not progressed sufficiently to qualify for political rights and social equality. Using the pen name "Helen H. Gardner," the suffragist Alice Chenoweth summarized the group's assertions concerning "Civil Law and Government": "Nowhere in all nature is the mere fact of sex made a reason for the fixed inequality of liberty." Amid readily available discriminations based on skin color and sex, and paralleling the pursuits of many of their Pan-Africanist contemporaries, the 1893 World's Congress of Representative Women marked a significant moment in the ensuing skepticism that biology could be used to support a denial of equal access to civil and political life.[13] Furthermore, the congress and its umbrella organization, the ICW, represented an international network of women who, while never escaping the need for prodigious documentation of progress, were agitating for social equality and political rights.

This agitation, while denying that biology could provide a litmus test for progress and concomitant political rights, also asserted that qualities unique to women could complement the characteristics of men in the public sphere. Stanton's essay, "The Ethic of Suffrage," begins, notably, with a direct plea for the "right of every citizen for self-government." It also argues that "masculine" civilization needs the "feminine element" to help in the "regulation of human affairs." If achieved, "we shall substitute cooperation for competition, persuasion for coercion." Instead of the "merciless" domination of the feminine element by male society, the recognition of the equality of women could only result in a "nobler type of men and women," with "two heads in council, two besides the hearth."[14] While rebuking the denial of rights and forcefully criticizing male domination, Stanton sought a cooperative relationship between the sexes, which she often expressed in florid language. Her essay delivered at this important international conference of women vividly illustrates how protests by marginalized people were compelled to document significant levels of progress in the pursuit of overcoming obdurate, often biologically based, prejudice. Its tone also demonstrates the need for caution when claiming inclusionary rights from mainstream society.

The theme of cooperation continued in words from the well-known reformer May Wright Sewall, the organizer of the congress and the editor of its proceedings. In her introduction to those proceedings, she argued that the event's "significance" lay in women's "claim of equality," which would be the groundwork for the "possible basis of permanent and satisfactory cooperation with [men]." Earlier in the introduction, she had asked if the congress would "date the hour of a new march—not for divided womanhood as against a separate manhood, but a new march for a unified, harmonious, onstepping [sic] humanity?" The need to establish union with men to achieve equality and rights was underscored in Sewall's opening dedication poem, which appeared prominently on the first page of the printed proceedings. It was addressed to both men and women, who, "having ears to hear," could only concur that the congress was the start of "The Ultimate Absolutely Equal Copartnership."[15] The ethos of copartnership flowed through the proceedings, not only revealing the relationship between female activism and male society but also shedding light on the link between mainstream female activism and female reformers of African descent.

The lens of race hindered the consistent involvement of African American women in the mainstream progressive feminist struggle.[16] The frequent appearance of the word *race* in the proceedings hints at this disconnect. Usually, the designation refers to the association among people of European descent. Indeed, while the text often touts the congress's constituency as "half the people of the world," the subtle but consistent reference to race belies this inclusionary language, demonstrating that a large majority of the activists at the event envisioned copartnership and equality primarily in terms of whiteness. The opening introduction of the ICW's text sets a divisive tone, stating that "any close observer of today's life, knows that between the changes made in the last half century in the condition, attitude, and outlook of men—which are indeed due to the general progress and improvement of the race—and the changes made in the same time in the attitude and condition of women, there is a fundamental difference." Here, the word *race* specifically applies to white people.

Although the introduction later complicates this statement by claiming that the presence of Native and African Americans at the congress was "magnificent proof of the capacity for forgiveness" of these "these two races," the passage maintains clear distinctions of racial difference.[17] This kind of racial division courses through the work. Thus, the copartnership mentioned in the dedication poem was intended to be union with white men. The unified message of the congress, like the larger progressive ethos of the late nineteenth and early twentieth centuries, was constrained by racial distinction. In this respect, the 1893 World's Congress of Representative Women can be read as a contribution to the construction of the global color line.[18]

Yet that line was always contested, even at the 1893 World's Columbian Exposition. In addition to Ida B. Wells, six other African American women—Frances E. W. Harper, Fannie Barrier Williams, Anna Julia Cooper, Fannie Jackson Coppin, Sarah J. Early, and Hallie Q. Brown— gave papers or offered responses at the World's Congress of Representative Women. All were active reformers, and, along with women such as Mary Church Terrell and Pauline Hopkins, they provided crucial leadership long after the event was over.[19] Their contributions complicated the association of female reform with white exclusivity.

The congress gave Harper, a novelist and a reformer, a spot on a panel considering "The Civil and Political Status of Women."[20] An editorial comment before this section of the proceedings argues that participants' testimony will help add "public spirit" to the "catalogue of womanly virtues." It also directly mentions civil rights and the ballot as goals of female activism, as does the opening essay in the section, "The Origins of the Women's Franchise League of Great Britain and Ireland," which claims equality "of political rights and duties" as its first objective.[21] The testimonies delivered in "The Civil and Political Status of Women," while not foregoing the documentation of progress or abandoning the deferential tone of copartnership, make an urgent and overt plea for political rights.

The fact that Harper was the only person of African descent on a panel agitating for political rights suggests the minimization of racialized and gendered distinctions. And her essay shifts the congress's racially restrictive sense of copartnership to invoke a standard mantra of abolitionism. Her introductory sentence bemoans the gap between men and women and, in keeping with the tone of the gathering, argues that bridging that distance is central to progress. The piece then, however, immediately shifts away from racial difference. Instead of using the single word *race*, which at the congress generally meant racialized exclusion, Harper argued that female participation in securing progress—"social advancement and moral development"—is crucial to the "*human* race." She cemented this inclusionary statement by relying on a well-known abolitionist phrase, arguing that the "present age" is marked by "recognition of the brotherhood of man."[22] At a congress dedicated to the women's movement, Harper challenged white-only overtones of access to political rights by using language that denied restrictions based on race. By marshaling key memorable phrases from the abolitionist movement for support, she created a potential segue into a consideration of the post-emancipated search for social equality and political rights.

Despite the abolitionist references, the bulk of the congress proceedings indicate little consideration about denying political rights to males. Although Florence Fenwick Miller argued, "The days of slavery should be over for women as well as for the black race," it remains unclear whether she meant to condemn post-emancipated conditions or to make the common comparison between the plight of women and the conditions of slavery. Still, every African American female activist at the congress explicitly drew attention to the denial of rights in the southern United States. Harper's entry, in particular, goes beyond denouncing discriminatory conditions and the denial of rights to citizens of African descent, instead reflecting an emerging central tactic employed by activists. By holding those responsible for lynching to a standard of civilization, she was able to call for the revocation of their rights and condemn the injustice perpetrated against African Americans: "Today there are red-handed men in our republic who walk unwhipped [*sic*] of justice, [men] who richly deserve to exchange the ballot of the freeman for the wristlets of the felon; brutal and cowardly men who torture, burn and lynch their fellow men."[23] Like many other anti-lynching activists, she made reference to the precepts and the legal code of civilization not only to claim rights but also to revoke them from transgressors.

Harper also endorsed aspects of preparedness for the realization of rights. While foregoing biological essentialism as the measure, she offered character as a criterion for full participation in political life. "It is not through sex but through character," she said, "that the best influence of women upon the life of the nation must be exerted." Furthermore, she made it clear that she did "not believe in unrestricted and universal suffrage for either men or women."[24] Though virtually all reformers in her time accepted measurements of progress, the use of character as a cultural and social indicator loosened the denial of progress based on biological determinants such as sex and skin color.

Harper's major contribution to the 1893 World's Congress of Representative Women was her criticism of the white-only hold on the inclusionary promises of progress, which at this gathering, consisted in the crafting of exclusionary copartnership. She also condemned the desultory aspects of race relations, shifting attention to more concrete standards of basic human rights. She ended her address with a plea, not for female suffrage but for basic justice: "O women of America! It is yours to create a healthy public sentiment; to demand justice, simple justice, as the right of every race; to brand with everlasting infamy the lawless and brutal cowardice that lynches, burns and tortures your own countrymen."[25] For Harper and the Pan-African activists I study in this book, "brutal cowardice"—the practice of racial discrimination and violence—was emphasized as the primary cause of the "Negro problem."

Other African American female activists at the congress participated in a session titled "The Solidarity of Human Interests," which addressed conditions in Spain, Latin America, Great Britain and her colonies, Poland, Iceland, and Syria. Additionally, and perhaps owing to its cosmopolitan composition, the session countered the exclusionary meanings of *race*. Indeed, the panelists explicitly expressed their opposition to the restrictive implications of the word, and the editorial comments that preface the text of the session note that the "woman question" is not "the curious culminating expression of the insane passion for independence characteristic of the Anglo-Saxon race." Rather, the comments mandate that "organized effort"—which does not create distinctions—is the best path for activism: "In this chapter greater significance lies between the lines than upon them, and it is commended to those 'who have eyes to see.'" As the session's title implies, its contributors were challenging the white-only progressivism generally projected by both the congress and the exposition. Echoing Harper's use of the term *human race*, the reformer Anna J. Cooper's brief remarks reiterated the pursuit of progress and rights unmoored from static distinctions and open to all, "not till race, color, sex, and condition are seen as accidents, and not till the substance of life; not till the universal title of humanity to life, liberty, and the pursuit of happiness is conceded to be inalienable to all." Frederick Douglass, who was in attendance, followed her remarks with a comment that spoke to his post-emancipated hopes. Recalling his long experience as an activist, he spoke of seeing his "old world" closing and a new period "dawning" in which "all discriminations against men and women on account of color and sex [are] passing away, and will pass away."[26]

Importantly, the session's introduction describes the contributions of the African American female participants as coming from "women of African descent in the United States." The distinction demonstrates that reference to Africa was one available description; and because these women were part of the testimony of the so-called civilized world, the connections to the continent were not completely obscured by connotations of savagery or the ethnographic other. Fannie Barrier Williams's contribution to the session, "The Intellectual Progress of the Colored Women of the United States Since the Emancipation Proclamation," invoked the goal of citizenship and referred to the experience of slavery as a common source of post-emancipated identity in the modern world.[27] She argued that slavery was a period of "long-enforced degradation" and that the "mean vocabulary of slavery" offered "no definition of any of the virtues of life." The moment of emancipation and the subsequent achievements of African American female progress, she asserted, provided a unique case study on the meanings of "freedom and citizenship."[28]

Sarah J. Early and Hallie Q. Brown made connections to places outside the United States, emphasizing the African American female commitment to Christianity and invoking "Ethiopia," an important reference to the significance of Africa in Pan-African thought. Early called on the "grand sisterhood" of post-emancipated women in the United States to continue "the spread of the gospel" to other people of African descent and detailed the contribution of women to church missionary efforts in the Caribbean and West Africa. Brown referred to the story and language of abolitionism. She connected Henry Wadsworth Longfellow's 1842 poem

"The Warning" and its ominous mention of the violent road to emancipation—"A shapeless mass of wreck and ruin lies"—directly to the Haitian Revolution and "the horrors of St. Domingo." However, Brown followed those warnings about violence with a reference to Frances Harper's poem "Ethiopia." Alluding to Psalm 68, the poem opens with a powerful statement that was relevant to both abolitionism and post-emancipated activism: "Yes! Ethiopia shall stretch / Her bleeding hands abroad." The biblical reference to Ethiopia had long been a staple of hope and redemption for Christian people of African descent. Brown augmented Harper's thesis by reminding listeners of the violent path taken by some enslaved peoples but, in the end, chose to elevate the religious tones of "Ethiopia" in her memories of abolitionism, thus demonstrating how some Pan-Africanists imbued their protests with a providential sense of race destiny.[29]

The World's Congress of Representative Women emphasized that the denial of social equality and political rights based on sex was arbitrary and unjust. African American female activists at the congress emphatically agreed with this platform but also saw the obvious connections to larger questions of race relations and opposed essentialist views. These women continued to have strained relations with mainstream women's movements. Perhaps motivated by these ongoing difficulties, and certainly due to a sense of race destiny that included references to Africa and the modern slave trade, they were at the forefront of the African American female club movement in the United States. Through these organizations, African American women continued to offer distinct commentary on post-emancipated issues. Additionally, some of them understood the transnational nature of the global color line. Many maintained an association with international organizations, including the ICW, and attended other international gatherings such as the first Pan-African Conference in London in 1900.

Congress on Africa (1893)

While still not part of the official exhibits of the United States, many people of African descent participated in the 1893 Congress on Africa held at the World's Columbian Exposition. Several aspects of this gathering are important. First, the participants were well aware of the standard of civilization established at Euro-American imperial conferences such as those in Berlin and Brussels. Second, the Congress on Africa simultaneously supported the civilizing mission projected in those imperial conferences and condemned practices that violated its tenets. Third, unlike the situation in Berlin and Brussels, where there were no colonized peoples represented, people of African descent made significant contributions to this congress. Finally, the Congress on Africa articulated that people of African descent should lead the redemption of the continent, and several prominent backers of this strategy, such as Alexander Crummell and Bishop Henry McNeal Turner, participated.[30] To be sure, people of African descent at the 1893 congress were aware of the international norms projected by Euro-American imperialism. Instead of only suggesting correctives to the practices that violated those norms, they began also to assert their claims to control aspects of the civilizing mission in Africa. These claims only enhanced awareness of Africa and the participation of its peoples in modernity.

Viewed as a continuation of the Berlin Conference of 1884–85 and the Brussels Anti-Slavery Conference of 1889–90, the Congress on Africa accentuated a progressive agenda. First, organizers invited Alfred Le Ghait, the Belgian ambassador to the United States, to open the first day of discussions. Le Ghait had published an overview of the Brussels Conference in the *North American Review*, ending his article by expressing admiration for the work of the conference and for the "civilizing" efforts of King Leopold of Belgium in Africa.[31] In Chicago, he continued this tack, adding that the United States had also contributed to the promotion of "commerce, Christianity and civilization." The U.S. representative to the Berlin Conference, John Kasson, sent an essay that was read at the Chicago congress. In it, he argued that the Congo was still an important "factor in the redemption of Africa" and that, through both nation-to-nation and religious cooperation, "African civilization will make strides to which history offers no parallel."[32] Both Le Ghait and Kasson offered a standard Euro-American template for Africa. By reducing friction between imperial powers and presenting Christianity as the best path to civilization, they hoped to ensure that the continent would remain open to Euro-American commerce. Neither man mentioned the rights of native Africans. Attendees in Berlin had taken an ambivalent position regarding missionaries and had clearly invoked ideas about self-determination and rights. Yet in Chicago, both Le Ghait and Kasson, who were well aware of the Berlin proceedings, remained silent about rights in their comments.

This omission was duly noted. After the reading of Kasson's essay, Reverend L. P. Mercer argued, to applause, that extension of the civilizing mission must take into account the rights of native Africans.[33] Other participants at the Congress on Africa also expressed discontent with the effectiveness of the Berlin and Brussels conferences. Horace Waller, a member of the Great Britain's Anti-Slavery Society, doubted the honesty of the civilizing mission. "A Berlin treaty or Brussels act on paper is one thing," he said, "the letter and spirit worked out with sincerity is another." Frederic Perry Noble, one of the organizers of the congress, also noted that the "Berlin and Brussels conferences have conferred but slight protection upon African aborigines." More critical was the testimony of a "Mr. Cherry" that directly followed the comments of Le Ghait. According to the transcript of the proceedings, "Mr. Cherry, just back from three years in the Congo, asserted that the State is free only in name, [and] is a Belgian colony exploited for Belgium's benefit." Prince Massaquoi an indigenous African, testified that many African "heathens" were aware of the Chicago congress and had performed a "blessing of the spirits" with the hope that it would not "take away their country from them." In response, the editorial notes exclaim, "What a comment upon the character and career of 'Christian' stewardship toward Africa!"[34]

Participants in the Congress on Africa not only critiqued the civilizing mission on that continent but, like the African American women at the World's Congress of Representative Women, took the opportunity to comment on conditions in the United States. The session chaired by Bishop Alexander Walters of the African Methodist Episcopalian (AME) church (he was later the secretary of the 1900 Pan-African Conference) catered to the mandate of progress reports and opened with an overview of the achievements in "negro education" in the United States since emancipation. William Hayes Ward of the New York newspaper the *Independent* argued that the best course for race relations in the United States was "absolute equality and actual fraternity," including the repeal of laws against interracial marriage and those that segregated public services and educational facilities. Douglass, again, unequivocally denounced any notion of the inferiority of African Americans. "There is no negro problem!" he said. "The only problem is whether there be enough Christian character and fidelity in white people to live up to their professions and Constitution."[35]

These arguments about domestic conditions in the United States reflected the ongoing discussion of comparative race relations. Much of the commentary at the congress alternated between attention to conditions in the United States and considerations of the international world. Bishop James T. Holly reminded participants of the historical importance of the Haitian Revolution: "In 1804, these self-emancipated freemen took their place among the nations." In a session chaired by Alexander Walters, participants considered the case of Liberia, arguing, "The negro is as capable of development as the white."[36] Other commentators noted that native Egyptians were "tending" toward self-government, that the Bantu had demonstrated self-government, and that indigenous central Africans were apt manufacturers and tradespeople. Prince Massaquoi argued that his native Vai Africans had long known the nature of God and that "no intelligent African" would believe the "jargon" of different denominations.[37] Yet the prince's use of the word *heathen* alongside his positive comments about the characteristics of native Africans was a reminder that the Congress of Africa still viewed the continent through the lens of uplift and the civilizing mission. While some of the commentary complicated the obdurate connotations of darkest Africa and her people, the congress as a whole still consistently used the descriptor "dark." The real discussion focused on the influence of the civilized and how they could draw out the potential of Africa and Africans.

Without question, Euro-American churches and their missionary wings continued to be at the forefront of this effort. Indeed, a large section of the congress proceedings analyzes their religious activity on the continent and includes extensive reports on British, French, Dutch, and U.S. missionary work. Virtually all of the reports from the different bodies comment on the contributions of natives, and many laud the development of freestanding African churches. Congress participants also reported extensively on the efforts of the AME church, which was at the forefront of African American evangelism in Africa. Although partially reflecting the widespread belief that people of European descent had a difficult time surviving in tropical zones, the report from the English entities concludes with an important concession: "By Africans must the Gospel ultimately be proclaimed in Tropical Africa."[38] The congress clearly demonstrated that people of African descent were claiming ownership of the Christian civilizing mission and the traditional missionary efforts that were long associated with the imperial mission. This momentum from the redemptionist message established at Chicago helped generate another Congress on Africa held at the 1895 Cotton States and International Exposition in Atlanta.

The 1895 Atlanta Cotton States and International Exposition

Conceived directly after the 1893 Chicago world's fair, the 1895 Cotton States and International Exposition, held in Atlanta, highlighted the economic and industrial progress of the South after the Civil War. Organizers saw it as an opportunity to demonstrate how the South was not only part of a reconstituted union but also a forward-thinking region primed for participation in the global political economy. The exposition was a reflection of this New South and was intended for both domestic and international consumption.[39] Inevitably, its statement of progress had to address the issue of post-emancipated race relations. In his official speech, George Brown, speaking as a representative of Georgia's governor, William Atkinson, pointed out the exhibition's Negro Building: "As an evidence of the absolute justice and fairness with which we have treated our colored citizens, we point you with pride and satisfaction to the exhibits contained in their building."[40] The platitudes about justice and fairness, however, belie the deep conservativism about race relations expressed in Atlanta. Not only was the Negro Building not integrated into the official exhibit halls of the fair, but the gathering also provided the forum at which Booker T. Washington issued his Atlanta Compromise.[41]

This conservatism was made clear during boosters' successful appeal before the U.S. House Appropriations Committee for federal funding for the event. The discussions before Congress demonstrated the continued complexities of integrating the progress of people of African descent into a nation-state's world's fair. Among those who testified in Washington on behalf of the Atlanta delegation were Booker T. Washington, Bishop Wesley J. Gaines, and Bishop Abraham Grant of the AME church. As reported in the official history of the exposition, Gaines commented that, in the South, blacks and whites "understood each other." Grant agreed that blacks and whites were on a path of "increasing friendship" and that, due to an expertise in cotton, the "negro" was the "finest laborer on earth" and, by nature, a "conservative element" in society.⁴² Washington testified that he had urged African Americans to eschew politics and concentrate on the accumulation of property. These three testimonies show that specific representations of post-emancipated race relations in the southern United States were used in the appeal to the nation-state for funding.

Clearly the conservative tone of the appeal to Congress anticipated Washington's later Atlanta Compromise speech. However, all three men believed that the end goal of progress would be the realization of legal and political rights for African Americans. A congressman from South Carolina, George W. Murray, himself of African descent, emphasized this goal more forcefully in a speech before the U.S. House of Representatives. Twice in his short address, he used the term "fellow white-citizen" when addressing the wider white population. He felt that the Atlanta exposition would make "white men" reconsider depriving the "colored man" of his right to participate in the "government of the country." Further, he argued that it was time to show the rest of the world that "colored people" were "part and parcel" of the United States, a "civilization which all the nations of the world look up to and imitate." While certainly accommodating the requirement that the Atlanta exposition would remain conservative regarding race relations, these appeals reveal that citizenship was always part of the aspirations of the African American reform movement. They also show, as Murray argued, that an international audience was searching for the supposed progressivism of the United States. In the end, funding was approved for the exposition. Yet in an echo of the struggle for integration at the Chicago event, an amendment later segregated the Negro Building away from the official Government Building.⁴³

Creation of a separate space for the Negro Building dovetailed with Washington's message at the Atlanta exposition. His speech, delivered at the opening ceremony, expanded on the themes in his short address during the House appropriations hearing. The commentary in the official guide of the exposition notes that there was hesitation about giving a "negro" a role in the opening exercises due to fear that such inclusion would suggest "social equality and prove offensive to the white people." However, the discussions concerning Washington's address allayed such fears, and the stage was set for his Atlanta Compromise. In that speech, Washington offered a compromise to white America. "Cast down your buckets" to assist the "8,000,000 negroes," he said, and in return African Americans would forego "the agitation of social equality." As a result, "you and your families will be surrounded by the most patient, faithful, law-abiding and unresentful people that the world has seen." To promote the guarantees regarding social equality, Washington delivered his now-famous line: "In all things that are purely social, we can be as separate as the fingers, yet one as the hand in all things essential to mutual progress."[44]

Washington's speech remains a fundamental marker of the African American approach to rights and equality during the late nineteenth century. Often dismissed as obsequious and fawning, the Atlanta Compromise was not a statement of complete acquiescence to white supremacy but offered a practical path that reflected contextual realities. Faced with social conditions marked by inequality and racialized violence, Washington and his exhibition at the Negro Building intended to show that post-emancipated people were industrious and contributing to the material progress of the nation. Because the documentation of material gain was an oft-referenced measurement of progress, many leaders, including W. E. B. Du Bois, praised aspects of his talk. Further, the address argued that of all the "material benefits" exhibited by progress were less important than the "higher good," which included "a determination even in the remotest corner to administer absolute justice, in a willing obedience among all classes to the mandates of law and a spirit that will tolerate nothing but the highest equity in the enforcement of the law."[45] Without question, this passage refers to the violations of justice experienced by people of African descent. Washington was a life-long critic of lynching, and the Atlanta Compromise was not a capitulation to racialized violence. He was also concerned about Africa. He argued for the continued sovereignty of Liberia, sponsored emigrationist movements, and stressed his model of manual training, which influenced many evangelizing efforts on the continent. Indeed, the gradualism and material concentration he espoused were in some ways analogous to ideas of preparedness embedded in the progressive model. As such, aspects of his thought remained relevant to reformers of African descent.[46]

Without question, however, the offering of a compliant labor force combined with the foregoing of social equality was conservative. The reproduction of a labor force for white-owned capital, the acceptance of inequality in society, and the capitulation to a gradual timetable for rights indicated no urgency for progressive change. Nonetheless, as I will document, Pan-African activists transformed the conservatism in the Atlanta Compromise.

By dispatching a famous African American to deliver a plea for friendly relations based on gradualism and by creating a separate Negro Building to demonstrate the materialist progress of African Americans, the Atlanta Cotton States and International Exposition conveyed what its organizers saw as a positive answer to the question of race relations.[47] But Senator Benjamin Tillman of South Carolina projected a different sentiment at the Atlanta event. A noted white supremacist and a vocal advocate for the disenfranchisement of African Americans, he used his appearance at the exposition to launch a diatribe that conflated the "Negro problem" in the South with the immigrant problem in the North. He warned that the time would come when only the "Southern farmer" could save the nation. Clearly, despite the laudatory views espoused by the official voices of the exposition and the conservative compromise offered by Washington, the Negro problem was deeply affecting views on race relations.[48] This oppositional lens was reaffirmed through the display of the ethnographic other on the fair's midway. President Grover Cleveland, perhaps unwittingly, touched on the convoluted depth of the subject when he commented on the effect of the Old Plantation exhibit (the only one he visited): "It was what its name signifies. With real negroes as the actors, and was as much superior to negro minstrelsy by white men as real life is to acting."[49] The Cotton States and International Exposition promoted the South as a modern economic region even as it imbued race relations with not only the vision of the post-emancipated compromise guaranteeing a conservative labor force but also a heavy dose of collective memory of the "good old days" of contented slavery.

Congress on Africa (1895)

Undoubtedly, the Cotton States and International Exposition projected a commitment to segregation. The *Negro Exhibit* was given space but not integrated into the official halls of the fair, and it symbolized accommodation as evidenced by Washington's call to "cast down your buckets" in the spirit of compromise. However, like the Chicago fair, the exposition also housed a Congress on Africa as a forum for reformers of African descent to project a message that was different from these lasting images of Atlanta Compromise. The momentum from Chicago carried over to Atlanta, and many African Americans took part, including John Wesley Edward Bowen, who served as secretary of the congress and editor of its proceedings. Bowen was an Methodist Episcopal minister and had received a PhD from Boston University in 1887. In 1893, he was hired as the chair of historical theology at Gammon Theological Seminary (a sponsor of the congress), a position he retained until 1932.[50] The congress received many contributions from people of African descent, including several from people who resided in Africa.

Rather than critiquing the failed civilizing intentions of the Berlin and Brussels conferences, this Congress on Africa offered more pronounced denunciations of European actions on the continent and suggested that a new platform was in order. The proceedings' "Opening Remarks" lambaste the evils of slavery—*the stealing of Africans from Africa*—and argued that a "curse" remained as European nations were now making *"efforts to steal Africa from Africans."* Yet as one would expect at a conference sponsored by a theological institution and its missionary foundation, the remarks go on to remind attendees that "God is stretching forth his hands to Ethiopia."[51] Like the Chicago proceedings, they express little confidence that people of European descent can provide the requisite leadership and clamor for people of African descent to lead the religious civilizing mission in Africa, pressing the claim of "Africa for Africans."[52]

Bowen's Africa for Africans sentiment emphasizes an emigration theme that was another strand of Pan-African thought articulated at both the Chicago and Atlanta congresses. While such discussions were not new, the most provocative leader of this movement in the 1890s was Bishop Henry McNeal Turner, who participated in both congresses. In Chicago, he opened his commentary with the bold declaration that Jesus was black. In Atlanta, Turner bluntly stated, "For the Negro to stay out of politics is to level himself with a horse or a cow." He argued that, regardless of strategy, social equality and political rights could never be achieved for people of African descent in white-led societies. This "chasm" between white and black, according to Turner, was apparent not only in the United States but also in the Caribbean, South America, and western Europe. In his discussions of the United States, he directly referred to the sentiments of Senator John Tyler Morgan of Alabama, who had forthrightly stated that whites would never grant social equality to the Negro.[53]

Turner believed that people of African descent should own the Christian civilizing of Africa, and he endorsed wholesale emigration as the only solution to the problem of widespread discrimination. In Atlanta, he articulated his long-standing hope that "the Negro should, therefore, build a nation of his own"—that is, return to Africa. Given the overt racism of white supremacists like Senator Tillman, he did not think that Washington's compromise or any other strategy would work. Rather, he argued that the construction of the Negro problem in the United States demonstrated that white society was adamantly opposed to post-emancipated social equality and political rights. His approach to argumentation made for odd connections, including some agreement with the white supremacist Senator Morgan, who also fervently supported emigrationist schemes.

Turner's arguments for emigration were part of his larger pursuit of race pride, which for him spurred hopes for a nationalist project in Africa. Other manifestations of race pride did not exclusively involve a defensive posture or arguments for emigration-based nationalism. The notion was a broad ideological disposition that recognized the connections between Africa and modernity, denied crass depictions of people of African descent, and celebrated their awareness and progress. As Du Bois declared in his 1897 "The Conservation of Races," race pride was fundamentally a cultural statement that was beginning to emerge from long-standing biological understandings of race.

During this era, belief in biological essentialism was widespread, and at times Pan-African discussions of race pride could take on its hues. Nowhere was this more evident than in Turner's disputes with T. Thomas Fortune during the Chicago and Atlanta congresses. Fortune vehemently disagreed with emigrationist strategies, arguing instead that "the inevitable destiny of the European whites in Africa is absorption and assimilation by the African blacks as surely as the ultimate destiny of the African blacks in the United States is the absorption and assimilation by the American whites." Fortune saw this absorption as a reiteration of the "unity of the human race"; and although his beliefs about emigration took on biological overtones, he consistently spoke up for the integration of people of African descent into U.S. society and polity. He and others, including Turner, extended their feud into a battle over skin color and appropriate nomenclature. Turner, for instance, was committed to the use of the word *Negro* and its association with blackness, while Fortune preferred *Afro-American* and its connotation of lighter skin color. Their discussions were heated and, at times, devolved into name calling. Indeed, in his Atlanta address, Fortune referred to emigrationists as "ravens."[54]

There were more sophisticated understandings of black nationalism, including those of Martin Delany and Alexander Crummell, who were seminal figures in Pan-African discussions during the mid- and late nineteenth century. Delany was a colleague of Douglass's, active in the abolitionist struggle (the two worked together at the influential newspaper, the *North Star*), and a major post-emancipated intellectual until his death in 1885. As early as 1852, he had denounced the prospects for integration in the United States and suggested emigration to Africa. In 1859, Delany was part of a fact-finding mission to the Niger valley to evaluate the prospects for a self-governing colony in the region. After the Civil War and emancipation, he worked for the Freedmen's Bureau, was involved in Reconstruction politics, and supported emigration efforts to Liberia. He also added to the recovery of African history with his 1879 work, *Principia of Ethnology: The Origin of Races and Color*. At the Atlanta congress, Delany's voice was a bridge between abolitionism and post-emancipated reform.

Both public awareness and historiography accord Delany a seminal position in the pantheon of black nationalist leaders.[55] His supposed radicalism is usually juxtaposed against Douglass's conservatism. In this usage, the notion of radicalism reflects a deep discontent with white society and suggests an embrace of black nationalist separatist strategies and the elevation of racial pride. In contrast, conservatism is demarcated by the adoption of integrationist platforms. Yet while these categories can be helpful, they should not be used to simplify the complexity of the actors and the context, as Delany's case makes clear.[56] The tumultuous experiences of his life—his flight across the Mason-Dixon line, emigration to Canada, the abolitionist struggle, his participation in emigration organizations, his travels to Africa, his role as a Union recruiter during the Civil War, his association with the Freedmen's Bureau, his disappointment with post-emancipation, his unsuccessful bid for federal employment—all contributed to his wide-ranging intellectual shifts and explorations.[57] He was undoubtedly committed to emigration and the development of race pride, but his active emigrationist phases ebbed and flowed, and his arguments for racial distinction often took on pluralist overtones. At times, he even looked toward inclusion into American society. Thus, the tendency to divide reformers into categories does not adequately capture how Pan-Africanists maintained an awareness of Africa that could promote emigration and also struggled for political and social rights within domestic contexts. Further, it does it reflect the complexity of intellectuals such as Delany or the less-studied figure of John Smythe.[58]

At the time of the Atlanta congress, Smythe was a former U.S. ambassador to Liberia, and he contributed a lengthy essay titled "The African in Africa and the African in America," which stressed the recovery of race pride through emigration back to Africa.[59] Although he was a committed emigrationist, he had spent much of his life in the United States and would be an early member of Alexander Crummell's American Negro Academy (ANA), established in 1897 to promote the "attainment of culture, at home or abroad."[60] Like Delany, Smythe argued for better domestic conditions for people of African descent in the United States and promoted emigration strategies. In 1897, he founded the Negro Reformatory Association of Virginia, an institution dedicated to providing manual education for African American minors convicted of criminal behavior.[61] Hence, he was not disconnected from conditions in the United States and actively took a role in progressive causes, especially those connected to people of African descent.

The Influence of Alexander Crummell

As his Atlanta essay makes clear, Smythe had a close relationship with Alexander Crummell, who, like Delany and Douglass, was a leading intellectual whose life bridged abolitionism and the post-emancipated reform movement. Crummell's contributions to the Atlanta congress were noteworthy and reflected some of his basic ideological tenets. As an ordained

Episcopalian minister, he used his first essay, "Civilization as a Collateral and Indispensable Instrumentality in Planting the Christian Church," to endorse the redemptionist mission in Africa. The piece emphasizes the links between the spiritual and the secular in the missionary movement, arguing that the teaching of "repentance and faith" in preparation for salvation is only one aspect of the missionary task. Crummell continued, stressing that Christianity is not "exclusively individualistic in its purposes" or limited to "celestial and external interests" but "reaches out to temporal regards and achievements." For Crummell, the twin missions of Christianity and civilization not only elevated the spiritual life of Africa but also raised the "mental, physical and governmental life" of many Africans on the continent.[62]

In his second essay, "The Absolute Need of an Indigenous Missionary Agency for the Evangelization of Africa," Crummell directly endorsed a major plank of the Atlanta congress: the stimulation of indigenous control of the church in Africa. The piece reveals his long-standing support for the British civilizing mission, applauding how "the church and people of England have uplifted the peoples of India to a plane of elevation never known before in all their histories." Nevertheless, it goes on to argue that native converts are best suited to propagate the message to their fellow Africans. While Crummell's position did not rule out Euro-American direction of the Christian civilizing mission, it critiqued its results and endorsed native agency in its dissemination.[63]

Crummell, as evidenced by his testimony in Atlanta, had long focused on the ideological constructions of emigration as well as its practical application.[64] Moreover, like virtually all of the other reformers, he assessed the problem of race relations in the United States in ethical terms. His 1888 essay, "The Race Problem in America," cuts through the "answers" of racial extinction and "amalgamation" by stating that the race problem "is not a carnal question—a problem of breeds, or blood or lineage" and later "that nations are no longer governed by races, but by ideas." Rather, the race problem is a moral issue best "dealt with as an ethical matter by the laws of the Christian system." For Crummell, this ethos advanced a Christian platform that planted the "idea of human brotherhood" into the movements of nation-states toward democracy. His argument embodied a central aspect of Pan-African activism: "The democratic spirit I am speaking of is that which upholds the doctrine of human rights; which demands honor to all men; which recognizes manhood in all conditions; which uses the State as the means and agency for the unlimited progress of humanity."[65]

Crummell asserted that, in the United States the "crucial test is the civil and political rights of the black man" and declared that "this country should be agitated and even convulsed till the battle of liberty is won, and every man in the land is guaranteed fully every civil and political rights and prerogative."[66] His position demonstrates how reformers of African descent used the readily available discourse of civil and political rights to inform their post-emancipated protest. Yet there were limits and exclusions built into his ideology. As the previous quotation demonstrates, Crummell, like Delany, consistently linked constructions of manliness to claims on rights. This emphasis constrained the role of female reformers; but as the 1893 World's Congress of Representative Women at Chicago had proved, it did not prevent female activism. While Crummell pressed for civil and political rights, he was more circumspect about the issue of social inequality that had excluded people of African descent from the official halls of the Chicago and Atlanta expositions. Despite his arguments in favor of human brotherhood, he dismissed the need for "amity" and social relations between African Americans and wider society. For him, the realization of civil and political rights was the primary objective, and time spent on developing social contacts was "ignoble," especially in places where a "wide divergence" of races existed. Crummell's arguments for the retention of unique traditions within communities, together with common civil and political rights, implied some level of cultural pluralism. However, this view also endorsed separatism, which, in the context of the 1890s, often worked as the primary mechanism for the denial of commonly shared rights. Washington's Atlanta Compromise was separatist—"in all things social we can be as separate as the fingers"—and acquiesced to the demands of white society for accommodation in terms of social equality. This position unduly compromised Crummell's urgency with regard to the realization of civil and political rights. While he retained his belief that "whining and crying," for social relations missed the larger point, after Atlanta he became a vocal critic of Washington and his ideology.

Despite his disagreements with Washington, Crummell recognized his stature as a reformer and invited him to the initial convening of the ANA in 1897. Washington declined the invitation. While his lack of attendance could have stemmed from a number of causes, including impracticality, his absence reflected a growing dissatisfaction with Washington's ideology. The Pan-Africanist Crummell never denounced manual training, economic strength, or material advancement, but he steadfastly denied that intellectual pursuits should be deadened in any strategy of material progress. While he advanced separatist ideologies, he never endorsed a separatism that placed people of African descent in servile positions of labor. This servility compromised his concept of unique race destiny by minimizing an ideological, spiritual, and educational engagement with the world. Crummell argued that intellectual uplift, not concentration on material pursuits, was of vital importance to people of African descent. Further, he advocated the leadership of the "talented tenth" to consistently document the contributions of peoples of African descent to "civilization" in order to provide a model for progress. Certainly, his uplift prescriptions had deeply providential and elitist overtones that mediated his calls for immediate political rights and social equality. Yet his activism fundamentally advanced the position that people of African descent were thinking, subjective agents, a position that contrasted starkly with Washington's materialist strategies. In the wake of Douglass's death in early 1895, that year's Atlanta Cotton States and International Exposition marked an important moment in Pan-African thought. Exposition participants continued to consider Africa and the international standard of civilization, and the much-publicized Atlanta Compromise invigorated alternative platforms such as Crummell's and the ANA's. These counternarratives helped resuscitate the struggle for the post-emancipation crowning of abolitionism that was slipping away during the 1890s as conditions worsened and influential abolitionists faded.

Crummell died in 1898, having influenced a cadre of intellectuals who bridged the gap between the dying abolitionists and a new generation of post-emancipated activists, including W. E. B. Du Bois, Anna J. Cooper, and John E. Bruce. Both Du Bois and Bruce were members of the ANA, and Cooper was one of the few women to deliver a paper before members of that organization. She was present at the International Women's Conference in Chicago and was a highly visible reformer striving for both racial and gender equality. Du Bois was perhaps the most famous reformer of African descent in the twentieth century, and his 1897 article, "The Conservation of Races," delivered at the ANA is a summative statement on the status of Pan-African reform at the turn of the century.[67] Bruce, while not in attendance at either the Chicago or Atlanta congresses, was a prolific journalist committed to reform and rights for people of African descent. Both his commentary and his archive (held at the Schomburg Center for Research in Black Culture) describe a vibrant community of Pan-African activists.

During the Atlanta exposition, Du Bois was teaching at Wilberforce University in Ohio and completing his doctoral requirements at Harvard. (Eventually he earned the first PhD granted to an African American by the university.) His dissertation became *The Suppression of the African Slave Trade*, published in 1896. Meanwhile, Crummell was growing more dissatisfied with the material focus of Booker T. Washington. When he created the ANA, he included Du Bois on his list of invitees for membership.[68]

That same year, Frederick L. Hoffman, a statistician and an executive with the Prudential Life Insurance Company, published his article "The Race Traits and Tendencies of the American Negro."[69] The piece argued that African Americans were biologically inferior, which led to serious health conditions and social problems. Hoffman's immediate goal was to provide evidence for denying insurance coverage to African Americans, but his piece, rife with the language of science and published by the respected American Economic Association, became one of the most influential racist works of the late nineteenth century.[70] While most of the contemporary academic community accepted Hoffman's findings, African Americans severely criticized the tract . Du Bois, by this time a respected social scientist, published a negative review in a leading journal of the social sciences, and Kelly Miller, an original member of the ANA and a professor of math and sociology at Howard University, critiqued it in the first paper ever delivered before the ANA. Both reviews pointed out methodological and statistical flaws in Hoffman's work, and Du Bois and Miller continued to invalidate the presuppositions of biological essentialism informing sociological scholarship—most notably in Du Bois's 1899 *The Philadelphia Negro: A Social Study.*

Du Bois's "The Conservation of Races," delivered before the ANA immediately after Miller's critique of Hoffman, flipped Hoffman's script, arguing that African American social problems were not the function of biology but the result of the sociohistorical effects of slavery. Beyond reflecting the references to the dislocations of slavery echoed at the Chicago and Atlanta congresses, the essay elucidates the contemporaneous state of Pan-African protest after the publicizing of the Atlanta Compromise. In line with the emphasis on Pan-African awareness demonstrated at both congresses, it explicitly calls for the "race ideal" to rise in both "America and Africa," suggesting a path of race destiny that emphasized unique, group-wide contributions and development. Prefiguring his later, more overt discussions of the global color line, Du Bois opened the essay by denouncing what he saw as the disingenuous adoption of the abolitionist platform of "human brotherhood." He argued that the belief that "of one blood God created all nations" not only reduced the search for the history of African peoples but encouraged the false hope that the promises of human brotherhood were "already dawning to-morrow."[71] Contextualized against the construction of the white-dominated global color line, such a mantra, in his view, contributed to the inability of people of African descent to challenge prevailing perceptions of inferiority.

For Du Bois (and for many attendees at both of the Congresses on Africa), a distinct understanding of the "negro" as a race was central for unified "striving" and realizing the "ideals of life." Connection to Africa and an understanding of African history were central to this racial identity, but the recovery of "Pan-Negroism" did not necessitate emigration back to Africa. Instead, Du Bois argued for participation in the United States in ways that did not mandate "absorption" by or "servile imitation" of white society. He denounced the absorption logic embedded in ideas of race mixing as well as what Crummell and the ANA feared could result from Washingtonian accommodation: pandering and servile behaviors. Du Bois held that an institution such as the ANA could serve as "an intellectual clearinghouse," supporting the "positive advance" of racial destiny and providing "negative defense" against the proliferation of threats to its realization.[72]

In its reflections on the construction of the "race ideal," "The Conservation of Races" demonstrated the growing challenge to biological essentialism. The essay details what was, in the late nineteenth century, a standard account of "differentiated races" and argues that the "eight great races of to-day follow the cleavage of physical race distinctions." Yet it also argues that, over the course of human history, the proximity of human interactions reduced physical difference; the "ideal life" replaced "purity of blood" as the primary indicator of group belonging. As these connections "began to coalesce into nations," physical distinctions were incorporated into the "sociological and historical races of men." Given the power of biological essentialism in the late nineteenth century, Du Bois was not able to completely dismiss physical differences but claimed that they were transcended by "spiritual" and "psychical" differences that demarcated the "conscious striving together for the certain ideals of life."[73] Hence, the "race ideal" demanded an understanding of how the specific sociohistorical path of race empowered "striving" to contribute to modern civilization.[74] Du Bois's language and argumentation must be considered within the deeply racialized context of the late nineteenth century, and his appeal to unique racial identity reflected a common strategy for battling the prevailing construction of global whiteness. Of course, the reassertion of the "race ideal" in the context of the global color line takes race as the defining category and thus informs practices of exclusion.[75] However, Du Bois's denial of biological essentialism was a crucial step away from the harsher overtones of racial difference that denied progress and its fruits on the basis of skin color. In what is one of the earliest statements of a culturally pluralist position, he declared, "We must strive by race organization, by race solidarity, by race unity to the realization of that broader humanity which freely recognizes differences in men, but sternly deprecates inequality in their opportunities of development." Near the end of his essay, he suggested that the main work of the ANA should be to advocate for a "social equilibrium" that would "give due and just consideration to culture, ability, and moral worth, whether they be found under white or black skins."[76] Du Bois's essay is a powerful statement on how reformers of African descent were debunking the building blocks of racism based on biological essentialism.

Despite exposing the disingenuous effect of human brotherhood at the start of the piece, Du Bois came full circle near its end, exhorting that the activism must continue until "the ideal of human brotherhood has become a practical possibility." He invoked the figure of the famous abolitionist William Lloyd Garrison to urge, "I WILL NOT EQUIVOCATE, I WILL NOT RETREAT A SINGLE INCH, AND I WILL BE HEARD."[77]

"The Conservation of Races" explicitly calls for people of African descent to develop "race destiny" and a group identity. Yet Du Bois and the wider Pan-African reform movement always appealed to what they saw as the unadulterated meaning of the abolitionist ethos—human brotherhood—and injected a sense of immediacy to a protest denouncing that skin color alone could be the basis for the denial of rights and humanity.

Anna J. Cooper also argued against biological essentialism, notably in the short paper she presented at the ICW session at the Chicago Columbian Exposition in 1893. Cooper was an important intellectual, the author of an 1892 collection of essays titled *A Voice from the South*, and she too participated in the ANA. She also was in attendance at the first Pan-African Conference in London in 1900 and remained an active voice of reform for people of African descent throughout the late nineteenth century and beyond. Born in 1858, she lived an astonishing 105 years.[78]

Consideration of Cooper and other voices of women of African descent deepens an understanding of the gendered dynamics informing Pan-African protest. As I will discuss, the connection of manliness to experiential vitality and active political rights pervaded the discourse of late-nineteenth- and early-twentieth-century reform. This ideal suffused through post-emancipated reform, often resulting in pronouncements that linked the struggle for rights and equality to the achievement of commensurate levels of manliness.[79] As a result, pervasive emphasis on manliness largely constrained the civic contributions of women of African descent to the traditional roles of motherhood and the home. Although not detailed in the earlier analysis of the Congresses on Africa, the connection of manliness to Pan-African identities and prescriptions filtered through the gatherings, and intellectuals such as Delany and Crummell made significant contributions to the construction of post-emancipated masculinity.[80] They also crafted arguments that placed women in roles emphasizing the creation and maintenance of the virtuous home. However, they acknowledged the importance of women in their uplift strategies and did not dismiss them as unimportant. Indeed, representative women who exhibited progressive womanly virtues were often central to the uplift project itself.

Cooper admired both Delany and Crummell and agreed that women had unique capacities that were not shared by men. She argued, however, that women were not overshadowed by men, and they should not be constrained to remain at home. Rather, she believed that their efforts complemented the pursuit of manliness. Using language similar to that of the mainstream women's movement at the ICW in Chicago, she sought a "copartnership" with male figures of African descent in the struggle for racial equality and rights. Her important 1886 essay, "Womanhood: A Vital Element in the Regeneration of the Race," which became the first chapter in *A Voice from the South*, is in direct conversation with Delany and Crummell. Cooper did not agree with their view that men were the voice of African American women. Further, she did not accept the implication spinning from authoritative constructions of manliness that women were in a subservient role in reform activism. "Only the BLACK WOMAN," she argued, "can say when and where I enter, in the quiet, undisputed dignity of my womanhood, without violence and without suing or special patronage, then and there the whole *Negro race enters with me.*"[81] Furthermore, she believed that the absence of female voices rendered race pride incomplete and damaged the fortunes of reform and progress.

Crummell also influenced the work of John E. Bruce. Bruce's life (1856–1924) bridged the gap between abolitionism and post-emancipated reform, and his membership in the ANA, like Du Bois's, was connected to his long relationship with Crummell. However, Bruce was not a typical member of the group. He had little formal education, worked far from the circles of academia, wrote for popular audiences, and contributed no essays to the ANA. Under the journalistic pseudonym of "Bruce Grit," he was an influential newspaperman with a reputation as a hard-hitting advocate for people of African descent. Bruce was also at the center of a vibrant print culture that linked together a variety of reformers.[82] Born a slave, Bruce would end his life as the "grand old man" of Marcus Garvey's Back to Africa movement and, through his prolific writings and connections, was an important contributor to Pan-Africanism.[83]

By the mid-1890s, Bruce was not only writing about the domestic struggle for racial equality in the United States but was also extending his critique to the international world. His ongoing conversations with Crummell and others had shifted his thought toward the like conditions brought by modernity to people of African descent, especially those in the British Empire and the United States. Like Crummell, he looked to the idea of African unity as a source of empowerment. (The West African Mojola Agbebi signed his letters to Bruce with the epithet "Yours from Africa.") Even by 1891, Bruce had started to recognize the potential of African unity as captured in an oft-repeated expression at both the Chicago and Atlanta congresses: "Ethiopia shall stretch her hands unto God."[84]

World's fairs provided a window on modernity, globalization, and imperialism and consistently presented images of the ethnographic other in the 1890s. However, the international text of the standard of civilization also destabilized the fixities of the ethnographic other by offering progressive tests as a measure for the achievements of the civilized and their accompanying benefits. Many people of African descent understood their unique position in modernity and the importance of the post-emancipated struggle to make claims on modern rights. At the world's fairs at Chicago in 1893 and Atlanta in 1895, reformers of African descent were denied full inclusion in the celebration of modern progress. Washington's speech on separatist accommodation, itself a product of discussions about the world's fairs before the U.S. Congress, only reaffirmed the post-emancipated distance from the crowning of abolitionism. Yet despite the exclusionary hurdles, people of African descent articulated crucial aspects of a growing Pan-African critique at both expositions.[85]

CHAPTER 2

THE SUMMER OF 1900

The American Negro Exhibit and the Pan-African Conference

I n 1898, after what would be his last trip to England, Alexander Crummell noted in a letter to John Bruce that, during his time in London, he had spoken to "three law students (negroes)" about an "African organization." Enthusiastic about the meeting and wanting to put "his finger in that pie," Crummell told the students about the "movement" that he and Bruce had initiated.[1] While he did not identify the students in his letter, it is safe to assume he was speaking to Henry Sylvester Williams or other members of the small population of students from Africa and the West Indies who were studying in London in the 1890s. The organization he discussed with them was likely the African Association that Williams had founded in September 1897—the progenitor of the 1900 Pan-African Conference.[2] Crummell's reference to the movement that he and Bruce had founded was certainly the American Negro Academy, which subsequently issued a motion announcing the organization of the African Association. Bruce would later imply that articles written by his friend John Cromwell, also an ANA member, had influenced the formation of the association.[3] Clearly, ANA leaders were taking the opportunity to connect the Pan-African association to their reform organization in United States. Yet Crummell and Bruce were not simply self-aggrandizing; they had long stressed the international nature of reform and the importance of using Pan-African identity as a platform for protest.

The Congresses on Africa held during the 1890s, Crummell's and Bruce's work to connect the ANA to Williams's movement, and the prolific correspondence between Bruce and a host of people of African descent all demonstrate that an active Pan-African network was firmly in place by the turn of the twentieth century. Indeed, the summer of 1900 was a notable time of global Pan-African engagement. At the American Negro exhibit at the 1900 Exposition Universelle in Paris and at the contemporaneous Pan-African Conference in London, Pan-African activists staged an international challenge to the harsh dichotomy of the ethnographic other that was a staple of world's fairs. Unlike the situation in Chicago and Atlanta, where people of African descent had created counterpublic spheres that were not included in the official expositions, the American Negro exhibit was part of the official exhibits of progressivism in the Musée Social. In that same year, the Pan-African Conference was held as a stand-alone event in the heart of London. Together, the two intensified the Pan-African interrogation of the promise of progress embedded in the continuum of racial difference and implied by the standard of civilization, with the goal of broaching discussions of racial equality and political rights.

The American Negro Exhibit

The Exposition Universelle was a culminating turn-of-the-century expression of the modern world and was, at that time, the most popular world's fair ever held, attracting almost 50 million visitors. As with all world's fairs, imperialism was central to the showcasing of the modern experience, and the Exposition Universelle included exhibits from the colonial encounter, including those dedicated to the viewing of the ethnographic other.[4] However, the Paris event did more than uncritically celebrate Euro-American mastery of the modern world. Burgeoning late-nineteenth-century progressivism saw itself as providing solutions for social problems, and this was the first world's fair to have an entire building—the Musée Social—dedicated to transatlantic progressivism's response to the dislocations of modernity. Situated prominently in that building, Thomas Calloway's and W. E. B. Du Bois's American Negro exhibit challenged stark depictions of the ethnographic other.

The American Negro exhibit was only one aspect of U.S. participation at the Exposition Universelle. In this visible international venue on European soil, the United States formalized its imperial standing through its exhibits on Cuba and Hawaii in the Colonial Hall. The U.S. Department of War allocated $25,000 for the Cuba exhibit, and the government took a direct role in its preparation, sending Lieutenant Commander A. C. Baker to instruct the organizers, Gonzalo de Chuesada and Ricardo Diaz Albertini, about the nature of the exhibition. Ultimately the Cuba exhibit included information about primary instruction in arithmetic and grammar, study guides on U.S. history, a treatise on English pronunciation, and assorted essays by Cuban authors on the arts, medicine, and sociology. It also dedicated a substantial section to the progress of agriculture and the mineral and chemical industries on the island. For the Hawaii exhibit, the organizer W. G. Irwin, under the auspices of the territorial governor, Sanford B. Dole, concentrated on themes similar to Cuba's. Both exhibits represented the official stance of the United States and advertised the nation as a modern, progressive, imperial power.[5]

As the United States continued to claim status as an imperial power, it also participated in the exposition's Musée Social, where it and numerous European nations displayed a series of exhibits that demonstrated advances in the social economy.[6] The American Negro exhibit was one of the first that visitors would see as they entered the U.S. section, and it demonstrated its links to the ethos of social advancement by documenting African American post-emancipated progress. Europe had long been interested in the "Negro problem" in the United States; and as imperialism drew the world closer together, race relations was becoming a significant international question. As the Colonial Hall exhibits on Cuba and Hawaii trumpeted the nation's imperialism, the popular American Negro exhibit furthered American claims to progressive imperialism. The message was that successful handling of the Negro problem could stand as a model for positive international race relations.

The exhibit's organizer, Thomas J. Calloway, had been overwhelmed by images of lynching, which, he believed, made the "Old World" conceive of African American males as a "mass of rapists." Thus, he saw the

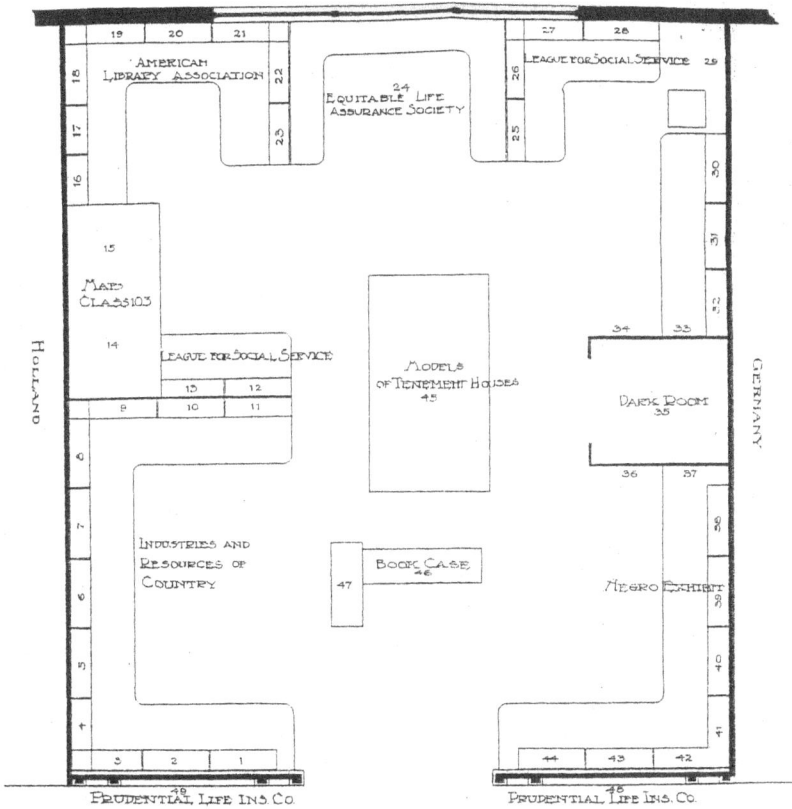

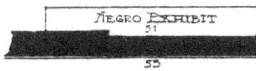

PARIS EXPOSITION OF 1900
PLAN OF INSTALLATION IN UNITED STATES SPACE
PALACE OF SOCIAL ECONOMY

Figure 2. Map of the American Negro exhibit, in *Report of the Commissioner-General for the United States to the International Universal Exposition* (Paris, 1900), 328.

exhibit as a chance to change Europeans' perceptions.[7] While his writings do not detail his reasoning, his dramatic description of his audience's preconceptions shows that he intended to follow the lead of an established counter-narrative, one that lambasted lynching apologists and their gendered arguments that condemned males of African descent as savage, sexual threats. Calloway shaped the exhibit into an international demonstration of post-emancipated progress in trade, industry, and education, and in that way he certainly helped the United States tout its approach to race relations as successful. However, the exhibit can also be read as an endorsement of African American progress *despite* the deep-seated racism that was perpetuating sensationalist assumptions around the world.[8] The American Negro exhibit offered the international audience an alternative understanding of race relations in the United States. It subpoenaed the scales of progress and complicated the generalized template of world's fairs that objectified ethnographic others, often in stark hues of savagery.

Du Bois's contributions to the exhibit extended those claims into the arena of subjectivity. His decision to incorporate images into the exhibit was one of the first instances of his articulation of the concept of "double consciousness."[9] For Du Bois, the ability to label the Negro as a problem not only lay at the heart of racism but also deeply affected the ability of the people who were thus objectified to realize their own subjectivity. He challenged such objectification by creating an exhibit that "encourage[d] viewers to participate in new ways of looking and seeing."[10]

Du Bois's engagement with sociological theory influenced this approach. He emphasized that sociology was not an abstract science but a practical tool to help advance society.[11] His portrayals of the statistical progress of African Americans were offered as proactive documents. Like the other pieces in the American Negro exhibit, they can be read as ways to obfuscate the gaze of difference based on savagery. Du Bois commented that, "above all," the exhibit was "made by themselves," meaning that people of African descent had shared in its creation. He noted that one of the its goals was to show the "history of the American Negro" in order to insert African Americans into modern notions of time and rescue them from the assumption that people of African descent could be lumped into a generalized narrative of the dark continent.[12]

The most striking aspect of the exhibit was its pictorial section. Here, dozens of photographic portraits defied the easy, consumptive gaze of the

Figure 3. Photograph of a young African American woman, in the American Negro Exhibit Collection, Library of Congress, Washington, DC. Courtesy of Library of Congress, Prints & Photographs Division, LC-USZ62–121109.

viewer and suggested that people of African descent had similar levels of conscious awareness. The exhibit offered a "multivalent aesthetic" presentation of African Americans that denied the standard portrayals of the savage ethnographic other and projected a "gnostic" sense of subjectivity that pressed for inclusion in modernity.[13] In other words, Du Bois's goal in this venue—and, more broadly, in his long career as a reformer—was to declare the equality of man and assert the awareness and agency of African people.

Figure 4. Photograph of a young African American man, in the American Negro Exhibit Collection, Library of Congress, Washington, DC. Courtesy of Library of Congress, Prints & Photographs Division, LC-USZ62–116617.

The Pan-African Conference

The momentum of the American Negro exhibit carried over to the London Pan-African Conference, which attracted many notable figures. Both Calloway and Du Bois played major roles, and Booker T. Washington attended an early preparatory meeting. (Bruce, though well aware of

the conference, was not present.) Other notable organizers and participants included Bishop Alexander Walters, Anna J. Cooper, and Frederic
J. Loudin from the United States; Mojola Agbebi from West Africa; John
Tengo Jabuvu and F. Z. S. Peregrino from South Africa; Benito Sylvain
from Haiti; and J. Robert Love from Jamaica. The conference report
lauded the event as the "first assembling of members of the African race
from all parts of the globe"; and while its stated subject was the controversial South African (Boer) War, the event focused on much more than
this conflict. Rather, it highlighted the international nature of its activism,
targeting practices in Africa, the Caribbean and the United States.[14]

As evidenced by Du Bois's address "To the Nations of the World"
(which was sanctioned by the conference and signed by its officers), participants linked race relations to the construction of the global color line.
Scholarship on international race relations has often overlooked the way
in which the Pan-African Conference elaborated correctives to battle the
color line. Some aspects of those strategies reflected paternalist strains
of imperial progressivism. For instance, the conference (perhaps because
of the South African War) supported the idea of a benign British civilization. "There are good friends in England yet, and though we wade
through the mire of the evil curses of civilisation in the Colonies," the official report stated, "their voices will blend with ours, that righteousness
and justice will be the ruling words of British civilisation." The conference proceedings also evoked religious arguments that had long characterized activism on behalf of African people, twice noting that reform
efforts were "for Christ and humanity"; and organizers deliberately
set the conference dates to follow on the heels of the World's Christian
Endeavor Conference. The report also included an official memorial to
the Reverend Bishop James Johnson of Lagos, recommending that every-
one follow his example and "glorify the cause of our common Master,
Jesus Christ." Organizers also thanked the Society of Friends for teaching
Africans "a true sense of civilisation calculated to bring them to Christ."[15]
As was the case with virtually all forms of activism concerning African
people, notions of civilization, religion, and the glory of God all informed
the 1900 Pan-African Conference.

Du Bois's "To the Nations of the World," however, argued that the
"cloak of Christian missionary enterprise" should no longer provide a

PROGRAMME OF SUBJECTS

·· FOR ··

The Pan-African Conference

TO· BE HELD ON THE

22ⁿᵈ, 23ʳᵈ, & 24th JULY, 1900,

··· AT ···

WESTMINSTER TOWN HALL,

LONDON, S.W.,

Under the Auspices of the AFRICAN ASSOCIATION.

Committee

REV. H. MASON JOSEPH, M.A.	REV. THOS. L. JOHNSON
T. BOWDEN GREEN, ESQ.	R. E. PHIPPS, ESQ.
REV. H. B. BROWN.	H. S. WILLIAMS, ESQ., *Hon. Sec.*

HECTOR MACPHERSON, ESQ., *Treasurer.*

On this occasion the famous JUBILEE SINGERS, under the Management of Mr. J. LOUDIN, hope to be present.

Figure 5. "Programme of Subjects: The Pan-African Conference," in *Programme of Subjects for the Pan-African Conference* (London, 1899), 1. Reproduced with the permission of Senate House Library, University of London.

cover for exploitation. Both he and the conference invoked the pantheon of abolitionists—William Wilberforce, Thomas Clarkson, William Lloyd Garrison, and Frederick Douglass—to assign a moral ethos that stressed protections before God and "crown abolitionism" with political rights.[16] While this call retained certain paternalist timeframes, it also reflected the emphasis of the American Negro exhibit, using African American progress to press for the consideration of rights of subject and citizen. Combined with the conference's denunciation of color as a distinction among men and thus as the basis of the global color line, the invocation of political rights marked a crucial moment in the evolution of Pan-African protest. The documentation of progress, the assertion of agency, and the call for political rights contrasted with the era's typical image of the ethnographic other. Hence, while Pan-Africanism at times invoked long-standing links to religion, looked to strategies of uplift, and supported so-called good imperialism, it also connected the struggle across boundaries and began to appeal to the rights-based script available in the secularizing modern moment of the late nineteenth and early twentieth centuries.

London was a vibrant site for international gatherings, and the first Pan-African Conference took advantage of its setting.[17] It was held at Westminster Town Hall, only months after the Greater Britain Exhibition was held at nearby Earl's Court. Given that exhibition's emphasis on the ethnographic other (in the Savage South Africa exhibit), the Pan-African Conference confirmed there was a wide diversity of thinking on race and empire at the turn of the century. It passed resolutions honoring several British reform groups that were central to the abolitionist cause—notably, the Aborigines' Protection Society, the British and Foreign Anti-Slavery Committee, and the Society of Friends—not only thanking them but also appealing for further assistance during this "acute period" of transition.[18]

Yet the conference was not content merely to subpoena its usual allies. "We have morality, religion, and perseverance on our balance sheet," the official report stated. Echoing the challenge of the American Negro exhibit, organizers reasoned that it was time to appeal to the "deep sense of justice of our age."[19] In its coverage of the conference, *Justice*, the official publication of the Social Democratic Federation, London's largest socialist body, asked, "Is it possible that the much-despised negro race may yet come to the front and lead in the march to a higher stage of human development?"[20]

Williams was certainly familiar with late-nineteenth-century notions of justice, and Du Bois's "To the Nations of the World" articulated them. His urgent appeal from the "metropolis of the modern world" challenged the global color line as a looming problem of the twentieth century. As I have discussed, conditions in the United States were often used in international discussions of race relations. The American Negro exhibit had demonstrated progress and displayed the subjectivity of African Americans. Now "To the Nations of the World" followed through on those implications of progress, arguing for full rights for African Americans based on their advancement from "slavery to manhood."[21]

Pan-Africanism, while certainly dedicating significant energy to conditions in the United States, extended its arguments beyond those borders. By 1898, the African Association had articulated a plank that recognized rights as a core objective, describing its intent "to protect the interests of all British subjects claiming African descent, wholly or in part, in British Colonies and other places, especially in Africa, by circulating accurate information on all subjects affecting their rights and privileges as subjects of the British Empire and by direct appeals to the Imperial and local governments."[22] Its descendent, the Pan-African Association, formed after the 1900 conference, used an overtly international approach in its objective to "secure the civil rights and political rights for Africans and their descendants throughout the world." Moreover, it endorsed an interventionist, practical approach to "secure effective legislation."[23]

Yet in "To the Nations of the World," Du Bois exhibited some hesitation about the immediacy of political rights. He qualified his appeal to Great Britain for responsible government in the "black colonies" with the phrase "as soon as practical." He commented that "the darker races" were not as advanced as the white ones. At the same time, however, he questioned biological essentialism and offered evidence of the changing attitudes about race. Restating aspects of his 1897 article "The Conservation of Races," he asked how differences based "chiefly in the colour of the skin and the texture of the hair" could provide the basis for denying participation in modern society. And he delivered a statement that had lasting significance in the search for racial equality: "Let not mere colour or race be a feature of distinction drawn between white and black men, regardless of their worth or ability."[24] While Du Bois and Pan-Africanism would claim race destiny as a source of identity and pride, the provocative "To the Nations of the World" exemplifies the loosening of racialized essentialism. Pan-Africanists struggled to convince the turn-of-the-century world that skin color was not the reason for either lack of progress or the realization of progress. Their movement, in its cultural sense of unity and identity and its overt calls for political rights and equality, was actively questioning the ideologies underwriting the global color line.

Transatlantic Reform

Changes affecting reformers on both sides of the Atlantic were also providing context for shifting discussions of race relations and rights.[25] The press of empire and the progressive impulse of reform affected Pan-African protest. This demonstrates that the continuum of thinking regarding post-emancipated people was far more complex than that contained in simplistic depictions of the ethnographic other. As the late nineteenth century brought a new sense of modernity, an emphasis on secular change affected reformer strategies. This emphasis, in connection to marginalized peoples, worked to augment earlier protest based primarily on religion and equality before God.

The challenges of the modern world appeared especially troubling to late-nineteenth and early-twentieth-century transatlantic reformers. In response, they adopted a perspective dedicated to progressive social politics that differed from the approaches of traditional Victorian reform.[26] Specifically, the continuing pressure of science and empiricism as prominent sources of authority challenged the belief that religious tradition, faith in the individual, and the workings of an abstract marketplace could provide the surest path to social reform. These reformers, in a fast-paced, secularizing world, endorsed an empirical worldview that cooled the acceptance of established truths, whether that be faith in God, belief in the sacrosanct individual, or trust in the invisible hand of laissez-faire. While certainly retaining significant attachment to religion, the individual, and the marketplace, the era's reformers recognized that modernity demanded new approaches. As such, they began to look for solutions to the perceived ills of modernity with a decidedly secular approach, and this "new liberalism" partially jettisoned the earlier reformer standbys.[27] Linked by transportation and communication advances (among them a burgeoning print culture), a broad network of people, ideas, practices, and sympathies adopted aspects of this progressive ethos in the turn-of-the-century Atlantic world.

While there were many layers to the transatlantic progressive bent, several provided important background for Pan-African activism. One of the most important was the endorsement of social holism. In response to the perceived failings of traditional laissez-faire individualism, transatlantic reformers began to emphasize that humans were, foremost, part of wider society and should be primarily committed to mutual responsibility. In a post-Darwinian world, these reformers invariably adopted a language of science, and advocates of social holism conceptualized society as an organism with a number of related parts integral to the whole. Those holding this position argued that only by recognizing the organic, connected nature of all in society could humans regain agency in a modern world that launched forces seemingly beyond individual control. This emphasis on social holism signaled, at the minimum, a partial paradigm shift that altered the path of transatlantic activism and had significant implications for reformer strategies.[28]

The movement away from the individual and competition toward approaches of social holism and cooperation also contributed to shifting conceptions of the nation-state. In contrast to classical liberal theory, the state was no longer the enemy of the individual but had evolved into a potentially benign force empowered to deal with the dislocations of a modern world and equipped to promote mutual responsibility and social cooperation.[29] The traditional fear of the state as a concentration of power detrimental to the individual did not disappear, but reformers weighed the potential benefits of statist intervention to social health. Laissez-faire, if ever completely realized historically, realigned to a question of appropriate levels of statist intervention relative to individual freedom. Of course, this debate would become a main topic across the North Atlantic in the twentieth century and, at the turn of the century, was already vigorously eliciting differing views on the appropriate levels of statist intervention and the state's responsibility to its citizens. In combination with the nation-state surge of imperialism, this deep questioning of the state's role in progressive politics reinforced the nation-state as a node of unity, authority, identity, and power in the flush of late-nineteenth-century modernity.[30]

A transatlantic ethical movement provided an intellectual rationale for the broader shift in reform.[31] Led by Felix Adler, Bernard Bosanquet, and Josiah Royce, the movement founded two new journals, the *International Journal of Ethics* and the *Ethical World*, which featured articles by notable reformers, including the political economist John A. Hobson, the Labour Party politician Ramsey MacDonald, the positivist Frederic Harrison, as well as Du Bois. In 1898, the *Ethical World* ran a piece titled "The Eclipse of Liberalism," which summed up the era's shift from the elevation of the individual to the authority of social interrelatedness:

> The reason why we should recognise our position as citizens is, in short, that it alone includes all the other interests and associations, and makes them possible. The association to which we belong as citizens is the only one to which we ascribe the right of compulsion, i.e. the only one which we accept as having natural authority—that is, again, as fully representing our own greater self, or our whole conception of a common good. All others are partial, and leave out the whole provinces of our lives, and whole masses of our fellow-countrymen; and the sign of this is that they are voluntary, except in as far as the State delegates authority to them. Thus it is the State, or civic community, in which alone society is focused as a whole, that represents the connection and adjustment, the criticism of all other interests and relationships so as to form parts, in a many-sided good life.[32]

The proponents of social holism did not feel that human society was subject to the same survival-of-the-fittest, "red in tooth and claw" evolutionary conditions as were other forms of animal life. Instead, they argued that human evolution was a progressively sophisticated demonstration of cooperation, not incessant competition. In the secular context of the era, social holism tied into the evolutionary language of science. Social holism, however, did not endorse competition-based mentalities that underscored displays of the ethnographic other, which often informed harsh, even violent, treatment of marginalized people.

The British positivist Frederic Harrison was a vocal critic of imperialism in the late nineteenth and early twentieth centuries.[33] Even before Hobson's articulation of the "taproot" critique of imperialism, positivists had denounced the jingoistic argument that empire was a safety valve for industrial problems at home. "[We] refuse to be lured from the pursuit of industrial changes at home by the delusive bait of more extended markets abroad," argued an 1894 article in the *Positivist Review*.[34] Similar to what Hobson would later contend, positivists argued that empire was exploitation by a relatively small class of profiteers who used the language of jingoism to dupe the working class into an ignorance of imperialism's damage to their fortunes. "While workmen show their aversion for Imperialism by simply ignoring it," the article asserted, "greedy speculators, restless soldiers, and jingo journalists have everything their own way. It is all very well for workmen to let the Empire alone; it will not let *them* alone."[35]

Positivists reserved particular reproach for popular writers such as Benjamin Kidd, who stressed racial competition in the endorsement of imperialism. To them, international platforms of group-wide racial competition threatened the social holists' emphasis that humanity was an organic whole composed, like many aspects of the natural world, of interrelated parts. The *Positivist Review* consistently berated Kidd and others for modifying Darwinism in ways that they believed were incomplete and disingenuous: "It is surely a very arbitrary sort of canon which recognizes that the struggle for existence is modified by the social spirit with the advantage to the family, to the tribe, to the nation, to the European race, but stops short of the conclusion that this modification will apply with similar advantage in the case of Humanity as a whole."[36]

Indeed, to the positivists, human agency depended on a *distancing* from Darwinian ideas of biological, racialized competition. Although they appreciated Darwin's contribution, which elevated empiricism and scientific inquiry, they also sought to rescue human agency from what they saw as crass applications of his theories. "The appearance in 1859 of the *Origin of Species* will remain an epoch in the history of science," declared the *Positivist Review* in August 1894. "But the theory will be supplemented by the incorporation of other factors. . . . Far greater caution will be used in the application of the Darwinian theory to the solution of human problems."[37] Instead of evolution through competition, cooperation among humans was the only path to progress, according to the positivists.

These thinkers questioned survival-of-the-fittest mentalities through their consistent exposure of imperial violence. In 1902, the *Positivist Review* condemned imperial "acts of aggression," from the transgressions against the Irish in the 1880s to the South African (Boer) War at the turn of the century.[38] Further, it recognized similarities between the American South and the British Empire and included lynching in its criticism of imperial transgressions: "The sufferings of the natives of India, the practical slavery of thousands in South Africa, the lynching in America, the horrors of the Congo, must make the most convinced optimist hesitate and qualify his statements."[39] Positivists' critiques challenged the jingoistic overtones of racialized Euro-American triumphalism that was vital to the construction of the global color line.

Beyond their consistent condemnation of imperial violence, positivists were also part of the changing landscape of race. One of their often-used phrases–"Unity, but not uniformity"–stressed an appreciation of not only social holism but also cultural relativism.[40] In 1895, the *Positivist Review* called for an anthropological understanding of other civilizations and argued that the future must offer a larger role to nonwhite divisions of humanity. By 1901 positivists were claiming that, although Europe and America had much to teach the world about progress, they could also learn much from places such as China and Japan.[41]

Boas and Biological Essentialism

"Unity, but not uniformity" coincided with a turn in anthropology that began to separate culture from biology, a shift best exemplified by the work and legacy of Franz Boas. Specifically, anthropology broke with the seemingly inescapable association between culture and the single track of evolution defined within the notion of civilization, which invariably dovetailed with claims of the biologically superior Anglo-Saxon "race."[42] The Boasian tradition influenced the transition away from acceptance of racialized hierarchies that informed monolithic standards of culture toward the use of the nonsingular term *cultures* that is at the heart of pluralism.

Thus, the turn of the century was, for mainstream reform, a transitional period in the dismantling of derogatory approaches to race. Like Du Bois's, Boas's separation of culture and biology evolved over time. In his 1894 article, "Human Faculty as Determined by Race," he was beginning to develop his ideas about culture, but he remained partially beholden to the traditional methodologies that measured difference vis-à-vis physical characteristics.[43] Yet Boas always denounced heavy-handed assertions of racial hierarchies, such as those foisted on the scaffolding of physical difference—for instance, in phenotypes displayed in exhibitions of the ethnographic other. As the historian Carl Degler points out, this shift gives credence to the idea of Boas as an antiracist pioneer. "Boas, almost single-handedly . . . developed the concept of culture," he argues, "which, like a powerful solvent, would in time expunge race from the literature of social science."[44] Boas and his influence demonstrate that alternative narratives were expanding the continuum of racial thought in the late nineteenth and early twentieth centuries.[45]

Boasian appreciation of environmental factors and historical conditions pushed a counter-narrative against prevailing schematics of racial superiority and inferiority based on essentialized biological difference. While biological rationales remained obdurate and arguments stressing cultural superiority were soon summoned to replace biological essentialism, the shift to environmental conditions was powerful. Indeed, by emphasizing the here-and-now secular environments of subject, citizen, and state, the clamor for rights based on the political standing of people of African descent as subjects and citizens of the British Empire and the United States continued to not only augment religiously grounded morality but also challenge color-based control of the measurements of progress.

Despite the fits and starts that accompanied promising changes in mainstream progressive reform for post-emancipated people, the implications of that reform, combined with the Boasian questioning of essentialized notions of racial superiority, were an important backdrop to the Pan-African protest challenging the global color line. The dislocations of modernity questioned traditional reformer certainties, and the resulting invigoration of transatlantic progressivism had obvious relevance for Pan-African protest. All people in the British Empire and the United States were subjects and citizens. Thus, because all parts of society were crucial to the health of the whole, Pan-African protest could press the obligations of fellow humans and the state to the state's subjects and citizens. The combination of a growing secularized society, the notion that political rights cohered around citizenship and the state, and the augmentation of traditional appeals to religion all invigorated the Pan-African search for post-emancipated equality. Moreover, the emphasis on the secular state and the civic community as engines of reform echoed a broader shift away from the primacy of religion.

Of course, the Boasian approach to culture and ideas of cultural pluralism were not the dominant narratives at the turn of the twentieth century, especially in relation to people of African descent. While the positivists demonstrated some appreciation for peoples and cultures other than the Anglo-Saxon, they were decidedly restrained when discussing the merits of people of African descent. Frederic Harrison echoed many in British society when he argued that African peoples were so far removed from the standard of civilization that the civilizing mission was hopeless; in his view, Great Britain and other European powers "should keep out of Africa altogether."[46] The *Positivist Review* argued that the British should pull up stakes in the West Indies and let the United States administer a separatist emigration scheme:

> If the United States would relieve us of our West Indian islands they would confer a great benefit upon the British taxpayer. We are now doling out large sums of money to these worse than worthless possessions without any prospect of return. [Auguste] Comte long ago suggested that the slave population in the United States should be emigrated there. The first step toward carrying out this proposal would be that the British flag should be withdrawn.[47]

Although they had certainly contributed to a new reformer ethos that brought hard questions to imperialism, their racial thinking in relation to people of African descent, at times, minimized calls for post-emancipated political rights or suggestions of racial equality. While these positivists and other reformers had jettisoned the appeal to God in favor of a secular spiritualism, a social gospel movement integrated enough secular ideology into its religious message to remain a leading force in turn-of-the century transatlantic reform. Indeed, with its clear connections to religious morality (akin to the moral ethos of abolitionism) and its emphasis on secular change, the movement may have been the best one prepared to promote change for people of African descent.[48]

The Social Gospel and Social Darwinism

The social gospel was represented in the U.S. section of the Musée Social in the displays of the League for Social Services, a branch of the American Institute of Social Services. Josiah Strong, the president of that institute and a leading architect of the social gospel movement, was in attendance at the 1900 Paris exposition; and provocatively, his league's display was located directly across from Du Bois's and Calloway's American Negro exhibit. Strong had extended the social gospel to the international realm, arguing in his influential 1886 text, *Our Country,* that Euro-American imperialism had provided an opportunity to Christianize the world.[49] By 1898, he was a luminary in social gospel circles. The success of the American Institute of Social Services, which was dedicated to a standard progressive cause (urban working-class reform), helped solidify his standing as a reformer and pursue his publishing career. He was a contributor to the monograph series that accompanied the U.S. exhibition in the Musée Social, and his lengthy essay, "Religious Movements for Social Betterment," considers the merit of ecumenical association, the importance of progressive reform, and the promise of the social uplift. Nonetheless, it quickly reverts to a familiar position on racial uplift, depicting "negroes and Indians" as "late slaves and savages" who would best be elevated through material improvement.[50]

The U.S. victory in the Spanish-American War empowered Strong's opportunism about the Anglo-Saxon imperial Christian mission, and in September 1900 (during the Paris exposition) he published *Expansion under New World Conditions,* an updated, more confident version of *Our Country.*[51] In it he argued that the volatile international situation was confirming the pressing need for Christian Anglo-Saxon imperial control and uplift. Considering this timeline and the depth of Strong's Anglo-Saxon commitment, one wonders how disorienting the American Negro exhibit might have been for him. The prominence and physical location of the exhibit alongside his own may have been troubling. Because much of the American Negro exhibit focused on African American people who were performing manual tasks—printing-press operation, agricultural labor, and other work that documented progress—he may have interpreted the exhibit as evidence of the genius of the Anglo-Saxon uplift model. He may have even sensed Du Bois's real challenge of demonstrating evidence of subjectivity. Yet Strong let the moment pass and neither lauded the exhibit as evidence of successful Anglo-Saxon uplift nor praised it as a statement of African American agency. In fact, he made no written comment on the American Negro exhibit in any of his later writings.

Still, over time, Strong backed away from his insistence that Anglo-Saxons should mold the world into their liking. In 1905, he lauded efforts that did not try to make Africans into Caucasians and supported independent "civilizations." Toning down the racialist overtones of his message, he maintained his belief that a common Christianity could join men into a harmonious brotherhood. Yet with the races unified through Christ, Strong and his institute found it easy to forego political integration and endorse separate institutions for people of African descent.[52] Ignoring interrogations such as the American Negro exhibit, he fell back onto a social gospel message of conservative, paternal Christianity in his discussions of race. While that gospel clamored for God's work on earth, it also asserted a platform of Anglo-Saxon triumphalism and Christianity that many Pan-African reformers saw as worn and untenable in a progressive new century. Often this triumphalism took on a social Darwinist tone: that is, it conceived of the international world as an evolutionary competition among different racial types that would require survival-of-the-fittest mentalities and behaviors.[53] In an 1898 speech, Great Britain's prime minister, Lord Salisbury, divided the people of the world into the "living and the dying," implying that the stronger races would push the weaker into extinction.[54] Others toned down the urgencies of racial extinction but still saw the world through a hard-edged lens of racial distinction.

In "Religious Movements for Social Betterment," Strong directly referred to the British author Benjamin Kidd, a popular proponent of Euro-American imperial control.[55] Kidd's works are representative of the social Darwinism adopted by many in the late nineteenth and early twentieth centuries. His 1894 work, *Social Evolution,* was popular in both Great Britain and the United States, where it was reprinted multiple times and translated into ten different languages.[56] In that work and a later book, *Control of the Tropics,* Kidd argued that Anglo-Saxons were best equipped to lead the international world. While he made obligatory reference to uplift and never called for overt violence in the survival-of-the-fittest struggle, he endorsed the strong hand of Anglo-Saxon rule over nonwhite people as the crucial component of the competitive struggle for world-wide progress. Kidd's popular tracts echoed the racialized essentialism portrayed in the ethnographic displays of world's fairs. In their prescriptions for international race relations, both Strong and Kidd reverted to conservative positions of Anglo-Saxon superiority and control. That they were luminaries in many circles is a reminder that the construction of the global color line was alive and well, despite the provocative challenges conveyed in Du Bois's American Negro exhibit and promising shifts in transatlantic reform.

Boasian anthropology and the Musée Social exhibitions illustrated the international possibilities of transatlantic reform. It is crucial to remember, however, that Euro-American views of the international world were intimately connected to imperialism. Thus, both Great Britain and the United States often perpetuated stark juxtapositions of racial difference to elevate their own triumphalism. Strong failed to acknowledge the American Negro exhibit's demands that viewers understand humanity beyond the lens of skin color. This startling oversight documents that, on one level, the Paris exposition was part of the triumphalist tradition of world's fairs. Yet the award-winning American Negro exhibit was integrated into the official exhibitions; and this success, alongside the contemporaneous Pan-African Conference, demonstrates that, by 1900, there was a visible stream of Pan-African protest.

CHAPTER 3

JOHN BRUCE'S
PAN-AFRICAN NETWORK
AND THE CONDEMNATION OF
WHITE CHRISTIANITY

O n March 4, 2017, Thabo Mbeki, a former president of South Africa, addressed an audience at Addis Ababa University in Ethiopia during a commemoration of the 121st anniversary of the Battle of Adwa.[1] In his speech, Mbeki argued that Emperor Melenik II's defeat of the invading Italian forces at Adwa in 1896 was an important moment of connection among African peoples, strengthening Pan-African beliefs in the symbolic promise of Ethiopia and inspiring the struggle against the global color line. Mbeki's speech emphasized that the notion of Ethiopia cannot be underestimated as a source of empowerment for peoples of African descent.

As I have discussed, the 1893 and 1895 Congresses on Africa endorsed the recovery of Ethiopia and motivated new understandings of Africa and its connection to the redemption project among people of African descent. Certainly, the victory at Adwa only enhanced the sense that, as noted in the 1900 Pan-African Conference report, "Ethiopia was awakening."[2] Emperor Melenik II himself had recognized the importance of the conference and sent his Haitian-borne confidant, Benito Sylvain, to be his official representative at the gathering.[3] Ethiopia as a symbolic framework segued with the broader cohesions of Pan-Africanism at the turn of the century. This activism offered critiques of imperialism and white-led Christianity and sought to recover historical agency for African peoples.

Critique of Imperial Practice

The Congresses on Africa illustrated how thoughts about the global color line had evolved since the Berlin and Brussels conferences. Likewise, the protests associated with the Aborigines' Protection Society (APS), one of Great Britain's most respected humanitarian organizations, also evolved into a more sustained critique of the civilizing mission in Africa. Shortly after the Berlin Conference of 1884–85, the APS joined the chorus of civilization in commending King Leopold of Belgium's intentions on the continent, even making him an honorary member of their society by the time the Brussels Anti-Slavery Conference convened in 1890.[4] Yet later in the 1890s, the APS's position on Leopold had changed completely. Led by Secretary H. R. Fox Bourne, the society emitted a mounting stream of protest against imperial practices. Making direct reference to the Berlin and Brussels conferences, it maintained that the standard of civilization was not a measuring stick to use in denying rights and autonomy to the "uncivilized" but a normative template for the conduct of the "civilized" powers. Shortly after the Berlin gathering, the APS interpreted the session's General Act as a step toward "strictly defined rules of international law" that would prevent "gunboats or armed expeditions" against native Africans.[5] The society also directly quoted the Act, which endorsed the commitment of nations involved in the imperial surge to "watch over the preservation of native tribes and to care for the improvement of their moral and material well-being."[6] Fox Bourne, in 1896, wrote to the prime minister, Lord Salisbury, arguing that King Leopold was in violation of the accords of Berlin and Brussels and was subject to the enforcement of the conferences' official mandates. "The time has surely arrived," he said, "when the Powers that agreed upon what was supposed to be a great and necessary philanthropic work, and sought in the Brussels General Act to improve upon their plan in the Berlin General Act, should insist on the terms of the agreement being carried out."[7] His protest against Leopold's rule in the Congo culminated in his 1903 work, *Civilisation in the Congo: A Story of International Wrong-doing.*[8]

Fox Bourne was not concerned simply with the actions of Belgium and other nation-states involved in imperial aggression. Indeed, he often integrated these protests into the APS's more traditional focus, the critique of British imperial practices, as his writings—*Matabeleland and the Chartered Company* (1897), "Black and White 'Rights' in Africa" (1898), and *Blacks and Whites in South Africa* (1900)—make clear.[9] In *Blacks and Whites in South Africa,* Fox Bourne hoped that a British victory in the South African (Boer) War would usher in improved conditions for all subjects under British rule. However, he argued that this amelioration for the "indigenous races" would not come automatically with the removal of Boer control but was dependent upon improved British policies in the region. In all of these works, he pressed for just treatment of natives by all imperial nation-states and introduced a language of civil and political rights for the native and "kindred communities" of fellow British subjects.[10]

Of course, Fox Bourne and the APS saw these improvements as a function of empire itself and thus were unequivocal supporters of the "civilizing" work of imperialism: "[Few] . . . will doubt that there would be immense advantage, if it could be honestly and truly done, in rescuing myriads of people scattered over vast portions of Africa from squalor and degradation, the base superstitions and cruel customs, the human sacrifices, the cannibalism, the slave-raiding and many other abominations that now affect them."[11] However, he also voiced his dissatisfaction with the empire's historic violations, made in the name of civilization, against African populations.[12] Fox Bourne accused the chartered companies of making a sham of bringing good government to native populations. Commenting on the actions of the British South Africa Company in Rhodesia, he lambasted its wanton self-interest and excoriated the white settlers who prodded the native rebellion of 1893 as a pretext for the appropriation of land, cattle, and labor. Further, he contended that white Rhodesians were consumed with self-interest. Instead of promoting good government and respect for native populations, they were proud that, in the wake of another "rebellion" in 1897, "at least eight thousand natives were killed off by Maxim guns, dynamite, destructions of grain causing widespread starvation, and other 'resources of civilisation.'"[13]

Fox Bourne understood that empire often equated to wanton land and resource grabbing, disregard for native labor and property, and unrestrained violence toward native populations. Yet he was not calling for the end of empire, and the APS had long supported uplift. In the conclusion of *Blacks and Whites in South Africa*, he wrote that he approved of the dismantling of indigenous land tenure (without "arbitrary and tyrannical interference"), supported a "moderate" hut tax, and accepted the concept of separate native reserves. Nonetheless, he argued that a "Magna Carta" for South African natives should recognize their "right to live their own lives in their own way" and that, when involved in European towns and settlements, they should have, "in every respect, rights and privileges equal to those accorded to white residents."[14] His reference to the Magna Carta highlighted his deep faith in the British tradition and reflected what he saw as best in British imperialism:

> [In Africa] Great Britain claims to have some authority, for the most part, doubtfully acquired and often unjustly exercised. Admitting that we can, and should, do much to extend to these fellow-creatures "the blessings of peace and civilization" and to this end there may be an advantage in inviting and enabling them to become fellow-subjects, is it not high time for us to fully and faithfully recognize, in theory as well as in practice, that they, as well as we, have absolutely the same rights?[15]

The timing of the issuance of *Blacks and Whites in South Africa* is also noteworthy. It was originally printed in January 1900 and reprinted in late May of the same year, shortly before the start of the first Pan-African Conference, which Fox Bourne attended. His involvement in reformer circles, together with and his consistent stream of printed material, demonstrate the vocal criticism of imperial practice emanating from the center of the British Empire at the turn of the century.

People of African descent also joined the protest against imperial practices in Africa—among them, George Washington Williams. A Union soldier in the Civil War, Williams wrote histories of African peoples, was ordained a Baptist pastor, and spent time as an attorney and a state congressman in Ohio. In 1890, he attended the Brussels Anti-Slavery Conference and soon thereafter went to the Belgian Congo to witness the civilizing project first hand. Almost immediately upon arrival, he penned "An Open Letter to His Serene Majesty Leopold II of the Independent

State of Congo." He opened the letter by noting how "inspired" he was by Leopold's commitment to run the Congo based on "the enduring foundation of *Truth, Liberty, Humanity and Justice.*" He went on, however, to lampoon Leopold's efforts to meet those mandates. Williams ridiculed the king for his part in the Congo's unequal treaties, its lack of medical care, the burning of towns, enslavement and forced labor, cruelty, murder, and lack of a justice system—problems that, according to the writer, were all smoothed over with "a few boxes of gin." To Williams, this rapacious example of the civilizing mission directly violated both the spirit and the language of the Berlin and Brussels conferences. He referred to article 36 of the General Act of the Conference of Berlin, which expressly calls for "modifications and ameliorations" to correct practices that violate the standard of civilization. Further, he appealed to "Philanthropists, Christians, Statesmen, and to the great mass of people everywhere, to call on the Governments of Europe to hasten the close of the tragedy your Majesty's unlimited Monarchy is enacting in the Congo."[16] Williams's denunciation of imperial practice, based on his firsthand knowledge of the situation, appealed to shared norms and nation-state power in its pressure for international change.

Theophilus E. S. Scholes also commented on imperialism and race relations.[17] Of African descent, Scholes was born in Jamaica and emigrated to Britain, where he trained as a Baptist missionary and successfully qualified and practiced as a medical doctor. His commitment to missionary work never wavered, and he traveled to Africa on many occasions, including to the Congo, where he, like Williams, wrote letters of protest to the leadership of his mission.[18] Scholes became an expert in international affairs, particularly those involving the British Empire. Like Josiah Strong, he recognized the geopolitical strength of the United States and wrote his 1899 work, *The British Empire and Alliances or Britain's Duty to Her Colonies and Subject Races*, partially to consider the possible advantages of international cooperation between the United States and Great Britain.[19]

According to Scholes, the issue of race relations was central to the consideration of cooperation. His chapter "The White and Dark Races" detailed the arguments of J. A. Froude and E. A. Freeman, both noted contributors to the construction of "global whiteness," who asserted that people of African descent were inherently inferior.[20] Touching directly on issues of citizenship, Scholes quoted Freeman: "You may give him citizenship by law; you can never make him the real equal, the real fellow of citizens of European descent. . . . The negro may be a man and a brother, in some secondary sense; he is not a man and a brother in the same full sense in which every Western Aryan is a man and a brother."[21] Scholes argued that this commentary was nothing less than a construction of "hatred amounting to absolute loathing."[22]

Scholes denounced Freeman's notion as "absurd" and commented that his absurdity was only equaled by the popularity that such notions enjoyed. As counter to this sentiment, he mentioned a host of other observers, including the English intellectual James Bryce, to document the progress of people of African descent and denounce the assertions of "inherent inferiority" as "clumsy and reckless."[23] Condemning the "preventing of equal rights" in the British Empire and "the ignoring of equal rights" in the United States, he connected the inequities of race hatred to an international denial of rights to peoples of African descent.[24] In line with the Congresses on Africa, he cast doubt on the convictions of white-led Christianity: "It must not be thought that *all* Christians, in both hemispheres, hold and practice the unchristian sentiment of race hatred and race distinctions, but we do wish to state our conviction that the solid mass of them do." Scholes also echoed a popular notion in the era's Pan-African circles: "the sparks which grew into the blaze of European progress and advancement were originally produced in Africa (Egypt)."[25]

While the protests of Fox Bourne, Williams, and Scholes were not the dominant narratives of imperial practice, they show that reformers in both the metropole and the colonies were critiquing such practices. Their criticism did not call for the end of imperialism or for a retreat from the standard of civilization. They did, however, denounce practices that violated expected standards of behavior and continued to consider race relations, counter arguments of biological essentialism, and suggest that the attainment of rights was still a powerful symbol for post-emancipated peoples.[26]

Assault on White Christianity

The report of the 1900 Pan-African Conference stated, "If, by reason of carelessness, prejudice, greed and injustice, the black world is to be exploited and ravished and degraded, the results must be deplorable, if not fatal, not simply to them, but to the high ideals of justice, freedom, and culture which a thousand years of Christian civilization have held before Europe." The report went on to not only invoke the Christian standard but also directly assert that white-led Christianity was often an apologist for imperial aggression: "Let not the cloak of Christian mission-ary enterprise be allowed in the future, as so often in the past, to hide the ruthless economic exploitation and political downfall of less developed nations, whose chief fault has been reliance on the plighted faith of the Christian church."[27]

The Pan-Africanist J. Robert Love was one of the few non-Americans to have his picture displayed as part of the American Negro exhibit.[28] Born in 1839 in Nassau, Bahamas, he lived in the United States from 1866 to 1881. In 1877, he was ordained as an Episcopalian minister and, in 1881, became the first person of African descent to receive a medical degree from the University of Buffalo. Love began his ministerial career in Haiti under the direction of Bishop James T. Holly. Later, he became embroiled in a controversy with Holly over the construction of a medical center, and he drew the ire of the country's president, Florville Hyppolite, who deported him in 1884.[29]

Love went to Kingston, Jamaica, where he became heavily involved in island politics. From 1894 to 1905, he published the *Jamaica Advocate*, which championed the rights of people of African descent, and he successfully lobbied for representation of people of African descent in the Jamaican parliament.[30] He also served on the Kingston city council and supported Henry Sylvester Williams's 1900 Pan-African Conference as well as Williams's 1901 visit to Jamaica.[31] Love was elected to the Jamaican legis-lative council in 1906 (only the third person of African descent to hold such a position), and he was an important mentor to a young Marcus Garvey. The historian Mary Lumsden describes Love as Jamaica's "outstanding black politician [and] possibly the most prominent politician of any racial origin between 1890 and 1914."[32]

Love was a long-time correspondent and friend of John Bruce. His Pan-African dissatisfaction with white-led Christianity was common in their circle, and Bruce expressed frustration with it in his personal letters to Love and in his articles for the *Jamaica Advocate*. In March 1900 Bruce published "The White Man's Idea of Heaven" in the *Advocate*, a piece that mocked the "sacred song" voiced by people of African descent as they approached the gate of heaven:

> Give me Jesus, give me Jesus,
> You may have all this world;
> Give me Jesus[33]

This spiritual acquiescence, Bruce maintained, endorsed the transfer of discrimination to heaven and was analogous to the stripping of empowerment in the secular world. He argued that Christianity segregated Heaven to make it appealing and safe for whites: "Those on earth who contemplate visiting this Kingdom may now do so without the slightest fear of coming into contact with the blacks—this is white man's heaven."[34] Clearly his parody of blind faith, whether in Heaven or on Earth, was intended to disparage the schemes of white-led oppression.

Bruce used his questioning of religiosity as a scaffolding for his demands for secular rights. Like the Pan-African Conference's condemnation of imperial exploitation as a violation of Christian tenets, Bruce's invocation of God was intended to pressure the state to intervene in society to secure rights, especially as the U.S. government ignored the tightening of Jim Crow in the post-emancipated period. In "Blot on the Escutcheon," a vociferous piece condemning the failure of the United States to achieve equality with emancipation, Bruce brought the weight of religion full circle: "We invoke the gracious favor of almighty God to the end that Liberty, Justice, and toleration may become synonyms for unrestricted and unhampered citizenship."[35] His reform ideology, while clearly inspired by rational secularism, also incorporated Christian ethics, especially to lament setbacks in the world of political rights.

In even more direct terms than the Congresses on Africa did, Bruce lambasted white-led Christianity as part of the falsehood that supported white supremacy and the global color line. Through this denunciation, he described what he and his fellow Pan-Africanists understood to be the true meaning of religion. As a result, his call for political rights invoked tempered messages of religious assurance. Indeed, his appeals to religion ultimately incorporated what he saw as the true meaning of Christian egalitarianism into his protest, which was never intended to dislodge the secular immediacy of his cause.

Influenced by thinkers such as Love, Bruce was also a powerful critic of white Christianity, attacking white clergy in the United States for their silence about the denial of rights to African Americans. Regarding lynching, he argued that white society was barbaric and condemned the white church for not speaking out against acts of violence that "smeared the Caucasian" with the innocent blood of black men. Further, he connected the apathy of the white-led church toward African American suffering to the failings of the larger international civilizing mission. Bruce mocked the hypocrisy of a missionary going to Africa with a Bible and a bottle of rum to "conquer the world for Christ" while race relations in America were a "festering scab."[36] His and other voices in the Pan-African network vehemently argued that the white-led Christianizing mission was not a source of redemption or progress but a dangerous tool borne from racial discrimination and thus intimately involved with the construction of the global color line.

Bruce's discussions with other Pan-Africanist figures helped inform his views on white-led Christianity. John P. Jackson, the African editor of the *Lagos Weekly Record*, responded to Bruce's comments on the plight of African Americans, writing sympathetically: "The African is beginning to find out that the European or white man's Christianity is all a farce and tends to demoralize rather than improve the people."[37] Bruce's archive includes similar exchanges with many non-American people of color, especially in his deep dialogues with Edward Wilmot Blyden and Mojola Agbebi, both highly influential in the world of transatlantic ideas.[38] The three regularly corresponded and commented on one another's thought and work, and they often criticized white-led Christianity.

Blyden was influential among many Pan-Africanists. Born in the Danish colony of St. Thomas, Blyden migrated to Liberia in 1851, thanks to the sponsorship of the American Colonization Society. As a writer and an editor for the *Liberian Herald*, he soon gained considerable sway in Pan-African circles. Capitalizing on his newfound influence, he published *A Vindication of the Negro Race* in 1857, which articulated his refutation of commonly held perceptions of African inferiority, a major theme of his career. Blyden was appointed commissioner to Britain in 1861 and Liberian secretary of state in 1864. In these roles, he solicited funding from British and American philanthropists for the Liberian educational system and became a vocal supporter of African American emigration to Liberia. Due to his uncompromising support of the notion of the pure Negro, Blyden became politically embroiled with Liberians of mixed heritage and was forced to leave for Sierra Leone in 1871. There he supported British extension of its civilizing mission and clamored for the United States to create colonies in Africa.

Returning to Liberia in 1874, Blyden became ambassador to Britain and later the Liberian minister of the interior and secretary of education. In 1885, after a failed attempt to become president, he centered his activities in other parts of West Africa. Between 1896 and 1897 he was a British Native Affairs officer in Nigeria and was the director of Islamic education in Sierra Leone from 1901 to 1906. Blyden was a central figure in the development of a Pan-African identity in the late nineteenth and early twentieth centuries, and he constructed a complicated narrative that criticized white-led Christianity in Africa. In his 1887 work, *Christianity, Islam, and the Negro Race*, he argued that Islam, while ultimately inferior to Christianity, had many redeeming features and could be a helpful force in both the civilizing of the continent and the administration of colonial Africa.[39] Blyden remained a prolific intellectual, contributing to West African print culture and to periodicals in the United States and Great Britain until his death in 1912.[40]

Blyden's critique argued that Islam took a much more color-blind approach toward Africa than the Christian civilizing mission did. As early as 1875, he argued, "The Mohammedan Negro has felt nothing of the withering power of caste. There is nothing in his colour or his race to debar him from the highest privileges."[41] Blyden continued to express his belief that Islam accepted Africans without prejudice and, in 1902, wrote, "Mr. [James] Bryce, in his Romanes Lecture . . . confessed to the inability of Christianity on this subject as compared to Islam. 'Christianity . . . with its doctrine of brotherhood, does not create the sentiment of equality which Islam does.'"[42] Blyden called on race experts of the West such as Bryce as well as native African voices to express Islam's orientation. With direct reference to Quranic phrases such as *"Almuminuna Ikhwatun*—All believers are brethren," he argued that the religious situation in Africa needed to stress the brotherhood of man before God. To him, Islam practiced what Christianity only preached.[43]

Thus, for Blyden, Islam was a positive detour for the civilizing of the continent amid the failings of the Christianizing mission.[44] However, he was a dedicated Protestant who maintained that Christianity was the pinnacle of religion: "There is, we doubt not, one and only one Prophet for all times and for all nations—the immaculate Son of God; and the teachings which He inculcated contain the only principles that will regenerate humanity of all races, climes, and countries."[45] Blyden's indictment was saved for those who distorted the Christian message in Africa, and he saw the operation of Islam as much less offensive in the context of the continent. Yet, for him, Islam was only an interim solution that would help cleanse Africa of paganism to prepare for the realization of what he believed to be the true edicts of Christianity.[46]

Blyden not only criticized white Christianity in Africa for denying the inherent message of equality but also directly connected the usurpation of Christianity to the secular political realm. He held that white-led Christianity prevented African peoples from embracing the political virtue of the British system and kept them in a perpetual condition of dependency. As such, he attacked the connection between the uplift of political institutions and the uplift of the white Christianizing mission, applauding the attempts of the British government to distance itself from affiliation with Christianity in its administration of West Africa. Blyden reprinted Lord Salisbury's claim that the British government was working hard to convince "other nations that the missionary is not an instrument of the secular government."[47] He criticized the disingenuous nature of white-led Christianity and its connected failings, arguing that they compromised the benefits of political institutions. He denounced the missionary's usurpation of Christianity in Africa and offered a counter-narrative that, however steeped with confidences in the political systems of the British civilizing mission, helped move the conversation of civilization and progress away from its traditional overtures of religiosity to an investigation of the political realm.[48] Blyden's complicated embrace of Islam as transitory along with his emphasis on secular politics, along with the objections of Bruce and other Pan-Africanists to religious hypocrisy, shows that patience with white-led Christianity was clearly waning by the turn of the century. Moreover, many Pan-Africanists suggested that political action could be the primary solution.

Mojola Agbebi was also a prominent critic of white Christianity in the late nineteenth and early twentieth centuries.[49] Born David Brown Vincent to parents of Yoruba and Igbo ancestry (he assumed his African name in 1894), he was educated by the Church Missionary Society and had many connections in the religious and political worlds. Agbebi undertook missionary work with chiefs from many different African locales, consulted with British officials (including Frederick Lugard), knew the British explorer Mary Kingsley, and began corresponding with Bruce by at least 1898.[50] He received honorary degrees from universities in Liberia and the United States, wrote fifteen published works, and, by the turn of the century, was the president of the Baptist Union of West Africa, which stretched from Sierra Leone to the Congo.

Agbebi argued that the tenets of Christianity demonstrated the equality of Africans and contended that Christian belief in the inclusive brotherhood of humanity was not only the ultimate blow to inequality but also was a crucial step toward the realization of the destiny of African peoples. In a passage written shortly after the Berlin Conference, he juxtaposed the praiseworthy white missionary against the exploitation of European traders: "Missionaries, and Missionaries alone, are the real pioneers of African civilization. It was commercial Europe that invented slave labour and discovered victims of slavery, but it was the evangelical that promulgated the edict of universal emancipation. . . . Whatever these pioneers of civilization are, whether they are Belgians, Frenchmen, Germans, Portuguese, English or American, tell them we shall ever hail them with delight, and God shall bless them."[51] Like Bruce, however, Agbebi began to argue that white-controlled religion was part of the deception informing white supremacy, and he became an increasingly vocal critic of what he viewed as the usurpation of Christianity by the economic and material interests of colonialism. From this belief, he created a powerful reform impulse that called for African reappropriation of Christianity.

In 1902, Agbebi delivered the inaugural sermon at the first anniversary of the African Church in Lagos, Nigeria.[52] The *Sierra Leone Weekly News* published the lecture as a pamphlet, and it was circulated in West Africa, Great Britain, and the United States. Blyden read the piece with "surprise and delight," while Bruce thanked Agbebi for his "great sermon" and asked for a full copy and a photograph of the author to be published in the United

States.[53] Agbebi's sermon is an example of the growing criticism of western Christianity emanating from Africa and, in his case, was an expression that arose from years of experience with Christianity in an imperial setting.[54]

In his critique, Agbebi remained beholden to the emphasis on religion, and he made no distinction between the secular world of politics and economics and the spiritual world of Christianity. He delimited the power of faith in the everyday expression of agency and, unlike Bruce, did not temper the reliance on God with arguments that placed primary emphasis on secular political rights. He expressed a deep faith in God's plan, at times even stressing the limits of humankind's comprehension: "All nature is but unknown to us, All chance, direction which we cannot see, All discord, harmony, not understood, All partial evil, universal good."[55]

Despite his belief in God's will as unerring, Agbebi attacked what he saw as the clear failings of white Christianity. Agreeing with Blyden's assessment of Islam on the African continent, he commented, "Islam is the religion of Africa. Christianity lives here by sufferance."[56] Europeans' distortion of Christian doctrine, he argued, was responsible for the success of Islam in Africa. Both Blyden and Agbebi were profoundly disappointed with the path of Christianity on the continent, as the following comment by Agbebi makes clear:

Christianity has been derided by some of its European friends as a bloody faith, the doctrine of shambles and the executioner's creed. European Christianity is a dangerous thing. What do you think of a religion which holds a bottle of gin in one hand and a Common Prayer Book in the other? Which carries a glass of rum as a vade-mecum to the "Holy" hymn book? A religion which points with one hand to the skies, bidding you "lay up your treasures in heaven," and, while you are looking up grasps all your worldly goods with the other hand, seizes your ancestral lands, labels your forests, and places your patrimony under inexplicable legislation? . . . O! Christianity, what enormities are committed in thy name.[57]

Agbebi contributed to the Pan-African claim that Euro-Americans distorted religion, and he attempted to Africanize Christianity into a religion that could evoke the true merits of the faith.[58]

The criticism of white Christianity was part of a concerted effort by people of African descent to take charge of the missionary experience in Africa. Although Africa had long been the focus of European missionary work, the participation of people of African descent in the work had dissipated by the late nineteenth century.[59] Southern Africa was a particularly intense region for missionary work, with more than two dozen active societies. By the mid-1880s, African converts in the region were rejecting European tutelage and forming their own churches, including Mangena Mokone's invocation of the significance of Psalm 68 in the 1892 establishment of an Ethiopian church.[60] Mokone's Ethiopian movement gathered converts across southern Africa and unfolded alongside the concerted push of African American leadership to take over the missionary project to Africa, made clear at the 1895 Congress on Africa.[61] The AME church took the lead in southern Africa, and its efforts led to direct interactions between Bishop Henry McNeal Turner and Mokone, ultimately resulting in the amalgamation of his Ethiopian movement with the AME in 1896.[62]

This control over Christianity by people of African descent generated a storm of protest in imperialist settler societies, and Euro-American commentators denounced the dangers of Ethiopianism. The wide-ranging colonial South African Native Affairs Commission of 1903–5, which saw Ethiopianism and the AME-sponsored education of native Africans at places such as Wilberforce University in the United States as undesirable agitation, put forth a recommendation for state-sponsored native colleges.[63] Thus, control over Christianity by peoples of African descent directly resulted in the furthering of Ethiopia as a capacious term that had outstripped its biblical meaning; now it had become shorthand for white society's racialized fears. In his 2017 commemoration of the Ethiopian victory at Adwa, Mbeki made sure to note that, in 1906, John Dube, one of Bruce's correspondents and a future president of the South African Native National Congress (the forerunner of the African National Congress), was acknowledged by authorities as a "proud Ethiopian who ought to be watched."[64]

Pan-Africanists generally concentrated on white-led Christianity's effect on peoples of African descent in the Atlantic world. Bruce, however, extended his discussions of the civilizing mission to other parts of the globe, including China. In a letter to the Chinese diplomat Wu Tingfang, he lauded Wu's article "Christianity and the Chinese" for its "broad and catholic views" that, to Bruce, presented aspects of Confucianism as superior to white Christianity: "If as you say Confucianism is broad enough to permit all men to worship the efficient first cause whom we know and recognize as God . . . it has at least the merit of superiority in this circumstance over the narrow and bigoted thing denominated [as] Christianity and of which the Aryan race are the self-appointed custodians."[65] Amid the chaos of the Boxer Rebellion in the summer of 1900 (and shortly before the Pan-African Conference), Bruce published a front-page column in the *Colored American* titled "The Chinese Question." In it, he denounced Western aggression connected to the Boxer Rebellion and argued that the "spirit of narrowness and caste prejudice" contained in the Chinese Exclusion Act of 1882 was now "bearing fruit," as it had triggered the missionary effort to civilize the Chinese "heathens." He added that the Chinese had a "civilization which antedates, by thousands of years, the civilizations which are endeavoring to force themselves upon the people of that country." Connecting the issue to betrayal of Christian ethics in the United States, Bruce concluded, "There is vastly more consistency and urgency for a combined missionary effort to civilize and Christianize the barbarians in the Southern portion of the United States than there is to metamorphase [*sic*] the Chinese into Western Christian automatons."[66]

This Pan-African concern for people and areas outside the Atlantic world grew during the first decade of the twentieth century. In this regard, Wu Tingfang was a crucial contact for Bruce and others. The two continued to correspond, and the *Colored American* continued to refer to Wu's expertise. Wu also contributed articles to mainstream journals, including the *North American Review,* and maintained a working relationship with leading Ethical Society member Felix Adler. Adler would be a motive force behind the 1911 Universal Races Congress, where Wu gave an important address.

Recovery of Historical Agency

The struggle for control over Christianity was intimately connected to Pan-African opposition to white-controlled construction of the historical record of people of African descent. The visceral gazes displayed in the American Negro exhibit demanded that they be recognized as subjective actors with awareness of the past and as active participants in modernity—a stark contrast to the usual depictions of the ethnographic other and the stereotype of the dark continent without history. At the 1900 Pan-African Conference, Du Bois used his speech "To the Nations of the World" to argue that African peoples had a long history of civilization, reminding the audience that their current position as "least advanced" had not always been the case. Progress and history—despite, or because of, their close link to the construction of the modern Euro-American narrative—were contested terrains and had alternative discourses. Pan-Africanists often worked to rescue a past African history that was equal to or exceeded the modern standard of civilization. They also detailed the more recent achievements of people of African descent and continued to question the biological determinism of skin color. The 1900 conference explicitly called for the recovery of historical agency for people of African descent and asked institutions to support this endeavor: "it is our firm belief that we must employ our own talent and energy to (a) educate our young minds in the prolific possibilities of the race; (b) develop our own chroniclers; and (c) institute and support our own libraries and organizations."[67]

Bruce's archive documents how people of African descent were chronicling their history. For example, in correspondence about the Proclamation of Haitian Independence, Love described it as "an able literary and political document," and in 1893 he translated it into English and forwarded it to Bruce.[68] He believed it "would interest" Bruce and his audience and hoped he would publish it.[69] Bruce, for his part, agreed that it was an expression of political genius and wanted to disseminate its message of political empowerment to his readers.[70] Like Du Bois, these leading Pan-Africanists maintained that recovery of the historical record was a crucial component of subjectivity, self-awareness, and empowerment.

The Proclamation of Haitian Independence, written by Haitian revolutionary Jean-Jacques Dessalines in 1804, was eventually published in the September 1905 edition of the *Voice of the Negro*.[71] Love also contributed another piece to the issue: an article about the proclamation and Dessalines. Here, he directly confronted the way in which barbarity was often linked to the Haitian Revolution, which, he said, "Negrophobists" did in order to denounce Haiti and peoples of African descent. Love maintained that he did not endorse the abstract notion of violence and pre-ferred nonviolent approaches to bringing about change. Yet, in his view, the historical context of the struggle in Haiti made violence unavoidable. Not only did the urgencies of war force Dessalines to hang Frenchmen during the conflict, but the revolution's "harvest of whirlwind" was the result of centuries of oppression and tyranny.[72] By chronicling the condi-tions facing peoples of African descent, Love contextualized the revolu-tion's violence as a way to counter blanket denunciations of the conflict as evidence of inherent barbarity.

In Love's opinion, the pursuit of liberty linked the Haitian Revolution with the French and American revolutions, for the desire to achieve the "full rights" of citizenship underscored all three. Yet the Haitian Revolution was "pitched in a key higher" than the others. Sugar produc-tion in the French colony (then known as Saint-Domingue) required mas-sive amounts of slave labor, and the situation denied all rights to peoples of African descent and positioned them "in the lowest depths of social degradation." Thus, the Haitian Revolution involved a racial compo-nent not present in the American and French revolutions. For Love, it was a moment of "self-emancipation" without "parallel in the history in the ancient or modern world." Cutting through the paternalist language of preparedness, he concluded that the revolution and the proclamation were "perpetual testimony to [the peoples'] *constitutional* fitness for all the duties, requirements and responsibilities of human existence."[73]

Many of the era's Pan-African periodicals commonly chronicled impor-tant historical figures such as Dessalines. For instance, the *Voice of the Negro*, edited by John W. E. Bowen, the organizer of the 1895 Congress on Africa, opened its March 1907 issue with a full-page picture of Theophilus E. S. Scholes followed by Bruce's short biographical sketch of him.[74] Bruce detailed how Scholes's initial dedication to missionary work and the "Fatherhood of God" merged first with a more academic approach and then morphed into a more general message about the "Brotherhood of Man." Scholes, wrote Bruce, proved that "the Negro was born to scholar-ship." He suggested that Senator Henry Tillman (recall his derogatory commentary at the Atlanta Cotton States Exposition in 1895), should read Scholes's work because "it would very probably take some of the com-placent conceit out of his rantankerous [*sic*] hide."[75] Along with George

Washington Williams, Scholes, Bruce, and Love demonstrated the Pan-African commitment to rescuing the historical agency of people of African descent. Bruce was at the center of these efforts, founding the Alexander Crummell Historical Club in 1899 and, with his Puerto Rican–born friend Arthur Schomburg, forming the Negro Society for Historical Research in 1911.[76] Both Williams and Scholes contributed to the society, and Williams's two-volume *History of the Negro Race in America* was a staple of the early Schomburg collection.[77]

Clearly, growing critiques of imperialism, denunciations of white-led Christianity, and the recovery of the historical record of African people were staples in Pan-African thought. These concentrations challenged the biological essentialism that underwrote the global color line and pressed the normative standards of subject and citizen in both domestic and international contexts. The emphases on empire, religion, and history were long-term projects of Pan-African activism that gained significant momentum by the turn of the century. Likewise, the South African (Boer) War offered opportunities for Pan-African protest and seemed to hold the promise of immediate gains.

CHAPTER 4

MANLINESS, EMPIRE, AND LEGITIMATE VIOLENCE

The lynching of African American males haunted Thomas Calloway. As he wrote in an 1899 letter to Booker T. Washington, he believed that his "well selected and prepared" American Negro exhibit at the Exposition Universelle could help counter the consistent "slander" displayed in the narrative of lynching apologists.[1] In addition to the many graphs and charts documenting progress, the exhibit's pictorial section demonstrated that African American men were participating in a myriad of respectable pursuits, including education, the trades, and various business endeavors. These men were generally depicted in formal attire, and most of them were posed in ways that emulated the era's standards of manly deportment. For Calloway, demonstrating proper manliness could help discredit the stereotypes that informed the narratives of lynching and the ethnographic other. This emphasis on deportment and carriage was part of the "best foot forward tradition" that influenced Pan-African reformers at the turn of the twentieth century.[2]

John Bruce and his main journalistic platform, the *Colored American*, also adopted these standards of deportment. The *Colored American* usually featured a full-front-page picture of a leading male of African descent. Without exception, his appearance conformed to accepted standards of male bourgeois respectability: wearing a crisp coat and tie; his face clean-shaven or with a well-trimmed beard or mustache. In an echo of Du Bois's portrayal of gnostic awareness at the American Negro exhibit, the man's gaze in the journal photograph exhibited poise, confidence, and subjectivity. Nonetheless, manliness, always an important notion in transatlantic circles, was an especially charged issue for Pan-Africanism in the late nineteenth and early twentieth centuries.

Manliness, "Legitimate Violence," and War

In the transatlantic discourse of the era, manliness connoted a sense of experiential vigor that countered the perceived weakness of the cloistered Victorian gentleman. Whereas older ideas of manliness had stressed self-control and restraint, this new manliness emphasized vitality and action that often intersected with forms of violence intended to shake up the stultification of the overly internalized Victorian male. Late-nineteenth-century imperialism fed from these emphases. While the need to model proper self-restraint to the world's less-civilized peoples had long underscored the imperial mission, this experiential turn was infusing imperialism with a martial spirit that the strident tenets of social Darwinism only reinforced. Manliness and its manifestations, including violence, dovetailed with the prevailing Euro-American imperial ethos.[3] The notion was also linked to citizenship, especially in Euro-American republicanism, where male hegemony controlled access to the formal political sphere. Citizenship was now associated with political action. In virtually all reform movements, the action of protest entwined with the active sphere of citizenship as evidence of vitality and manliness. For Pan-Africanists, experiential manliness gave further urgency to their invigorated push for active citizenship.

Nonetheless, the idea of self-restraint never disappeared; there was always a line drawn between civilized and uncivilized actions. This demarcation was especially relevant for males of African descent, who were often represented as the savage ethnographic other. Lynching provides an example of this tension. Both those who performed the act and those who constructed the powerful apologetics for it argued that males of African descent were guilty of predatory sexual behavior toward white women. Because this so-called illegitimate violence was the most damning symptom of a savage character, many whites excused the violence of lynching. Yet lynching's extralegal nature threatened accepted forms of civilized violence, and the anti-lynching protests denounced the acts as uncivilized. Still, while anti-lynching protests were significant, the prevailing stereotype depicted the male of African descent as a wanton savage with the inherent tendency to commit uncivilized, illegitimate acts of violence. This asymmetry mercilessly constrained such men, especially in relation to active citizenship and political rights.

The participation of males of African descent in the state-sanctioned violence of war, however, offered a powerful demonstration of legitimate experiential manliness and appeared to be an especially promising avenue toward claiming the political rights of citizenship. Pan-Africanists recognized this promise, and the American Negro exhibit featured dozens of photographs of males of African descent in military uniform. The exhibit also included a mural dedicated to African Americans who had earned medals of honor in the Spanish-American War, which, as Du Bois noted, was "not the[ir] least interesting contribution to history."[4] Along with that conflict, the South African (Boer) War gave Pan-Africanists the opportunity to interrogate the language of freedom and rights embedded in the discourse of these military engagements and in the wider language of imperialism. Many hoped that the South African War would push Great Britain to fulfill the promise of its liberal tradition by ameliorating the conditions of African people, especially in the Cape Colony. Likewise, Bruce and others argued that the participation of African American males in the sanctioned violence of the Spanish-American War would show that they possessed the prerequisite levels of manliness that could translate to fuller rights of citizenship.

Even though material interests drove the aggressive international posturing that brought about these two wars, the Anglo-American language of freedom and political rights pervaded the discourse of both. Many Americans reasoned that the suffering and oppression inflicted on the Cuban people under Spain's antiquated colonial system validated the war as a continuation of the liberal revolution against authoritarian rule. Likewise, many people in Great Britain and the empire saw the denial of rights to *Uitlanders*—British immigrants living in the Boer-controlled Transvaal—as a violation of the liberal protection and enfranchisement of British subjects. Race relations intertwined with this discourse and was especially noticeable in the Cuban campaign, as the island's legacy of slavery and its population of millions of people of African descent segued into post-emancipated claims on equality in the United States. A subtext of the British approach to the South African War was the Boers' perceived ill-treatment of native Africans. In this narrative, not only would the British effort ensure the rights of the *uitlanders*, but the empire would also rescue native Africans from tyranny. The sinking of the battleship *Maine* on February 15, 1898, elicited a general upsurge of patriotism in the United States, but people of African descent remained conflicted about the Spanish-American War. Many supported a war with Spain to free fellow African peoples from the yoke of a repressive colonialism and to embolden claims for equality in the United States. Others, however, were suspicious that the United States' growing extra-continental imperialism was an extension of domestic white supremacy. Still others saw the war as an opportunity for soldiers of African descent to display their manliness and secure rights for their brethren.[5]

Initially, Bruce supported the Spanish-American War because he saw it as an opportunity to free people of African descent from oppression. He viewed the conflict as a testing ground for the use of legitimate violence to demonstrate proper manliness, which, in turn, could help realize the rights of citizenship in the United States. He believed that "the blot" (that is, the setbacks to the promise of the Fourteenth and Fifteenth amendments) stemmed from the fact that males of African descent were seen as inherently uncivilized, savage, and unprepared for citizenship. Despite his many criticisms of the American political climate, he believed in the larger promise of the United States as a liberator that could help people who were oppressed by illiberal forms of governance, as his poem "Cuba Libré" (published in the *Colored American*) makes clear:

> O bankrupt, proud and haughty Dons!
> Your hour of doom is near;
> And the oppressed of Cuba's isle
> As freemen then will shout
> The stars and stripes for them will be
> a sure and safe defense[6]

He and many others in his Pan-African network also linked Boer society in South Africa to retrograde practices and looked to the British Empire to deliver equality. In the July 1900 issue of "Bruce Grit's Melange," his regular column in the *Colored American*, he argued that Boer society was damaging the fortunes of native Africans. Emphasizing his dissatisfaction with white Christianity, he asserted that he had "no sympathy whatever with the Boers, believing as I have to, that they are a set of psalm singing 'nigger' baiting hypocrites."[7] Bruce referred to an array of non-American sources, quoting James Bryce's *Impressions of South Africa*, John Tengo Jabavu's Cape Colony newspaper *Imvo Zabantsundu* (Native Opinion), the *Lagos Weekly,* and the London-based *New Age*'s report on an interview by the Netherlands Women's League at The Hague regarding Boer treatment of natives. Like many Pan-Africanists, Bruce was both aware of and contributing to international forums in his censure of domestic conditions.

In the same issue, the *Colored American* ran an article reprinted from the African American–owned *Detroit Republican* that argued that a British victory in the South African War would "show that no nation can hope to systematically and persistently heap obloquy and injustice on subject peoples without some day, distant though it may be, having to pay the penalty for its misdeeds."[8] While this critique acknowledged the temporal distance of consistent international censure or penalty, it transmitted a sense of urgency borne from the claims of international civil society and intensified by warfare, and it applied that urgency to issues facing people of African descent. As Bruce argued, Great Britain should "rise up to the higher power of their mission" and "ensure for all men without any exception, equality of rights and equality of treatment."[9]

Participants at the Pan-African Conference also saw the South African War as an important moment for the pursuit of freedom and rights. The timing of the conference coincided with the British assault on the Boer republics in the summer of 1900, and one of the gathering's primary objectives was to call attention to the situation of native Africans in South Africa. Henry Sylvester Williams concurred with Lord Salisbury's 1899 statement blaming the war on the Boers' treatment of Africans and implied that a British victory would correct the inequity.[10] He also referred to legitimate violence when he documented the participation of African soldiers on behalf of the British Empire, arguing in a 1901 lecture that the "valor of our black soldiers" contributed to British successes in its West African colonies and territories.[11] Extending the argument to the South

African War, he argued that it was clear that African peoples were fighting for the British cause and that this effort, combined with the potential of the empire's civilizing influence, should secure improvements to racial conditions. His reasoning was the kind of merit-based demand for rights that coursed through the conference report, which even spoke directly to Queen Victoria about the need to correct the "evils" and foster "true civilization amongst your . . . native subjects."[12]

Many Pan-Africanists felt that the British Empire, despite its failings, had a powerful capacity to effect change in the international world. This worldview derived from a recognition of Great Britain's historical lead in abolitionism and the long-standing African American view of England as a more tolerant place than the United States was.[13] In an 1846 comment in the *Liberator* about his reception in England, Frederick Douglass wrote, "[I was] received as kindly as though my skin were white. . . . I breathe, and lo! the chattel becomes a man."[14] Here, again, Bruce's archive is instructive, as many in his circles endorsed not only the racial climate of England but also the British civilizing mission in the pursuit of equality. Further, as reflected in the gendered language of Douglass, Pan-Africanists consistently associated the civilizing process with manliness.

At the 1895 Congress on Africa, Alexander Crummell had argued that people of African descent should control the Christian civilizing mission, and he was a critic of imperial ventures driven by self-interest instead of intellectual and moral idealism. In an 1898 letter to Bruce, he denounced "the opportunists, spidery demagogues, both dead and living who, during the last 25 years have been riding on the back of Africa into 4th rate offices for self; and who have painted on the brazen foreheads 'statesman' while the devil has quietly plastered upon their backs—'shams.'"[15] Edward Blyden also believed that the civilizing mission in Africa should shift to African ownership. In his view, imperialism was most laudable if it incorporated a proper appreciation for African peoples, an approach that could help them retain and develop their own customs.[16] While both men criticized aspects of British imperialism, they believed in the potential of British-led interventionism to expand the rights of African natives. Blyden "accepted the efficiency of white colonization" and felt that the British were the best practitioners of empire, and Crummell always admired the empire's order and cultural ideals.[17]

Frederic Loudin, Samuel Coleridge-Taylor, and the Politics of Transfiguration

Frederick Loudin was the star basso in the original Fisk Jubilee Singers (1874–78), and he organized and performed in a variety of highly skilled, all-black Jubilee troupes during the late nineteenth century. In his travels, he toured the United States, Canada, England, Scotland, Ireland, Wales, Germany, Holland, Switzerland, South Africa, Australia, India, New Zealand, Hong Kong, and Japan.[18] Loudin recognized the modern dilemma of de jure rights and de facto racism and used popular culture to navigate the challenges that modernity posed to people of African descent.[19]

Spirituals dominated the Jubilee repertoire. They appealed to emotion and sentiment while emphasizing suffering and the promise of salvation. Even as they invoked biblical stories, they reflected an African hero tradition and followed African rhythms, patterns, and style.[20] In this sense, they were analogous to Mojola Agbebi's appropriation of Christianity for African peoples. Moreover, by comparing slavery to conditions of post-emancipated society, spirituals called on audiences to contemplate the continuing prejudice facing people of African descent and to recognize the hope embedded in freedom. As the Jubilee singer Theodore F. Seward noted, "The excellent rendering of the Jubilee Band is made more effective and the interest is intensified by the comparison of their former state of slavery and degradation with the present prospects and hopes of their race, which crowd upon every listener's mind during the singing of their songs."[21] While spirituals were not a direct call for immediate political rights, they were expressions of culturally rooted creativity. They gave performers a way to challenge the racist mockery of other popular forms of entertainment linked to people of African descent. In this way, they directly countered the displays of the ethnographic other available at world's fairs as well as those found in blackface minstrel shows.

Minstrelsy alleviated white society's anxiety about the threat of black people and allowed them to reaffirm racial boundaries. Through incessant mockery and ridicule, white producers and consumers of blackface "demonized and de-humanized" people of African descent, rendering them as characters who were outside the pale of white civilization.[22]

Minstrel shows were extremely popular during the era, not only in the United States but also in racially tense South Africa. Indeed, many white South Africans began to call their African laborers and servants "Jim" in direct reference to the Jim Crow stereotypes perpetuated by minstrel shows.[23]

In the face of such expressions, the Jubilee Singers gave people of African descent a sense of dignity and agency.[24] These performers were also vocal critics of racial inequality. According to the historian Andrew Ward, their singing tradition was not accommodationist but grounded in "militancy and fierce autonomy." This dissidence only increased as their worldwide fame grew. "In fact," writes Ward, "it emboldened them. With increasing vehemence and eloquence, they denounced racism wherever they encountered it." Loudin, in particular, "champion[ed] his people with a boldness and a sonorous eloquence worthy at times of Frederick Douglass."[25]

Members of the Virginia Jubilee Singers toured South Africa for almost five years during the 1890s and consistently challenged racialized norms in their daily behavior. When a white police officer suggested, in Zulu, that the singer Richard H. Collins was a native African and thus subject to a law that prohibited natives from frequenting bars, Collins refused to leave the establishment. "Who are you talking to?" he asked. "Talk English. I have as much right in the bar as you have." After the American consul in Durban intervened, all charges against Collins were dropped, and the *Times of Natal* expressed concerned about the "blunder" and its effect on diplomatic relations with the United States.[26]

Certainly, Henry Sylvester Williams felt that the Jubilee tradition was an important cultural aspect of Pan-African protest. As the program for the 1900 Pan-African Conference noted, "On this occasion the famous JUBILEE SINGERS, under the Management of Mr. J. [*sic*] LOUDIN, hope to be present."[27] For his part, Loudin praised England, recalling with fondness his first visit: "It seemed to me as if I had always been walking around blind before. We were astonished to find such freedom, such an entire absence of racial prejudice. . . . I gradually realized that I could do what anybody else could do, if I had the capacity enough; and I could go where I pleased and do what I pleased, without any prohibitions on the ground of my color."[28] He also commented on the connections between the United States and Great Britain. In a long letter written to Bruce in 1900, he noted that the work of Frederick Douglass and Ida B. Wells had helped many in England protest the treatment of African Americans in the United States: "This country had passed resolutions at large and influential meetings condemning lynching [and] the press has spoken out against it." Yet he argued that "white America" was assiduously working to diminish British concern for people of African descent in the United States: "in recent years . . . great efforts have been made to counteract that sentiment [anti-lynching], letters from Southerners and people from the north as well have frequently been published in various papers against us and to lead these people to believe they had not known the real facts in the case."[29]

Loudin, in the letter, used the example of the composer Samuel Coleridge-Taylor to compare the racial climate of the United States and England.[30] He denounced performances that denigrated people of African descent and lauded Taylor's success as evidence of England's tolerant racial attitude, especially in relation to the prejudice of "free" America:

> I need not tell you what Britain has been to us [the Jubilee Singers] and is the bare fact of the experience of Coleridge-Taylor the fact that there is a sentiment prevalent here to render such a thing possible says more than all I could write in months. Think of it, one of the most exclusive and aristocratic musical organizations in the world if not the most exclusive asking a Negro to write a work for it and then to conduct their performance of it in the finest and largest hall in Britain with an orchestra of over 150 pieces . . . and a singing of Negro music (not a Coon song) and that Negro conducting it. Think of that and then tell me if the President, members of Congress of the Supreme Court and all the legislatures would not resign if such a thing would occur in Free America.[31]

Both Loudin and Coleridge-Taylor participated in the Pan-African Conference and were officers of the Pan-African Association that spun from that gathering.

Coleridge-Taylor was born in London in 1875 to a native Sierra Leonean, and he later married an English woman. He attended the Royal College of Music and stormed onto the British classical music scene in the late nineteenth and early twentieth centuries. His 1897 *African Romances*, 1898 *African Suite*, and 1902 *Ethiopia Saluting the Colours* were infused with melodies and rhythms influenced by African culture. A traditional Jubilee standby, "Nobody Knows the Trouble I See," was the basis for the overture to his immensely popular *The Song of Hiawatha*.[32] Certainly, both Loudin's and Coleridge-Taylor's styles catered to aspects of prevailing Euro-American norms and were performed primarily for bourgeois audiences. Yet their music also reflected the experience of people of African descent, creating a voice for African peoples in modernity through music, association, and political organization.[33]

Like all of the Pan-Africanists I study in this book, Loudin and Coleridge-Taylor maintained cultural connections to Africa and established a shared sense of identity, and those actions informed their political sensibilities. They acted out Paul Gilroy's "politics of transfiguration" through their music while articulating a "politics of fulfilment" that pointed out the hypocrisy of liberal standards in their search for equality and political rights. In this way, turn-of-the-century Pan-Africanists "occupied" both spaces simultaneously and sought to connect them— undertaking what Gilroy calls "a provocative and even oppositional act of political insubordination."[34]

The South African (Boer) War and the Cape Liberal Tradition

Loudin saw the South African War as a charged political moment for Pan-African protest and connected it to race relations in the United States. The war stirred powerful reactions in England and was controversial in the United States, where many held pro-Boer sentiments.[35] In a letter to Bruce in April 1900, Loudin commented that people in England continually asked him about the conflict. He told them that Americans' sympathy for the Boers came from racial intolerance, which, to him, confirmed their continued refusal to support equality and rights. In his view, the United States "had turned her back" on African peoples after the Civil War, and sympathy with the Boer cause was a continuation of this betrayal.[36]

Nonetheless, Loudin also believed that the charged context of the war and its racialized commentary presented an important opportunity for protest on both sides of the Atlantic. This opportunity stemmed from what he saw as the positive British influence on worldwide race relations. Loudin argued that the British presence in South Africa prevented the Boers from enslaving native populations and that the long tradition of British dedication to antislavery and freedom in the face of this Boer oppression was responsible for the conflict. While "British rule in Southern Africa is not all that we want it to be," he thought it was "a thousand times better than the Boer administration." He continued, "Britain has her missionaries there and [is] doing something to uplift the race while the Boers with all this religious hypocracy [*sic*] don't believe we even have a soul to be saved and only look to repress and further degrade us." Loudin welcomed the promise of British civilization: "I have been under the British flag in nearly all the quarters of the globe and have never with the single exception of Canada—which draws its inspiration more from America than England—been denied any rights a white man enjoys."[37]

Loudin believed that the South African War provided a prime occasion for African Americans to show support for Great Britain. His position not only endorsed the widely held view that Great Britain was protecting native peoples from the degradation of the Boers but also implied that attention to the conflict could help contest the construction of the global color line. "I think we ought to speak out," he said; "there has been no time in our history when speaking out on this question will count for half so much as the present moment. No time when our words would have such weight for the good of our race in all parts of the world so far as Britain is concerned as just now. No time when we could make so many friends as now." He appealed to Bruce to engender support for the British cause and sealed his plea with this question: "But our time has come, now have we the *manliness* to prove it?"[38]

In South Africa, the belief that a British victory in the war held promise for native peoples was most apparent in the British Cape Colony. The Cape's liberalism originated in the British missionary tradition and was empowered by the work of broad array of British societies concerned about the welfare of native Africans, including the Aborigines' Protection Society. By the turn of the century, an economic platform and a language of political rights had developed around these attitudes. They were informed by a religious tradition, a commitment to modernizing capital exchange, and a belief in an evolutionary path to opportunity, including self-government.[39] Cape Colony franchise laws, in contrast to those in the British colonies of Natal and the Boer republics, extended the vote (with qualification) to African males; and as late as 1887, the native African vote was a significant force there.[40] Eventually, new voting requirements specified in the 1892 Franchise and Ballot Act and the 1894 Glen Grey Act whittled away at the native African franchise, significantly reducing political agency.[41] Still, the Cape Colony did offer the possibility for franchise, and many people saw the South African War as a chance to reinvigorate the struggle for full inclusionary citizenship, which would include improved conditions in the Cape and Natal colonies and the extension of rights in the Boer republics of the Orange Free State and the Transvaal.[42]

The Cape liberal tradition produced several reformers, including the journalists John Tengo Jabavu and F. Z. S. Peregrino. With the help of white liberals, Jabavu founded the South African newspaper *Imvo Zabantsundu* in 1884 and served as its editor. He may have been the most active African political voice in the Cape during the late nineteenth and early twentieth centuries. He worked with Henry Sylvester Williams, participated in the 1900 Pan-African Conference, and corresponded regularly with Bruce.[43]

Jabavu, like Crummell, praised Queen Victoria's 1897 diamond jubilee celebration in the Cape: "Natives who are so beholden to Her Majesty's beneficent rule might well take part in the excitement."[44] When the colony's supreme court overturned a lower-court ruling that had imprisoned the native Pondo chief Siocau, he declared, "Thanks a thousand times that the British Flag waves over us," and argued that "direct imperial control is the talisman engraved on the heart of every native in the land."[45] Yet in a letter to the secretary of the APS, he protested that "the rights of our people have not been safeguarded by Her Majesty's representative; they have been sacrificed to the tender mercies of a cruel and unreasoning majority of Dutch Boers, the eternal enemies of native political rights. . . . Can this be looked upon with indifference by Her Majesty's Government in this decade of reform, in this the end of the 19th century?"[46]

However, Jabavu's fealty to white patrons had, by the outset of the South African (Boer) War compromised his belief in the promise of imperial rule and his denunciation of Boer practices. Jabavu was indebted to moderate members of the Afrikaner Bond political party, which had helped sponsor many of his activities. Throughout the 1890s, the moderate wing of the Bond had balanced their assertion of Boer autonomy and objectives with British interests in the Cape. However, after the Jameson raid confirmed suspicions that British capital sought the mineral wealth of the Boer republics, the Bond became less cooperative and began to take a hard line against British objectives. These tensions contributed to the outbreak of the South African (Boer) War. Due to his loyalty to the Bond, Jabavu endorsed British reconciliation with the Boers during the war.[47] This position cost him significant support, and the Cape government retaliated by shutting down *Imvo* for more than a year during the height of the war. Jabavu responded to growing criticism from Cape liberal and native circles by arguing that harmony among the British, the Boers, and the Africans was the most efficient path toward an equitable society. This color-blind approach did not match the on-the-ground realities of South Africa, and others began to challenge Jabavu's leadership. For instance, Walter Rubusana, a correspondent and an agent for *Imvo*, started a rival paper, *Izwi Labantu* (the Voice of the People) in direct response to Jabavu's affiliation with the Afrikaner Bond. He became a serious rival to Jabavu and an important popular leader of native Cape politics.[48]

F. Z. S. Peregrino, who also corresponded with Bruce, agreed that Jabavu had chosen the wrong side in the South African War. Yet because he felt that Jabavu was a contributor to the voice of African peoples in the Cape, he supported the postwar removal of the ban on *Imvo*.[49] Born in Accra, Gold Coast, Peregrino had lived in both London and Buffalo, New York.[50] At the outbreak of the South African War, he saw an opportunity to improve conditions in southern Africa and left the United States for the Cape Colony. He arrived in Cape Town after a stopover in London, where he attended the Pan-African Conference. Soon after arriving in the Cape, he started his weekly periodical, the *South African Spectator*.[51] Despite many transgressions against the political rights of the colony's native Africans, the war was an opportunity to champion the perceived progressive racial policies of British rule. The *Spectator* became a prominent voice in this discourse.

Early in 1901, Peregrino reiterated his commitment to securing rights in post-emancipated societies. In his review of the objectives of the local Pan-African Society, he stated, "For the information of several correspondents who have written enquiring what are the aims and objects of the Society we append the following: To secure to Africans and their descendants throughout the world their civil and political rights; To ameliorate the condition of our oppressed brethren in the Continents of Africa, America, and other parts of the world, by promoting efforts to secure effective legislation; To encourage our people in educational, industrial, and commercial enterprises."[52] He felt that the United States was a crucial comparative case for race relations. In a column comparing the American Civil War to the South African War, he argued that the wars were similar because of the importance of their end result, which allowed people of African descent to "pass from the rod of oppression to the glorious heritage of free men."[53] Of course, Peregrino was also disturbed by the consistent violations of this heritage, and the *Spectator* paid particular attention to domestic conditions in the United States. Bruce was the paper's official U.S. correspondent, and the *Spectator* printed excerpts from African American periodicals and had a regular column titled "America" that commented on topics such as lynching, political rights, and church matters.[54]

Another regular column, called "Judge Lynch," listed all of the lynchings that occurred in America. Aware of the standard of civilization, Peregrino used the issue of lynching to criticize the U.S. denunciation of injustice in the world. In a feature titled "The Devil Convicting Sin," he noted that the United States had voiced its concern to European powers about the treatment of Jewish people in Romania. The "righteous horror" expressed by the United States at the persecution of Jews, he argued, was "well enough," but it was a "quixotic venture" considering that the government refused to intervene in the protection of its own citizens.[55] Prefacing Peregrino's commentary are side-by-side clips from other papers; the first details the U.S. appeal on behalf of the Romanian Jews, and the second describes the lynching of several black men that had occurred in the span of one week in Georgia, Virginia, and West Virginia. He criticized U.S. calls for international justice in the face of its refusal to intervene in the protection of its own citizens.

In a 1901 Peregrino ran a column in the *Spectator* that featured a letter from Bruce, who wrote, "It seems to us [in the United States] strange that there should be in any British Colony the occasion for a struggle such as the black people are now making for equality of rights and of opportunity."[56]

Clearly, like many of his Pan-African contacts, Bruce saw the British Empire as a powerful force for equity and justice, and his writing for the *Colored American* also reflected this position. In his commentary on the South African War, he held the Boers responsible for the transgressions against native peoples and saw the empire as the saving grace. In addition, Bruce's contributions to the *Colored American* documented the transatlantic nature and comparative tendency of Pan-African print culture. In one piece, for example, he reiterated the prevailing anti-Boer sentiment by referring to an editorial in the *Lagos Weekly* that itself had commented on a *Colored American* piece and an article from *Imvo Zabantsundu*. Further, Bruce, like Peregrino, conflated the Boers with white southerners in the United States: "these pious Bible reading and praying Dutchmen are as full of race prejudice and race hatred as our own Boers in the South." In the same article he wrote, "It is to be hoped that when the war is ended Great Britain will rise to an adequate conception of the higher purpose of her mission, and introduce in South Africa a system of government which will ensure for all men without any exception, equality of rights and equality of treatment."[57]

Peregrino also used the international standard of civilization to condemn actions in the Belgian Congo. He claimed that he had commented as early as 1878 that the native chiefs in the area would much prefer the British flag over those of other European powers. In 1902, he denounced the rule of King Leopold as one that had "pillaged and slaughtered [natives] in the thousands" and had violated the conditions of his supposed "philanthropic movement." Peregrino explicitly mentioned the proceedings at the Berlin Conference in his criticism. He noted that the Congo Free State was to be a "pro-Native power" and that all of the signatories at Berlin were committed to the protection of the natives. Now that these terms and conditions had been "systematically and unblushingly violated," he called on the international community to stop the abuses. Informed by the Pan-African editor of the London journal *West Africa* that the United States had become one of the first nations to recognize the Congo Free States, he called for international cooperation from Great Britain and the United States to "procure remedy for these wrongs" in the region.[58]

Peregrino saw this charged moment as an opportunity to battle for political and civil rights for African peoples, and his forays into the international world of Pan-Africanism were behind his move to the Cape Colony. After arrival, he founded the Colored People's Vigilante Society, which publicized transgressions against people of color in the Cape. The *Spectator* also published columns dedicated to the latest violations as well as articles that described abuses elsewhere. Peregrino drew on his Pan-African connections to construct this mix of local and international reporting, and he also relied on manliness to further his cause. For instance, he praised his cousin, Henry Plange, a native West African, for his achievements in the Gold Coast military. Plange had attained the highest post ever achieved by an African in the Huasa Force and was a representative to the African Association.[59] Peregrino also ran updates on the service of his son, L. G. H. Peregrino, who was involved in the U.S. Army's campaign in the Philippines.[60]

Peregrino felt that the British effort in the South African War was a form of legitimate violence that would benefit African peoples in the region. He saw participation in the war effort as a way to demonstrate manliness, which he hoped would segue into better conditions after victory; and he advocated a "best foot forward" approach to daily life in the Cape. In virtually every issue of the *Spectator*, he invoked powerful images of manliness to help sell his periodical: "Be a Man, buy, don't borrow the *Spectator*!" While this marketing strategy was certainly connected to his constant focus on financial gain, it was also part of a broader sensibility that emphasized the discipline of work, exchange, and integrity as opposed to vagrancy, alms, and dishonesty. Like many other reformers in England, the United States, South Africa, and the Caribbean, Peregrino connected manliness to not only the legitimate violence of the state-sanctioned military but also the quotidian values of uplift and progress.

Peregrino's commitment to traditional reform strategies was apparent in his involvement in a number of societies and committees. In addition to participating in the local Pan-African Society and the Colored People's Vigilante Society, he served as secretary of the postwar Colored Refugee Commission, which was set up to integrate native Africans back to society.[61] His protest also focused on animal rights.[62] Peregrino was not unusual in this; many Anglo-American reformers had a deep connection to animal rights. Indeed, by the early nineteenth century, protection of animals was part of the growing bundle of reform issues gathered beneath the abolitionist umbrella. Abolitionists often connected the protection of animals to the campaign against human bondage and pain. In fact, the abolitionist leader William Wilberforce had helped organize the Society for the Prevention of Cruelty to Animals in 1824.[63]

The implications of Darwin's evolutionary theory had radically shifted views on the relationship of people to animals, and the new notion of a common origin had created deep ethical concern for the protection of animals. By the 1870s, Victorian reformers often used the conditions facing animals as a gauge for the standard of civilization maintained by a society.[64] That shift also motivated a search for those uniquely human traits that could reestablish distance from animal life. One such measure was the capacity for self-restraint. Indeed, a definition of Victorian manliness was the ability to demonstrate command of animal instincts. The disavowal of acts of illegitimate violence, such as unrestrained sexual aggression, extralegal retribution, or the abuse of animals, also informed concepts of proper manliness. Transatlantic reformers' commitment to the protection of animals was always entwined with their pursuit of human rights and was linked to norms of proper civilized manliness.

Peregrino adopted these capacious meanings to inform his own protest. Almost immediately after arriving in the Cape, he started Friends of the Animal (FOA), a club for the *Spectator*'s young readers, and in the paper's recurring "Children's Corner" column he urged them to join. In his view, the Cape was rife with animal abuse, and he promoted general kindness to animals as a way to exemplify proper behavior. His depictions of illegitimate violence toward animals also allowed him to comment on the conditions facing the Cape's African peoples. In "The Burden of the Horse," a multipart story in the column, the narrator listens in on a conversation between horses who are lamenting the rough treatment they receive at the hands of their owners. In a telling reference, one horse comments, "Oh but there is a country where the horses are well-treated and men and women have banded together and their Society is known as the Society for the Prevention of Cruelty to Animals. They look after us and the brute that whips you is sent to prison."[65] The unnamed country is obviously England, and it is hard not to understand this commentary as a demonstration of Peregrino's hope that the empire would correct brutish behaviors and assuage the racial woes of Cape society.

Peregrino positioned violence at the center of his FOA discourse. He consistently detailed illegitimate violence and thereby created a template of civilized restraint for his youthful readership. All of his examples of animal mistreatment describe the perpetrators as "cowardly Big Brutes" or the like, and they are always male.[66] In this way, he constructed a code of conduct that endorsed a sense of manly virtue based on self-restraint and compassion. Although his FOA writings do not always attach the word *Boer* to the descriptions of the "brutes," they do consistently lambaste Boer society as "uncivilized." Likewise, in another recurring column, "Boer and Black," Peregrino, along with predicting a British victory in the war, made it clear that he believed that Boer men consistently violated the basic rights of fellow humans. Most of the entries in this column detail incidents in which Boers beat or murdered native Africans, and they describe Boer society's lack of concern for "Zwart dings" (black things).[67] In yet another column, "A Horrible List," Peregrino described the "treatment meted out by the unspeakable Boer to the black man" during the war.[68] His word choice—"murder," "shot dead," "brutal"—implies that Boer actions outstripped even the urgencies of war.

Female Protest and the Disappointment of War

The British suffragist Josephine Butler also argued that the empire was the best hope for people of African descent in South Africa. Her 1900 work, *Native Races and the War,* is a long review of the history of South Africa with a special concentration on the Cape Colony. It conflates a firm endorsement of British rule with the standard faith in the civilizing mission for natives in South Africa. Invoking the legacy of British abolitionism, Butler argued that it created a "straight line" to measure the "liberty of the natives" and that British rule was central to correcting the "deviation" in South Africa.[69] Siding with those who condemned Boer society, she quoted several native Africans, including King Khama of the Bechuanaland Protectorate, who both denounced Boer practices and proclaimed their fealty to the queen.[70]

According to the scholar Antoinette Burton, Butler's protest on behalf of native Africans was part of her press for equal rights for British women.[71] To Burton, the ability to understand the suffering of others was part of the construction of the empathetic subject that was central to liberal conceptions of political rights. Thus, Butler's sympathy for colonial peoples subject to oppression was implicitly connected to the protest for female citizenship in the metropole.

The war, however, quickly revealed brutality on both sides. Lord Kitchener's scorched earth policy of attacking the Boers' crops and homes displaced thousands of civilians who had no means of survival. The British massed these civilians into numerous concentration camps, and London-based reformer Emily Hobhouse's report on conditions in those camps elicited widespread condemnation. More than 20,000 women and children died in the camps and the conflict, a situation that deeply affected the Boer military and arguably led their leaders to negotiate for peace.[72] Hobhouse's reporting explicitly refers to the standard of civilization. In the introduction to her book *The Brunt of the War and Where It Fell*, she borrowed language directly from *The Manual of Military Law* issued by The Hague Conference of 1899, which denounced "gratuitous barbarities, and every description of cruelty and insult."[73] Although this passage applies specifically to behavior during the course of war, it nonetheless echoes an international critique of actions that fell outside accepted norms, which was also demonstrated by John Bruce's reference to the Netherlands Women's League interrogation of Boer practices.

Yet even as Hobhouse and other observers revealed the awful conditions in the camps filled with Boers, they failed to give equal attention to the roughly 115,000 native Africans who were either forcibly interned or sought refuge in squalid native concentration camps. According to the Native Refugee Department, the occupants were "generally contented," but the actual conditions were terrible, with little shelter, food, or medical care. Officially more than 14,000 people died in those camps, but historians estimate the number to be much higher. In the resettlement process that followed the war, the government focused on reintegrating displaced Boer peoples into the fabric of South African society but gave little attention to the thousands of native Africans released from the camps or displaced by the fighting.[74]

The South African War profoundly affected all peoples throughout the region.[75] While the British did eventually win the war, the peace settlement, known as the Treaty of Vereeniging, explicitly delayed the issue of political rights for nonwhites. Although it did extend a limited franchise in the Cape Colony based on wealth and education, it effectively prevented the majority of the nonwhite population from voting. Throughout the rest of the colonies, the franchise was vehemently denied. The treaty delayed any discussion of self-government, and the British Colonial High Commissioner undertook administration of the colonies. However, the momentum toward union and self-government within the empire gathered steam, largely due to the successful avoidance of any real form of majority rule. In 1908, the South African National Convention drew up a constitution and forwarded it to the British Parliament for approval. The proposed constitution allowed only white men to serve in the South African parliament and continued the individual franchise laws of each colony. (Again, only the Cape had any room for nonwhite franchise.) While some in Great Britain argued against restrictions on suffrage, Parliament approved the basic form of the constitution. Louis Botha, a leading Afrikaner general in the war, became prime minister; and after the union of South Africa in 1909, the now self-governing British dominion used its strong centralized state to continue white supremacy. In fact, it became more common to interpret references to the racial question as a query regarding the tension between British and Afrikaner whites.[76]

The Treaty of Vereeniging and the union of South Africa severely damaged Pan-Africanists' hope that a British victory in the South African War would usher in a new era of equality and rights for people of African descent. African Americans also began to doubt that the Spanish-American War would ameliorate the racial conditions in the United States. The *Colored American* ran multiple stories detailing the wartime contributions of African American males as well as pieces about their past military service. Yet as the war wound down (except for the continued conflict in the Philippines), many argued that their participation had made little tangible change in the racial climate. In fact, some felt that racial tension in America had increased during the war. The African American paper the *Richmond Planet* commented in July 1898, "It would seem that the war would tend to allay race prejudice and bring closer together the races in the South. It has had an opposite tendency for the number of lynchings has been steadily on the increase."[77]

The *Colored American* echoed this reaction in 1901 when it ran a full-page cover illustration titled "Uncle Sam look Behind You." The illustration includes a short passage by Albion Tourgee attesting to the blood shed by African American soldiers and reminding readers that "the Negro [is] first of all an American." The caption at the bottom asks, "The American negro . . . the most loyal and patriotic of citizens is being lynched, roasted, disenfranchised, and discriminated against in every way. Whither are we drifting?" Elsewhere in his quoted passage, Tourgee argued that African Americans had "sloughed off the African" and progressed to a position worthy of full citizenship. A second caption expresses dismay over the nation's interactions with (and possible incorporation of) "dark-skinned peoples, who do not understand the customs and religions of the United States."[78] These comments reveal the continuing prevalence of convoluted schematics of racial progress that were often burdened with paternalism and biological essentialism as well as oft-replicated arguments that denounced U.S. imperialism because of the possible inclusion of racialized others into the nation.[79] Nonetheless, it is clear that many were questioning if the manly demonstration of legitimate violence at the turn of the century could expand rights for people of African descent.

CHAPTER 5

LYNCHING, THE "NEGRO PROBLEM," AND FEMALE VOICES OF PROTEST

Women were contributing to the discourse of imperialism, rights, and the standard of civilization. In South Africa, for instance, F. Z. S. Peregrino's daughter, Florence, not only wrote for *Spectator* columns such as "The Children's Corner" but also was involved in many other aspects of the paper's operation. As I discussed in chapter 4, Emily Hobhouse and Josephine Butler had become important voices, and John Bruce and others recognized the importance of women to the Pan-African cause. Bruce corresponded regularly with Ida B. Wells and supported her anti-lynching tours of England. He used his primary mouthpiece, the *Colored American*, to publicize the activities of the National Association of Colored Women (founded in 1896) and share updates about leading African American feminists. The February 17, 1900, edition featured a front-page image of Mary Church Terrell, and its lead story focused on her contributions to the suffrage movement. According to the article, Terrell exemplified the way in which the suffragist had changed from a "mannishly attired, short-skirted, short-haired woman" who was "the butt of the satirist and the cartoonist" to a "cultured, womanly woman" who supported motherhood and the "home which she ennoble[d]."[1] While the *Colored American* supported her arguments for female suffrage and declared that her image was good for the larger struggle, its endorsement, like many documents in Bruce's Pan-African archive, reveals a patriarchal attitude that sought to keep discussions of rights for women within traditional bounds of republican motherhood.

These patriarchal overtones did not prevent African American women from contributing to reform. While many female intellectuals adopted respectable deportment, their voices were not confined to the realms of domesticity.[2] In venues such as the 1893 World's Congress of Representative Women in Chicago, they were sharing fundamental observations on important public issues central to Pan-Africanism, significantly bolstering the movement's stance on biological essentialism, race relations, and the pursuit of equality and rights. Further, they often embraced an internationalist perspective.[3]

Ida B. Wells and Catherine Impey

By the end of the nineteenth century, people of African descent who lived in the American South still maintained the de jure status of citizenship but had been marginalized in ways that reflected the situation in southern Africa and elsewhere in the British Empire. The region had become a case study on issues of race relations and post-emancipated rights amid expanding Euro-American imperialism. Usually bundled together as the "Negro problem," these issues were ubiquitous in transatlantic discourse; and by the 1890s, lynching in the South was a central topic in discussions of race relations. For many in white society, the Fourteenth and Fifteenth amendments had let loose a political, social, and cultural threat that was embodied in people of African descent. Lynching was one severe measure used to counter their possible intrusions into white society, and the number of males of African descent who were lynched rose dramatically in the post-Reconstruction years.[4] To lynching apologists, the act and the narrative surrounding it emphasized the inferiority of people of African descent. Ritually exorcising the black body from the psyche of the white community and confirming the belief that post-emancipated peoples were far away from the body politic and its conferring agency, lynching served as a dynamic symbol of exclusion.[5]

The ability to consign males of African descent to death struck at the core of subjectivity because it failed to recognize their individuality or selfhood. By acting out a performance ritual on the objectified black body, white society exploited the power of violence to affirm its own identity as the body politic.[6] This affirmation was a continuation of attempts by white individuals to designate people of African descent as objects that did not meet the standard of civilization and were thus outside the pale of citizenry.

Ida B. Wells began her lifelong crusade against lynching in 1892, after three African American males were lynched in Memphis, Tennessee. Through public speaking, newspaper articles, and three lengthy pamphlets—*Southern Horrors: Lynch Law in All Its Phases* (1892), *A Red Record: Tabulate Statistics and Alleged Causes of Lynching in the United States, 1892–1893–1894* (1895), and *Mob Rule in New Orleans: Robert Charles and His Fight to Death* (1900)—she mixed concrete detail with incisive analysis to challenge the constructions of race and gender that were used to support lynching. Unlike most of her contemporaries, Wells exposed lynching as a critical piece of the larger process that denied the power of citizenship to African Americans. She steadfastly argued that charges of rape against African American men were unfounded and that the miscegenation boundaries erected by white society were hypocritical shams in light of the years of sexual assault by white males upon black females. Combining an appeal to Christian duty, a secular critique of American civilization, and a message of political empowerment, Wells constructed a powerful anti-lynching counter-narrative in the 1890s and beyond.[7]

Discouraged by a weak response to her anti-lynching campaign in the United States, Wells decided to campaign in England: "The moral agencies at work in Great Britain did much for the final overthrow of chattel slavery. They can in like manner pray, write, preach, talk and act against . . . the hanging, shooting and burning of a powerless race. America cannot and will not ignore the voice of a nation that is her superior in civilization, which makes this demand in the name of justice and humanity."[8] Transatlantic Anglo-American affinities ran deep and American reformers such as Wells looked to the long tradition of British reform to help in the struggle for rights in the United States. Her successful tours of Great Britain in 1893 and 1894 uncovered a stream of protest that not only criticized lynching but also challenged the denial of citizenship in a post-emancipated imperial world.[9]

In England, Wells sought audiences with many influential British reformers, including those associated with the Aborigines' Protection Society. The society's mission was to protect the interests of native populations in the British Empire, and this agenda limited its commentary on the plight of people of African descent in the American South. Yet the APS could not countenance the violence of lynching, and its members met with Wells in the summer of 1894. In their discussions, Wells did not refute or even address the apologist argument that rape by African American men justified lynching. She noted only that "falsehoods were put about" and instead concentrated on the argument that all people deserved a fair trial. Before a proposed resolution was adopted, however, one male member of the APS argued that the laws in the South governing rape were weak and that this laxity demanded "self-protection." According to him, it was not fair to blame every "white man in America" for lynching. Another male member noted that "there was great fear on the part of the whites [in the South] that the negroes would become too strong and too numerous for them." Still, after airing these customary apologist arguments, both men agreed that they were no excuse for the "atrocities" discussed by Wells.[10] The fact that she chose not attack the apologetics of rape in front of the APS (or that the APS recorder chose not to acknowledge it in the report) shows that the apologist argument had great power. It also reveals the delicate path that Wells negotiated within the male-dominated British reform tradition. In the end, the organization's official resolution charged the United States with lawlessness and called for the right to protection under the law. In other words, while the APS criticized race relations in the United States on the grounds of protection and the enforcement of legal code, it stopped short of endorsing full participatory citizenship.

Wells's tours helped establish the British Anti-Lynching Committee, which met eleven times in 1894 and 1895, sent several letters to governors in southern states, and corresponded directly with newspaper editors in the United States. After 1895, the committee lost momentum, and its planned convention never took place. Nonetheless, it, along with the impact of Wells's tours and the coverage of British newspapers, provided an influential critique of American civilization that led to an upswing of both apologist and denunciatory commentary in the United States.[11]

The British activist Catherine Impey was another transatlantic voice of protest in the late nineteenth and early twentieth centuries.[12] Impey, who was a dedicated member of the Society of Friends, had ties to reform circles in England and the United States. She participated in the 1900 Pan-African Conference and was intimately involved with Wells's British tours. The scholar Marika Sherwood describes her as "remarkable," not least because she directly challenged the APS to take a more progressive course of action.[13]

Impey believed that "to deliberately choose a life of independence one has to carve out one's own path instead of following some beaten route."[14] She did indeed carve out her own path. In 1888, she founded the Society for the Recognition of the Universal Brotherhood of Man, which was "devoted to the interests of coloured races." Like most reformers in the late nineteenth century, she recognized the power of print, and she founded the monthly journal *Anti-Caste* in order to dismantle ideas of racial difference and demand the immediate recognition of all humans as equal under the aegis of God: "It is a solemn sublime fact—that Every man is by birth, by natural descent as it were, a child of God."[15] Commenting on an incident in which a young black man was turned away from a drawing class at the YMCA, she exclaimed, "It is not pretended that the rejected person is not a Christian. He is not only a church member but a member of the Young Men's Christian Association! If good enough to enter the kingdom, why should he not be good enough to enter the auspices of an association of Christians? No! It is not a question of character or religion, but really the old question of race and color."[16] Impey extended the implications of the abolitionist slogan "Am I not a Man and a Brother?" and applied its religious mandate to a platform that denied racial difference and clamored for post-emancipated inclusion.

She also argued that secular conditions guaranteed rights. In a December 1889 issue of *Anti-Caste* she not only called attention to the international character of the British Empire but also criticized its purpose: "How little realized by [the] English that England itself is a small part of a great empire." She continued, "The masses of [colonial peoples] have been brought under British rule sometimes voluntarily but more often, we fear by force and fraud, and for ends not purely disinterested." Yet despite her criticism, Impey recognized that British imperialism, in theory, promised colonial populations secular political rights. She noted the equal political status of all imperial populations, in the metropole as well as in the colonies: "We English are, as it were, but an inner cluster of the big crowd of British subjects." Moreover, as subjects, colonial peoples could call on the state to solve injustice: "Now they, like us, press around the same British Government with its mighty and cumbrous machinery of State, looking to it—though almost despairingly at times—for power to carry out the necessary reforms, for the redress of public grievances." Impey's statement reflected a standard belief among many Pan-African reformers that the British Empire had a sense of justice and was a potential vehicle of redress for conditions of oppression. Clearly, however, she had little hope that the British state would effectively honor the political rights of colonial subjects and make corrections to the inequalities of the imperial world: "One is led to wonder how long the slender fabric of Empire shall hold together? Especially does this thought press when the bitter cry of suffering and oppression reaches us from some outer part of the great crowd."[17] Impey recognized the construction of a global color line a decade before Du Bois's pronouncement; and although she acknowledged some potential for redress, she had serious doubts that secular mechanisms alone could solve its dislocations. Still, she was a prescient voice, balancing religious arguments with secular hopes in her activism for racial equality.

The "Negro Problem"

While Impey reached many in her reform circles, the most respected commentator on race relations was the prominent British intellectual James Bryce. He, too, interrogated issues surrounding racial equality and secular rights but, unlike Impey, hesitated to suggest the immediate realization of such equality. Bryce was well known among Anglo-American literati and a prolific contributor to its print culture, including the *Nation*, the *Forum*, the *North American Review*, and *Nineteenth Century*.[18] He wrote several books that were considered mandatory reading in the era, works that established him as not only the foremost British expert on democracy in the United States but also as a leading voice on international race relations.

"The Relation of the Advanced and the Backward Races of Mankind," a paper that Bryce delivered at the Romanes lecture series at Oxford

University, cemented his reputation as one of the world's leading experts on race relations.[19] In a letter to Bryce, Charles William Eliot, the president of Harvard University, commented on the paper: "Under these circumstances, it seems clear to me that we are dealing with a distinct stage of progressive development. You have looked at it from this point of view, and dealt with it seriously—not in the mercantile or philanthropic sense, but in a spirit truly scientific."[20] In the work, Bryce adopted standard arguments that endorsed aspects of racial hierarchy, paternalism, and temporal constraints on progress. However, he dismissed harsher ideas of international racial competition and relied on a language of social cooperation and progress with regard to post-emancipated issues. While offering historical background about the extinction of the "weaker races," he also argued that the era of competition-based imperial aggression was over. In his view, trade and balance-of-power dynamics guaranteed a relative international stability that could reduce strife and foster cooperation. Embracing the standard progressive approach to race relations, Bryce argued that the "world-process" of imperial expansion placed all races in permanent contact. Thus, it was incumbent upon the more "advanced races" to uplift the "backward races" in the next phase of this process.[21] Some of Bryce's views are similar to those held by the British and Foreign Anti-Slavery Society. In 1891, it expressed its opposition to emigrationist plans to send African Americans to Africa, arguing that doing so would not resolve the problem of the color line. According to the society, it was incumbent upon the "superior" race to help people of African descent prepare for the benefits of citizenship. Like Bryce, however, the Anti-Slavery Society thought that white society's prejudice based on physical characteristics precluded integration in the form of "miscegenation" as a solution to the problem of race relations.[22]

Bryce, however, fundamentally recognized that people of African descent in the empire and the United States maintained de jure rights of subject and citizen. As such, he had long considered race relations a crucial question for modern society. His 1888 tome *American Commonwealth* paid particular attention to the social milieu of the American South and, by 1891, he noted that most of the political issues of the day (tariff policy, money supply, railway expansion) "s[a]nk to almost insignificance" in comparison with the Negro problem in America.[23] In his 1897 *Impressions of South Africa*, he made direct comparisons between the racial milieus of South Africa and the United States.[24] Concerned with how the British Empire dealt with non-Anglo populations, he not only looked to America for understandings of race relations but also argued that, as the United States expanded internationally, it would face many issues similar to Great Britain's.

Although Bryce took a pessimistic view of the immediate integration of people of African descent into British and American political life, his writings reiterate that political rights were a distinct component of reformer discourse at the turn of the twentieth century. For him, a key to positive race relations was the immediate realization of full civil protections of person and property for peoples in the empire and the United States. He argued that there should be open access to professions and occupations; and in a period rife with lynchings and imperial transgressions against colonized peoples, he suggested that the realization of civil rights and a commitment to reducing occupational disparities could smooth tensions by creating respect for the "lower race" among the "higher" and allowing the "lower race" to feel a sense of "justice" in their daily lives.[25] On the question of political rights beyond the protections of civil rights, Bryce acknowledged that the exclusion of African American men from the right of suffrage was a direct breach of the constitution and the tradition of law. Yet he considered the admission of former slaves into the body politic to be a grave error of democratic excess: "The difficulty arises from the fact, not that colored men can vote, but that the majority of the colored voters are not capable voters, competent for the active functions of citizenship."[26] Here, Bryce gave momentum to the standard view of Reconstruction in America, reasserting standards of character and suggesting a theory of race repulsion that emphasized the biological essentialism beneath race differentiation.

By the turn of the century, Columbia University historian William A. Dunning and his political science colleague John W. Burgess had interpreted Reconstruction as a deeply flawed assertion of federal power that made the mistake of granting political rights to supposedly unprepared former slaves. Although immediately contested by Du Bois, the Dunning school was influential, giving scholarly weight to the general retreat from the post-emancipated realization of political rights.[27] Bryce reiterated this interpretation as he claimed that suffrage granted to "half-civilized" men unleashed the threat of democratic excess and created "two nations" destined for conflict. He warned that granting political rights to African Americans created a "tremendous problem" that would have to be dealt with elsewhere, offering the imperial hotspots of South Africa and the Philippines as examples. Although he argued that the "contrast between principle and practice, between the theoretical recognition of the rights of man and the denial of them to a section of the population will be palpable and indefensible," he contended that giving political rights to those "unprepared" for participation was a mistake. In other words, he believed that "there are cases in which the exclusion of the Backward race seems justified, in the interest of humanity at large, by the consideration that to admit that race would involve more of loss to the higher race than of gain to the lower."[28]

Despite the problems associated with political rights, Bryce suggested that the connectivity of the modern world was moving humankind toward "a new kind of unity." He argued that the phases of race extinction and absorption had largely passed and that the continued interaction among the civilized, semi-civilized, and uncivilized had two potential arcs: racial fusion or racial segregation. To him, the mixing of race, if deepened by intermarriage, often produced a progressively stronger race and civilization, and he contended that the "great people of the world are the result of the mixing of races."[29]

Basing his arguments on what he referred to as a sense of "physical repulsion," however, Bryce went to great lengths to deny that people of African descent could participate in interconnectivity through racial fusion. "Colour," he wrote, was the primary basis for this repulsion, which reached its highest level with the aversion of the "Teutons" to people of African descent. Further, in the American South, Christianity "ha[d] failed to impress the lesson of human equality and brotherhood upon the whites."[30] Bryce's tedious development of race repulsion and fears of democratic excess dominated his writing on race relations. Not surprisingly, his solutions for societies peopled with both whites and blacks was segregation, with educational and property measures mediating political rights. Of course, the prescriptions of segregation, education, and property requirements were all too typical. Thus, as a respected thinker on race relations, he most certainly contributed to the construction of the global color line.[31]

Nonetheless, in the course of these arguments, Bryce contributed other, more open-ended comments to the discourse. Despite his long exposition on race repulsion, he detached political rights from biological essentialism. In the concluding section of "The Relation of the Advanced and the Backward Races," he argued that "race and blood" should not be the grounds for discrimination against political rights, for "some of the races now deemed backward may show a capacity for intellectual and moral progress greater than they have been credited with."[32] This acquiescence demonstrates that the claims on agency and demonstration of progress made by the American Negro exhibit and Pan-Africanism were being seriously considered in other circles. This consideration, together with Bryce's delinking of race from political rights and his earlier remarks lauding "advance[s]" of the "negro race in America," shows that the discourse on race, rights, and progress was multifaceted and not represented only in the coarse hues of the ethnographic other.

Mary Church Terrell, Anna J. Cooper, and Pauline Hopkins

The National Association of Colored Women (NACW) offered an important challenge to obstacles facing people of African descent during the late nineteenth and early twentieth centuries. Established in 1896, it capitalized on the momentum that African American women had initiated at the 1893 World's Congress of Representative Women in Chicago.[33] As a consistent and influential contributing member to subsequent International Council of Women conferences, the NACW became one of the most vocal African American female reform movements of the era.[34] Hallie Quinn Brown, an NACW member and a participant in the Chicago congress, attended the 1899 ICW in London, and Mary Church Terrell delivered an address, "The Progress of the Colored Women," at the council's 1904 gathering in Berlin. Their contributions affirmed that African American women saw reform as both a domestic and an international issue.

A leading reformer and the first president of the NACW, Terrell spearheaded the organization's commentary on major public issues. Her 1904 essay "Lynching from a Negro's Point of View," published in the *North*

American Review, reiterated Ida B. Wells's dismissal of rape as the motive for lynching. Terrell also weighed in on the matter of social equality, which was a pressing issue in the American South that contributed to Booker T. Washington's decision to soft-pedal the issue at the 1895 Atlanta conference. Constructing distinctions among people of African descent, Terrell argued that most "ignorant negroes" had no understanding of social equality and maintained that those who were "educated," "as a rule," would not assault white women or commit crimes. In her view, the threat of social equality as an excuse for lynching was baseless.[35]

After discussing the brutality of lynching, including the murder of Sam Hose (which deeply affected both Wells and Du Bois), Terrell argued that the reason for lynching was "race hatred." She asserted that this hatred not only arose from fears of social equality but was also directly related to the "brutalizing effect of slavery." Terrell indicted Christianity for not doing enough to combat the horrors of lynching, suggesting that the church should pay less attention to foreign missionary work and instead "inaugurate a crusade against the barbarism at home, which converts hundreds of white women and children into savages every year." Invoking the standard of civilization, she declared, "If the wild and diabolical carnival of blood does not diminish, nothing can prevent this country from becoming a byword and a reproach throughout the civilized world."[36]

As corrective, Terrell argued that women were the moral center of society. For instance, she believed that the "purity and power" of southern "white women" could help reduce the violent actions of their "fathers, husbands and sons." In language denouncing biological essentialism, she warned that the practice would continue until the people of the South began to "respect the rights of other human beings, no matter what may be the color of their skin." This "renaissance of popular belief in the principles of liberty and equality" could shift the sympathy and attention of the "American public" away from the plight of other oppressed groups around the globe toward "the murderous assault upon Negroes in the South."[37] Thus, Terrell, like Wells, directly invoked the normative power of public discourse to censure the practices of violence against people of African descent. Both women remained active reformers well into the twentieth century and were later associated with Du Bois's National Association for the Advancement of Colored People.

Anna J. Cooper, like Terrell, did not allow the constraints of respectability to soften her commentary on pressing public issues. At the 1900 Pan-African Conference, she delivered an address on "The Negro Problem in America," which she followed up with a longer address on the same theme, given in 1902 at a Society of Friends meeting in New Jersey.[38] In her New Jersey speech, Cooper made direct references to Africa and used the descriptor "Ethiopian" to denote people of African descent. She invoked images of a "sunny" continent and denounced the slave trade that tore its peoples away from their ancestors. The experience of slavery, she asserted, was "chatteldom" that existed hypocritically in a nation "conceived in liberty" and that pushed African Americans further behind in development. While she conceded that progress was being made, she also included a standard Progressive Era denunciation of the "petrifying spirit of commercialism" that unduly stressed material measures as the test of progress. Cooper argued that the vagaries of "free labor and cut throat competition," combined with the biological trait of skin color, severely handicapped people of African descent. While immigrants could learn the language and the "white man" could project his "meanness" through the application of "burnt cork" (minstrelsy), African Americans were subjected to "colorphobia" that "show[ed] no quarter."[39]

Cooper saw lynching as the heinous outcropping of this colorphobia. She denounced the construction of African American men as immoral sexual predators and fought against their erroneous depiction as "beast[s] [that] must be kept under a reign of terror." Like Terrell, she mocked the "absurd" idea that the United States was in danger of "negro domination." These irrational fears, she declared, resulted in whites' widespread failure to recognize the humanity of people of African descent, which was conveyed by the American Negro exhibit. If they would, Cooper maintained, they would then understand that African Americans were "human beings capable of human emotions, human aspirations, human suffering, defeats and triumphs." She also denounced Bryce for denying the humanity of people of African descent and castigated him for arguing that they were a "peculiar and menacing problem" with no real chance of resolution.[40]

Cooper criticized the state for failing to protect the rights of its citizens. Playing on tropes often reserved for African people, she described the lynching of Sam Hose as "an outburst of diabolism that would shame a tribe of naked savages." She noted that, because lynching was performed "without court of jury," the case was deemed to have no "Federal aspects," which meant it did not qualify for the government's corrective intervention. Connecting this legal protective terminology to the imperial record of the United States, she said that a lecturer who had recently detailed the African American Tenth Cavalry's contributions to the victory at San Juan Hill during the Spanish American War was met by "hisses" from the crowd and forced offstage. She asked, "Don't you think we would find a way to give them Federal aspects if it were poor old Spain lynching her obstreperous islanders?" Reflecting the Progressive Era's turn to the state, Cooper sought government intervention to halt the lynching of African Americans. Moreover, using the standard-of-civilization template that supposedly guided imperialism, she denounced the violent domestic behavior of the United States. Ultimately, she argued that America needed to recognize that the "Negro question" was indeed "humanity's problem."[41]

Cooper's address used a language of norms to frame the question of race relations. She listed the "expediency" of issues such as free coinage, tariffs, and imperialism but argued that, instead of gains through "percentages and cash balances," the "Negro question" was the "one issue that says *ought*." This moral framing asked people to revisit Christian precepts that avoid the "blinding pride of race" as well as return to the basic abolitionist question "Am I my brother's keeper?" Her religious moorings imbued her understanding of "unalienable rights" with a commitment to Christian morality and practice. Yet she augments this ethos by stating that, for people of African descent in the United States, "citizenship is beyond question." Her conclusion reflected the basic normative premise of the standard of civilization: "The right to rule entails the obligation to rule right."[42]

Like Cooper, Pauline E. Hopkins was a well-known African American writer and reformer. At the beginning of the twentieth century, her fiction and nonfiction often appeared in the *Colored American Magazine*, which was a popular monthly with an international audience.[43] Shortly after the 1900 Pan-African Conference, she began writing a series of articles under the general title "Famous Men of the Negro Race." The project opened with Toussaint L'Ouverture.[44] Subsequent essays included an exposé of Kirkland Soga of South Africa, in which Hopkins referred to

F. Z. S. Peregrino as a leading newspaper editor in the region and argued that "there is no reason why both Negro in America and Bantu in Africa should not unite on larger questions, for their own safety and progress."[45] She immediately followed the "Famous Men" series with "Famous Women of the Negro Race." In a March 1902 contribution, she lauded Wells for her powerful public presence and the success of her anti-lynching tours of Great Britain.[46] Subsequent articles detailed the contributions of Terrell and Frances Ellen Watkins Harper.[47]

After a falling out with the *Colored American Magazine*, Hopkins began writing for the *Voice of the Negro*, where she began documenting the various activities of non-white peoples around the world. Her series "The Dark Races of the Twentieth Century" appeared in six installments during 1905 and demonstrates her quest to understand other peoples affected by the global color line. In the first installment, she argued that European peoples, "the sons of Japheth," created "perils" based on the "unreasoning insanity" of color. Invoking Martin Delany's writings about pigment as well as Acts 17:26, she asserted, "God hath made of one blood all of the nations of men to dwell on all the face of the earth."[48] The series moved through Oceania, the Malay archipelago, Southeast Asia, and Africa and ended with a discussion of native North Americans. She provided ethnographic summaries that considered physical characteristics, cultural and religious traditions, and social and political organization. While Hopkins did offer some evaluation of each group's position on the standard of civilization, she also argued for a cyclical understanding of history, noting that many peoples in the past had attained prerequisite levels of civilization. Concluding with a clear denunciation of biological essentialism, she wrote that, in the struggles of modern times, "the color of the skin, the curl of the hair, the development of the cranium will not count."[49] For Hopkins, "one blood" forced a recognition of common humanity and encouraged an understanding of darker peoples around the globe, which strengthened the resistance against the global color line.

Although manliness and patriarchal hierarchy pervaded Pan-African strategies, women were a formidable voice in the struggle to erode the global color line. Wells's transatlantic campaign against the illegal lynching of African American men was only one part of her life-long anti-lynching work. Terrell's outcry over the murder of Sam Hose was only one example of her life-long commitment to the condemnation of inhumane practices. Both reformers linked their protests to the larger Pan-African goal of citizenship for people of African descent worldwide. Impey's sophisticated fusing of religious and secular ideology to argue for racial equality questioned the assumptions of the civilizing mission of the British Empire. Cooper's prodigious writing in prominent Pan-African publications and her direct references to Ethiopia signaled a global call for equality for people of African descent. And Hopkins's chronicling of the accomplishments of leading people of African descent as well as her comprehensive documentation of peoples of color around the world developed pride and international awareness. These women (and many others) participated in reform organizations and global gatherings such as the World's Congress of Representative Women, the Pan-African Conference, and the NACW, thus reinforcing Pan-African positions on biological essentialism, race progress, and the struggle for equality. Both individually and collectively, they not only made substantive contributions to the international Pan-African effort to combat the global color line but also set the standard for future reform endeavors.

CONCLUSION

THE 1911 UNIVERSAL RACES CONGRESS AND PAN-AFRICAN ANTICOLONIALISM

I n June 1906, the front page of the Atlanta University *Bulletin* noted that the school had hosted a special event to recognize the anniversary of the 1899 Hague Peace Conference. Flowing out of a long-standing transatlantic peace movement, that conference had concentrated on reduction of armaments, arbitration of internal conflict, and laws for conduct during war. These objectives contributed to normative understandings of acceptable behavior for nation-states—the continuation of the standard-of-civilization discourse articulated at international forums. While the conference did not explicitly discuss political rights for people of African descent, it did continue to articulate accepted standards of human behavior and suggested that actions outside those norms were subject to international censure. It demonstrated the existence of what Geoffrey Best calls a "humming transnational civil society" committed to developing standards of international behavior.[1] As I noted in chapter 4, people of African descent were well aware of the conference and The Hague's symbolism as a center for international justice.

The June issue of the *Bulletin* also gave considerable attention to the university's recent graduation ceremonies and printed the full address of the commencement speaker, Franz Boas. In his speech, Boas argued that, while the "Negro race" might have "slightly different hereditary traits," it would be "entirely arbitrary" to assume them as an "inferior type."

He denounced "the arguments for inferiority drawn from the history of civilization." While he acknowledged, "instability and signs of weakness of primitive culture" in Africa, he contextualized these vulnerabilities within the broader evidence of "achievement" by African peoples. Boas detailed historic African aptitude in the measures of civilization: social organization, trade and thrift, political aptitude, and artistic innovation.[2] Leveraging his opportunity to speak to a group of college-educated people of African descent, he directly challenged biological essentialism and asserted that African history met the qualifying tests of civilization.

W. E. B. Du Bois, who was a professor at Atlanta University, had invited Boas to speak and commented positively on the address.[3] Over the course of the next few years, the two continued to work out their understandings of race and race relations, and both attended the 1911 Universal Races Congress held at the University of London. Truly a global gathering, the congress was a historic exchange of racial and cultural knowledge among nations from every corner of the world. Its connections to Pan-Africanism were clear. Wu Tingfang gave a paper about China, John Tengo Jabavu about South Africa, Mojola Agbebi about West Africa, and Du Bois about the United States. Boas and John A. Hobson also presented papers, and the bibliography in the congress report lists a host of contributions from intellectuals, reformers, and organizations, including Edward Blyden, James Bryce, Charles Dilke, E. D. Morel, the South African Native Affairs Commission, Kelly Miller, Booker T. Washington, and George Washington Williams. Many of the delegates to the second Hague Peace Conference, held in 1907, also supported the congress; and two important organizers, Gustav Spiller and Felix Adler, were part of the Ethical Society movement that had long focused on race relations.

As demonstrated by the size of the congress's executive committee, which was much larger than that of the 1900 Pan-African Conference, attention to Pan-African issues had increased substantially during the first decade of the twentieth century, and the movement was expanding beyond the Atlantic world. By 1911 a significant amount of interest was directed toward the Asian world. Events such as the Boxer Rebellion in China and Japan's advance onto the imperial stage with its 1905 victory in the Russo-Japanese War had attracted new attention. By 1912, the Pan-Africanist Dusé Mohamed Ali confirmed this outlook with his new journal, the *African Times and Orient Review (ATOR)*.

The Universal Races Congress

Held in London on July 26–29, 1911, the Universal Races Congress was an "extraordinary encounter" that brought together a wide array of global intellectuals to continue the consideration of race relations.[4] The object of the congress was to further "the general relations subsisting between the peoples of the West and those of the East, between so-called white and so-called coloured peoples, with a view to encouraging between them a fuller understanding, the most friendly feelings, and a heavier co-operation."[5] The qualifier "so-called" used before the identification of skin colors documented a crucial point in the growing questioning of biological essentialism, long a fundamental plank of Pan-African thought.

Gustav Spiller was the main force behind the conference, and his paper in the first session reiterates the denunciation of biological essentialism. It takes the standard foray through the documentation of progress, including a reference to Theophilus E. S. Scholes's work as evidence of the academic contributions of people of African descent. This evidence of progress, Spiller argued, helped show how the peoples of the world were, "for all intents and purposes, essentially equals in intellect, enterprise, morality and physique." Thus, "the deepest cause of race misunderstandings is perhaps the tacit assumption that the present characteristics of a race are the expression of fixed and permanent racial characteristics." Confirming what Pan-Africanist and other reformers had long argued, Spiller asserted that "the belief in racial superiority is largely due . . . to unenlightened psychological repulsion and under-estimation of the dynamic of environmental factors."[6] Although the scales of progress remained obvious, he disconnected them from biological essentialism.

Spiller's emphasis on environmental factors reinforced the importance of Franz Boas's work. In his paper "Human Faculty as Determined by Race," first delivered at the 1893 Columbian Exposition in Chicago, Boas had questioned the assumption that any biological deviation from the European standard "white type" constituted lower forms of "civilization."[7] By 1905, as demonstrated in his commencement address at Atlanta University, his questioning of biological determinism had expanded significantly. By 1911, it had matured, and his contribution to the Universal Races Congress was an important moment in his denunciation of the link between biology and racial superiority. The address concludes, "The old idea of absolute stability of human types must . . . evidently be given up, and with it the belief of the hereditary superiority of certain types over others."[8] The lack of progress toward the standard of civilization, Boas argued, was not primarily a function of biology but determined by environmental conditions.

His understanding of environmental conditions as determinant moved him to expand his idea of culture away from its previous conception as the progressive accumulation of civilization. Instead of measuring and summarizing culture within the framework of the advancement or retreat from the standard of civilization, Boas was, by 1911, suggesting that the Euro-American conception of civilization could no longer be used to understand the diversity of cultures. George Stocking notes that Boas's approach to culture "involved the rejection of simplistic models of biological or racial determinism" and the "rejection of ethnocentric standards of cultural evaluation."[9] Deeply involved in the attack on the racialist assumptions of biological essentialism, he provided the foundation for the field of modern cultural anthropology.

The paper that Hobson delivered at the congress reveals his general tendencies to view people using the measure of civilization and to warn against unrestricted capitalist monopoly and greed. Reflecting standard paternalist arguments, Hobson argued that the "semi-civilized" and "backwards" peoples of the world had "no natural or inalienable right" to withhold their resources but required the assistance of the "white man's knowledge, organisation, and capital." This learning curve, he said, would be slow and would require guidance and authority. Yet it could not be left to unrestricted private interests, which had long abused the privilege. Rather, the "civilized States" must develop a higher sense of justice, humanity, and economic wisdom in the international world.[10] Hobson's comments reiterate how obdurate the standard of civilization remained, despite the challenges from Boas and others.

Jabavu's important address begins by tracing the history of the Bantu people and then arguing that the initial European encounter with natives did not launch a dedicated effort to "improving the conditions of their new wards." Jabavu denounced the current categorization of the average South African of European descent as one rarely moving beyond the exploitation of native African labor.[11] Yet he believed that the current government was doing the best it could with a "peculiar" situation. For Jabavu, "uplift" and education remained the focus, especially given the lack of state assistance. He noted that the missionary schools had success-fully prepared some native students as leaders and argued that a dedicated educational institution could train a larger number of leaders to help con-tinue the uplift mission. Via his address at the congress, he subpoenaed help for funding what he envisioned as the first African college in South Africa; and in 1916, he did succeed in establishing of the South African Native College, becoming its first native African full-time lecturer. The college (later the University College of Fort Hare) became an important institute, and a host of future leaders were students there, including Nelson Mandela.

Mojola Agbebi's paper, titled "The West African Problem," argued that the only real problem was the tension between European rule and African conditions. In his view, African political institutions did not have an estab-lished coercive arm of rule similar to those of European institutions. Thus, social dislocation occurred because of the European "principle of might, from which the idea of force is inseparable." The answer to this problem, he believed, was a shift in the imperial worldview toward patience and understanding of African people. In his paper he described a host of African social traditions and issues, including interracial marriage, witchcraft, can-nibalism, and polygamy. These descriptions are not filled with compari-sons to the standard of civilization. Indeed, the only direct comparison notes that Africans saw European "spiritualism" as a form of witchcraft. Otherwise, Agbebi stressed the African context—noting, for example, that polygamy was a foundation of African domestic and social life. He con-cluded by stating that African people might be positioned as a "child-race" for the benefit of European "greed and aggrandizement," but each person was also "a full-fledged man in the "eternal providence" of the world.[12] As a central figure of African Christianity, Agbebi invoked religion in his denunciation of European practices and worldviews. In an international setting at the heart of empire in London, he eschewed the compulsive need to measure and began to present African culture on its own terms.

Du Bois's contribution to the congress was typical of his historical-sociological approach, mixing historical detail with statistical measure-ment and paying significant attention to educational and occupational indicators. In it, he continued his denunciation of biological essentialism by documenting the advances of people of African descent. He argued that Washington's Atlanta Compromise had resulted in further disenfranchisement and increased "race prejudice." This path of "silence and sweet temper," he declared, had run its course, and he used his platform at Universal Races Congress to call for continued "agitation" for full rights of citizenship.[13]

In August 1911, Du Bois published a review of the congress in the *Crisis*, the official journal of the National Association for the Advancement of Colored People. He noted that the mood in London had been "uneasy" as people "sens[ed] the strength and determination in the darker world." Yet he praised that environment in comparison to the "barbarity" of New Orleans and argued that participants met there as "men and equals in the center of the world." Summarizing the congress's dismissal of biological essentialism, Du Bois claimed that "America is fifty years behind the scientific world in its racial philosophy."[14]

The September 1911 issue of the *Crisis* featured the seal of the Universal Races Congress on its cover and included more commentary on the papers delivered there. It reprinted "A Hymn to the Peoples," which Du Bois had read at the gathering, as well as pictures of many participants, including Jabavu and Agbebi as well as Wu Tingfang of China and Tongo Takebe of Japan.[15] Such attentions underscored the importance of this international event and its focus on global race relations. The diverse composition of its attendees (in contrast to those at the Berlin and Brussels conferences, which were dominated by people of European descent) was obvious, and the number of people involved was much higher than the Pan-African Conference's. The Universal Races Congress was, in essence, a summative statement on more than two decades of Pan-African activism against the global color line.

Wu's contribution opened with the direct assertion that China's "civilization" was the most "venerable" in the world. Like Agbebi, he commented on a host of religious, social, and political topics, appealing for positive international relations and arguing that "fair play and mutual consideration should be the guiding principle of nations." He extended this logic to question what he called "White policy"—immigration rules that restricted entry by "colour." Wu believed that, as China was "forced" into opening to western powers, this lack of reciprocation would make the world more "narrow-minded." He said that the countries that followed these policies should take a page from Confucianism and recognize that all should be treated as "brothers and sisters." He concluded that China and other "Eastern nations" expected that their peoples should be treated "equally and equitably."[16]

In contrast to Wu, who appealed to the standard of civilization in his plea for equal treatment, the Japanese speakers at the congress delivered powerful statements about sovereignty. Teruaki Kobayashi and Tongo Takebe were professors at the Imperial University of Tokyo, and their joint paper argued that Japanese victories in the 1895 Sino-Japanese War and the 1905 Russo-Japanese War had led western countries to recognize that Japan had joined "the company of the Great Powers" and become their equal. Now, they declared, European nations needed to search for the "secret" of Japanese development. In their view, the unbroken Japanese imperial line had created a long-lasting respect for the sovereign. This strength, combined with a cultural tradition that did not distinguish among morality, religion, and politics, had created a "perfectly harmonised" society that treated all naturalized people in the same way and made them genuine subjects of Japan. Thanks to this unity, Japan was a "virile nation destined to play an important role in the history of the world." In ways reminiscent of positivist Frederic Harrison's pronouncement a decade earlier, the two professors argued that "Western civilization" could be enlightened "by the brighter features of a civilization which three thousand years of experience created."[17]

The Japanese defeat of Russia had dramatically affected the Euro-American world. Some saw the victory as evidence of heightened international racial competition, and others used it as an excuse to tighten the whites-only restrictive immigration policies that Wu noted in his speech. In many respects, the Japanese victory over a European power had reinforced the need for protection of global whiteness.[18] Yet as Kobayashi and Takebe made clear, world powers now recognized the sovereignty of Japan and were beginning to calculate and consider its geopolitical power, especially regionally.[19]

The Japanese victory had been important for people of color around the world. Students in Java formed a nationalist organization, newspapers in the Middle East celebrated the event, and a young Jawaharlal Nehru eagerly read of the victories as a student in England.[20] For people of African descent, it proved that white superiority was a fallacy. The *Voice of the Negro* argued that the war taught "arrogant" Europe about racial inferiority, and Johannesburg's *Rand Daily Mail* ran a letter expressing the hope that the victory would trigger racial equality in South Africa.[21] As evidenced by John Bruce's earlier criticism of Western actions in the Boxer Rebellion and his relationship with Wu Tingfang, Pan-Africanists were beginning to pay more attention to Asia, and the Japanese military victory—a form of legitimate violence—enhanced these considerations.[22]

The *African Times and Orient Review*

No figure better symbolizes how Pan-Africanism expanded beyond its Atlantic focus than Dusé Mohamed Ali does. Born in Egypt in 1866 to an Egyptian father and Sudanese mother, Ali traveled extensively before landing a position in 1909 as a reporter for the London-based weekly *New Age*, where he consistently denounced oppression.[23] Ali was at the Universal Races Congress and recognized the need for a new Pan-African and Pan-Oriental journal. His *African Times and Orient Review* debuted a year later, in July 1912.

In the first issue of the *ATOR*, Ali noted the importance of previous conferences but argued that they had not reflected the universality of the Universal Races Congress. He delivered an extensive report on its events and discussed the growing agitation of Pan-Africanists. Using the common tropes of Ethiopia and Psalm 68, he commented, "Pray by all means," but the "mere lifting of hands will not help you"; instead, "do something for yourself."[24] Subsequent issues of the *ATOR* produced a stream of reporting on topics relevant to people of color all over the world. The journal had correspondents in many different locales, including John Bruce and F. Z. S. Peregrino, and delved into British imperial policy, Indian politics, Egyptian nationalism, U.S. race relations, Japanese imperialism, immigration restrictions, and a host of religious practices and cultural traditions. Crucially, the *ATOR* criticized not only imperial policy that violated the standards of civilization but also imperialism itself and its attendant measures of progress.

PAPERS

ON

INTER-RACIAL
PROBLEMS

COMMUNICATED TO THE

FIRST UNIVERSAL RACES CONGRESS,

HELD AT

THE UNIVERSITY OF LONDON

JULY 26–29, 1911

EDITED, FOR THE CONGRESS EXECUTIVE, BY

G. SPILLER

HON. ORGANISER OF THE CONGRESS

LONDON

P. S. KING & SON

ORCHARD HOUSE, WESTMINSTER

BOSTON, U.S.A.

THE WORLD'S PEACE FOUNDATION

29A, BEACON STREET

1911

Figure 6. Title page, in *Papers on Inter-Racial Problems: Communicated to the First Universal Races Congress,* ed. Gustav Spiller (London: King, 1911).

The journal had a vibrant book review section, and its consideration of two works in particular are especially instructive for understanding Pan-Africanism in the years just before World War I: *Dawn in Darkest Africa* (1912) by John H. Harris and *Ethiopia Unbound* (1911) by J. E. Casely Hayford.[25] Harris was an English missionary who had documented the atrocities in Belgian Congo, often by using photographs shot by his wife, Alice Seeley Harris. Both were original members of E. D. Morel's Congo Reform Association.[26] Harris remained active in African and English reform circles throughout the first decade of the twentieth century and, in 1910, became the secretary of the now combined Anti-Slavery and Aborigines' Protection Society. *Dawn in Darkest Africa* mixes details about African customs and crop production with criticisms of imperial practice. For Harris, the improprieties of imperialism were rampant and especially damaging in Portuguese West Africa, where he contended that slavery and the slave trade continued to thrive. In his search for solutions, Harris referred back to the agreements in the Berlin and Brussels acts of the late nineteenth century. He argued that Great Britain should recognize these violations and intervene, though he acknowledged that such intervention was highly unlikely, given the nation's diplomatic relationship with Portugal.[27]

Writing of Harris's book, the reviewer in the *ATOR* noted that, while he was suspicious of the general missionary enterprise on the continent, he applauded Harris's plain-speaking evaluation of the subject and his commitment to "justice" for the "native." The immediate form of this justice, the reviewer wrote, must involve a groundswell of public sentiment to stop imperial mistreatment of African peoples and change the "exceedingly slow movement of the Colonial Office."[28] In his book, Harris invoked British responsibilities for the civilizing mission and maintenance of international norms. The work, typical of reform societies, was an effort to both generate public awareness and subpoena action from the state.

Yet while condemning imperial practice, Harris never wavered from his belief in the paternal uplift of African peoples. He denounced the increasing "autocracy" of rule and the rise of capitalist interests that "possess[ed] neither heart nor conscience" but praised the "benevolent tutelage of native races." However, Harris sometimes let his concern for the well-being of missionaries override his attentions to uplift. His chapter "The White Man's Burden" details how, in his view, a white person in Africa could avoid death by living in a proper dwelling, getting suffi-cient recreation, and gardening to "help keep his mind calm, provide him with healthy exercise, and a supply of fruits and vegetables." Elsewhere in the book, however, Harris calls for understanding and interacting with African peoples, arguing that "negrophobia" will be quickly cured by "staying a few days with an educated native."[29] This stress on education was central to Harris's worldview. He certainly felt that native peoples were entitled to full rights as subjects of the British crown, but this entitle-ment was subject to the paternal tests of civilization. Like many other reformers, he invoked the standard of civilization to protest violations of basic standards of humanity but also used the standard to empower the practice of paternalist tutelage.

The *ATOR* review of *Dawn in Darkest Africa* was positive, but in other issues the journal criticized Harris and the Anti-Slavery and Aborigines' Protection Society. In May 1914, for instance, Frank Hugh O'Donnell, an Irish anti-imperialist, echoed the earlier expressed sentiments of the *ATOR* that "the present Anti-Slavery and Aborigines Protection Society has, it would appear, become an unofficial wing of the Colonial Office."[30] O'Donnell, continued, arguing that while Harris and the society criti-cized practices of other nations, they remained silent on problems in the British Empire. Harris responded in a letter to the *ATOR* defending his practice of conducting protests in a "quiet and effective manner behind the scenes."[31] In the next issue of the *ATOR*, O'Donnell countered that the "Non-Protection Society" method was failing because it refused to publicly address the "horrors against humanity" occurring under British rule.[32] Referencing Harris's letter, the *ATOR*'s editorial section questioned the "secret" work of the society, noting that its results had been "infinitesi-mal." The writer argued that the society needed to foment public opinion on the issues, which would make the Colonial Office either attend to the problems or "face the wrath of the British people which loves justice and fair play."[33]

The *ATOR* also reviewed the work of the Ghanaian-born intellectual J. E. Casely Hayford. A leading critic of imperial practice, Hayford offered prescriptions for reform that vehemently denounced European paternal-ism while asserting the vitality of African political and cultural identity. He was intimately involved with the *ATOR* and had helped it weather a difficult downturn in 1912.[34] For its part, the journal frequently published articles by him as well as commentaries on his work, and in November 1912 it focused on his novel *Ethiopia Unbound*.

Despite being structured as a work of fiction, the book is a clear statement of Hayford's political, social, and cultural ideas. His authorial voice often sets up the context of the narrative, talks directly to the reader, and explains the conversations and speeches of the work's main character, Kwamankra. His chapter "The Black Man's Burden" flips the script of Harris's "The White Man's Burden," transforming concern about white mortality rates in Africa into a scathing rebuke of civilizing practices. The chapter describes white-led Christianity as a "fetish which they call civilization" and notes that "trade gin" is nothing but "vile stuff" perpetuated to economically benefit the bureaucracies of government. Referring often to the work of Edward Wilmot Blyden, the novel juxtaposes such descriptions against a portrait of the Muslim quarter, which combines "primitive simplicity and faith." Like Blyden, Hayford claimed that Christ was stronger than Muhammad but that internal divisions in the leadership of Christianity had made Islam a stronger force.[35] He stressed the Pan-African recovery of African history as a way to generate pride in the "customs and institutions of our forefathers" and he called for African Americans to return to the continent, not on the civilizing redemptive mission outlined at the Congresses on Africa but as cognizant people seeking to understand their natural African instincts.[36] This realization of authenticity, Hayford argued, was an educational process; and like most Pan-Africanists, he stressed that the ability to "acquire proficiency in the arts and sciences, in technical and industrial training" worked in dialogue with the recovery of African authenticity.[37] The *ATOR* reviewer celebrated the character Kwamankra as a "type to be reckoned with in forecasting the future of the coloured races." To that reader, his "spirit of rebellion" rails against the stereotypes constraining people of African descent and turns the premise of inferiority back onto their "erstwhile teachers." Kwamankra is able to take what is valuable from his European studies and reject what does not live up to his African standards. *Ethiopia Unbound*, the reviewer declared, is a "profound meditation" on the true "uplifting" for peoples of African descent and epitomizes the "the spirit of the leaders of young Africa."[38]

Pan-African Anticolonialism, Citizenship, and Human Rights

Amid the widespread deprivation and oppression of people of African descent as well as the violence committed against them during the late nineteenth and early twentieth centuries, Pan-Africanism challenged predominant theories of biological essentialism that denied social equality and political rights. Boas's speech at the Universal Races Congress signaled an important victory in this struggle. He argued that skin color was an invalid criterion for evaluating progress, and his definition of culture suggested that the standard of civilization was not a legitimate measurement for international law or imperialism. This shift away from traditional benchmarks of progress indicated that people of African descent could engage with African tradition and authenticity without capitulating to western standards.

Some Pan-Africanists, including Blyden, Martin Delany, and Alexander Crummell, had crafted a sense of race pride based on African tradition and authenticity. The Universal Races Congress, the *ATOR,* and books such as *Ethiopia Unbound* also worked to understand societies without resorting to western-derived standards. Accompanying this process was a growing unease with imperialism's standard of civilization. Even as Ali and Hayford continued to denounce imperial violations of that standard, they suggested that such practices were a result of deeper systematic problems within imperialism itself.

Although the *ATOR* predicted that young leaders would take on these issues, Du Bois was one of the first. The same June 1906 Atlanta University *Bulletin* featuring the address from Franz Boas also quoted Du Bois's "Credo," which demonstrates how he and Pan-African thought were becoming more strident in their condemnation of the global color line: "the wicked conquest of weaker and darker nations by nations whiter and stronger but foreshadows the death of that strength."[39] At the Pan-African Conference he had called on the ethos of abolitionism and the norms of liberal rights and equality to defy the global color line, but he was now less enamored of European standards. By the 1919 Pan-African Congress, he would express his discontent in a clear statement of self-determination.

Marcus Garvey was certainly one of the young leaders that the *ATOR* was looking toward. During his time in London in 1912 and 1913, he worked

briefly at the journal and considered it an important period in his education. According to the historian Adam Ewing, "no prewar organ did more
to sow the seeds of anti-colonial consciousness."[40] Prior to that point, one
of Garvey's biggest influences had been J. Robert Love, who continued to
engage in Pan-African activism and Jamaican politics until an illness in
1907 forced his retreat from public life.[41]

Garvey's Universal Negro Improvement Association and his Back to
Africa movement were powerful statements of anticolonialism for people
of African descent. Yet Garveyism did not attract only young leaders. By the
turn of the twentieth century, John Bruce had become disillusioned with
efforts to improve the conditions of people of African descent, especially
in the United States. Once again, he welcomed international conflict—
this time World War I—as an opportunity for African American men to
exhibit legitimate violence and earn their participation in the body politic.
In *A Tribute for the Negro Soldier*, he noted that 500,000 "black and coloured
men" were involved in the war for "democracy, brotherhood and justice"
and declared that they would, in the aftermath, demand a "place in the
sun."[42] Once again, however, Bruce was disappointed, and thus near the
end of his life he became the "Grand Old Man" of the Universal Negro
Improvement Association.[43]

Bruce's link to Garveyism illustrates a crucial continuity of Pan-
Africanism. Earlier Pan-African actors had found connectivity in the modern experience of African peoples and wrested the history of Africa from
connotations of darkness. They had argued for control of Christianity
in Africa and brought together the providential and secular meanings
of Ethiopia. Further, they established clear political agitation with their
consistent exposure of the fracture between the legal status of subject
and citizenship and the de facto exclusionary conditions endemic to the
global color line.

A major focus of turn-of-the-century Pan-Africanism was a push to
claim the benefits of modern citizenship. Now, however, the *ATOR* and
others were beginning to question the imperial project itself even as they
remained attached to claims of citizenship within the empire. In March
1914, an *ATOR* opinion piece titled "Imperial Citizenship" argued that
inclusion in the empire should be the defining test of citizenship and that
this status could not be subject to restrictions by self-governing dominions

in the empire. Anyone who was born a subject of the crown "shall be a citizen of the British Empire everywhere in the world, with all the rights and privileges of a British citizen." This privilege "would give the coloured subjects of the King-Emperor an assurance that their rights as British citizens would be respected in all regions under the British Crown."[44] Rights for post-emancipated people remained a powerful symbol, and the benefits of modern citizenship—shorn of measures of progress—remained a fundamental plank in decolonization and the civil rights movements of the twentieth century.

Thus, turn-of-the-century Pan-African activism contributed significantly to the modern understanding of citizenship as the process of rights accumulation. As the noted British sociologist T. H. Marshall argued, the evolution of citizenship from duties to rights was an important marker of modern society, and he set up a framework, based on English history, for the realization of civil, political, and social rights. For Marshall, civil rights asserted individual rights that contrasted against older systems of rank and hierarchy. Political rights formalized authentic belonging and participation in the political community, which implied access to basic social and economic entitlements. The remaining aspect of modern citizenship, social rights, gave all a share of the "concrete substance of civilized life," delivering the substantive realization of the social and economic rights implied in the political.[45]

To Marshall, the central aspect of the shift to civil rights was the right of free labor: the ability to sell one's labor in the marketplace as well as the accompanying ability to acquire private property. Political rights symbolized by the vote gave citizens membership in a community, viable avenues to the exercise of political power, and participation in aspects of civilized life. This civilized life, in turn, gave access to education and basic social and economic entitlements. The continuing evolution of these rights was crucial to the goal of modern citizenship—achievement of, and interaction among, the civil, the political, and the social. This achievement could temper undue inequality and produce a civilized liberal society with fair and appropriate standards for all citizens. "A modicum of legally enforceable rights may be granted," Marshall wrote, "but what matters to the citizen is the superstructure of reasonable expectations." While his typology seems to imply that one set of rights must be accomplished before the next becomes available, he in fact argued that the three strands of rights did not have to occur sequentially and that the political and the social strands had "considerable overlap."[46] Rights accumulation was a powerful ideal in the post-emancipated context, and its template was generally accepted by Pan-Africanists. Denial of such accumulation was at the core of their protest.[47]

The human rights scholar Jack Donnelly offers another perspective on rights accumulation, one that gives insight into the types of social interaction that involve rights. For him, the optimal stage of rights is "objective enjoyment," when the right is ingrained to the point of not being discussed or even contemplated in social exchange. While objective enjoyment should be the standard of societies, Donnelly also discusses two other forms of social exchange: "active respect" and "assertive exercise." Active respect refers to the consideration of rights when determining behavior, without the right being directly claimed. "Assertive exercise" is the process of claiming a right, which is then respected or violated. Donnelly argues that rights are most important when either active respect or objective enjoyment does not occur. It is this "possession paradox"—possessing a right without enjoying it—that often motivates assertive exercise.[48]

Marshall's and Donnelly's frameworks assist the understanding of Pan-African, post-emancipated protest. First, emancipation moved former slaves into positions of free labor. Second, upon emancipation in the British Empire and the United States, the state enacted legal definitions of subject and citizen, which, because they were open-ended, generated understandings about the reasonable expectations of citizenship. Finally, despite these shifts, people of African descent did not generally experience objective enjoyment of rights or their implications. Therefore, Pan-African activists found themselves constantly reminding mainstream society to consider the template of subject and citizen, directly asserting claims on rights, often in the wake of their violation.

As discussed, Pan-Africanists were conversant with the standard of civilization and used transnational networks and forums to critique the processes of rights accumulation occurring within particular nation-state frameworks. Thus, their network of activism contributed to a normative discourse that had "a quality of 'oughtness' and shared moral assessment" that set standards for appropriate behaviors.[49] It influenced the domestic and international norms that defined citizenship and helps to understand the process of norm development on both domestic and international levels.[50] This normative "oughtness" was brought into relief when activists addressed practices that violated accepted norms. Moreover, the appeal to the nation-state for redress compromised the applications of protest, which became particularly evident as Pan-Africanists subpoenaed individual nation-states who were slow to recognize the international censure of their own domestic practices. This conundrum remains salient in the current struggle for human rights.

In the history of modern human rights, there was a long hiatus between the republican revolutions of the seventeenth and eighteenth centuries that established modern rights within the framework of the state and the twentieth-century culmination of these rights in the transnational 1948 Universal Declaration of Human Rights (UDHR).[51] In their studies of the interregnum nineteenth century, scholars identify the moral campaign of abolitionism as a form of human rights activism. The literature, however, emphasizes that it was not until the twentieth century that secular-based demands became significant enough to shape the modern notion of human rights, which combines basic morality with the pursuit of Marshall's checklist of civil, political, and social rights.[52] This holistic interdependence and indivisibility are the cornerstones of modern human rights.[53] While some locate the antecedents to the UDHR in the interwar period, others argue that there were, at the minimum, turn-of-the-century bridges connecting the moral campaigns of the nineteenth century with the modern notions of the mid-twentieth century.[54]

Human rights theorists believe that the success of advocacy is found not only in its direct influence on practices and behavior but also in the difference that advocates make in the normative environment in which all actors operate.[55] Pan-Africanists' post-emancipated pursuit of social equality and rights did not overturn racism or stop the marginalization of people of African descent. However, their struggle revealed powerful layers of thought that influenced later reform movements, contributed to the normative meaning of human rights, and helped to uncover the processes that denied those rights.

NOTES

INTRODUCTION: PAN-AFRICANISM, THE SAVAGE SOUTH AFRICA EXHIBIT, AND THE STANDARD OF CIVILIZATION

1. On whiteness in this context, see Marilyn Lake and Henry Reynolds, *Drawing the Global Colour Line: White Men's Countries and the International Challenge of Racial Equality* (Cambridge: Cambridge University Press, 2008).

2. Robert O. Keohane and Joseph Nye, Jr., characterize this intensity within the valences of "thick" and "thin" (*"Globalization*: What's New? What's Not?" *Foreign Affairs*, no. 118 [Spring 2000]: 104–19). For a powerful historical perspective on globalization, see Emily S. Rosenberg, ed., *A World Connecting: 1870–1945* (Cambridge, MA: Belknap Press of Harvard University Press, 2012).

3. See Thomas Bender, *A Nation among Nations: America's Place in World History* (New York: Wang and Hill, 2006).

4. The social contract provided an edifice for the authority of the modern nation-state in certain geographic areas. Of course, the depth and breadth of representative government is always subject to context, and state building did not have to occur along republican lines. However, the two nation-states at the center of this study, Great Britain and the United States, were substantiated by the republican model. For an excellent discussion of "the long century of modern statehood" (defined as about the 1850s to the 1970s), see Charles S. Maier, "Leviathan 2.0: Inventing Modern Statehood," in Rosenberg, *A World Connecting*, 29–40.

5. Robert Vitalis has long argued that race relations deeply influenced international relations in practice and as a discipline. See, for example, *White World Order, Black Power Politics: The Birth of American International Relations* (Ithaca, NY: Cornell University Press, 2015).

6. In *Drawing the Global Colour Line*, Lake and Reynolds open their introduction with Du Bois's observation, 1. Their book not only details the construction of the global color line but also explains how many saw its development as a time of crisis.

7. *The Report of the Pan-African Conference* (London, 1900), 11, 10.

8. Rosenberg, *A World Connecting*, 887.

9. See Raymond Corbey, "Ethnographic Showcases, 1870–1930," *Cultural Anthropology* 8, no. 3 (1993): 338–69. and Gwendolyn Wright, "Building Global Modernisms," *Grey Room* 7 (Spring 2002): 124–34.

10. Frederick Cooper and Ann Laura Stoler, eds., *Tensions of Empire: Colonial Cultures in a Bourgeois World* (Berkeley: University of California Press, 1997), 4.

11. Seminal works include Robert W. Rydell, *World of Fairs: The Century-of-Progress Expositions* (Chicago: University of Chicago Press, 1993); Robert W. Rydell, *All the World's a Fair: Visions of Empire at American International Expositions, 1876–1914* (Chicago: University of Chicago Press, 1984); Paul Greenhalgh, *Ephemeral Vistas: The Expositions Universelles, Great Exhibitions, and World's Fairs, 1851–1939* (Manchester, UK: Manchester University Press, 1988); and Bernth Lindfors, ed., *Africans on Stage: Studies in Ethnological Show Business* (Bloomington: Indiana University Press, 1999).

12. As Robert Wald Sussman makes clear, the attachment to biological understandings of race remains a fundamental aspect of our modern world (*The Myth of Race: The Troubling Persistence of an Unscientific Idea* [Cambridge, MA: Harvard University Press, 2014]). Also see Jerry Gershenhorn, *Melville J. Herskovits and the Racial Politics of Knowledge* (Lincoln: University of Nebraska Press, 2004); Stephen Jay Gould, *The Mismeasure of Man*, 2nd ed. (New York: Norton, 1996); Tommy Lott, *The Invention of Race: Black Culture and the Politics of Representation* (Malden, MA: Blackwell, 1999); Audrey Smedley and Brian Smedley, *Race in North America: Origin and Evolution of a Worldview*, 4th ed. (Boulder, CO: Westview, 2012); George Stocking, Jr., *Race, Culture, and Evolution: Essays in the History of Anthropology* (Chicago: University of Chicago Press, 1982); and Vernon J. Williams, Jr., *The Social Sciences and Theories of Race* (Urbana: University of Illinois Press, 2006).

13. See John A. Hobson, *Imperialism: A Study* (New York: Pott, 1902), 225, 227, 233, 234.

14. See David Long, "Paternalism and the Internationalization of Imperialism: J. A. Hobson on the International Government of the 'Lower Races,'" in David Long and Brian C. Schmidt, eds., *Imperialism and Internationalism in the Discipline of International Relations* (Albany: State University of New York Press, 2005), 71–92.

15. On Earl's Court and the construction of the Empress Theatre, see Ben Shepard, *Kitty and the Prince* (Johannesburg: Ball, 2003), 36–38.

16. *Official Catalogue of the Greater Britain Exhibition* (London: Spottiswoode, 1899), 2.

17. See Lake and Reynolds's analysis of Charles Pearson's 1892 *National Life and Character: A Forecast*, in *Drawing the Global Colour Line*, 75–94.

18. On the dominion movement, see John Darwin, "A Third British Empire? The Dominion Idea in Imperial Politics," in *The Oxford History of the British Empire*, vol. 4, *The Twentieth Century*, ed. William Roger Louis (Oxford: Oxford University Press, 1999), 64–87. On the concept of Greater Britain, see Duncan Bell, *The Idea of Greater Britain: Empire and the Future of the World Order, 1860–1900* (Princeton: Princeton University Press, 2007).

19. *The Times* of London announced that the Greater Britain Exhibition was a "high-sounding title" for an exhibition dominated by collections from Australia (May 9, 1899).

20. On the key to the map of the grounds, the Empress Theatre is labeled with the description "Frank Filliss's Savage South Africa." The key attaches no similar description to any of the other buildings (*Official Catalogue of the Greater Britain Exhibition*, 4–5).

21. Shepard details the performance in *Kitty and the Prince, 76–79.*

22. There are several full-page advertisements for Savage South Africa in the *Official Catalogue of the Greater Britain Exhibition* that were surely posted in public places.

23. Henry Sylvester Williams, letter to Joseph Chamberlain, CO (Colonial Office) 417/279, 1, 2.

24. As Duncan Bell argues, "binaries" such as *civilized* and *savage* were "complemented, supplanted, and occasionally undermined by other attempts to classify and order the world" ("Empire and International Relations in Victorian Political Thought," *Historical Journal* 49 [March 2006]: 283).

25. John Gallagher and Ronald Robinson, "The Imperialism of Free Trade," *Economic History Review* Second Series, 6, no. 1 (1953): 1–15.

26. The seminal work is Gerrit W. Gong, *The Standard of "Civilization" in International Society* (Oxford: Clarendon, 1984).

27. General Act of the Conference of Berlin, art. 6, in Arthur Berriedale Keith, *The Belgian Congo and the Berlin Act* (1919; reprint, New York: Negro Universities Press, 1970), appendix.

28. "Report of the Secretary of State on the Independent State of the Congo," in Alpheus Henry Snow, *The Question of Aborigines in the Law and Practice of Nations* (1919; reprint, Northbrook, IL: Metro, 1972), 151, 152.

29. Although Kasson signed the Berlin Act, it was not ratified by the U.S. Senate due to worries that an international treaty would weaken the unilaterally established Monroe Doctrine. The United States did ratify the General Act of the Brussels Conference of 1890. Most view Brussels as an extension of Berlin. On the relationship of the United States to the Berlin Conference, see Peter Duigan, "The USA, the Berlin Conference, and Its Aftermath: 1884–1885," in *Bismarck, Europe, and Africa: The Berlin Africa Conference, 1884–1885, and the Onset of Partition,* ed. Stig Forster, Wolfgang J. Mommsen, and Ronald Robinson (London: Oxford University Press, 1988): 321–31.

30. Snow, *The Question of Aborigines,* 109.

31. Ibid., 110–11.

32. See Neta Crawford, *Argument and Change in World Politics: Ethics, Decolonization, and Humanitarian Intervention* (Cambridge: Cambridge University Press, 2002), 209.

33. Snow, *The Question of Aborigines,* 111.

34. On the gap between imperial liberal promise and practice, see Uday Singh Mehta, *Liberalism and Empire: A Study in Nineteenth-Century British Liberal Thought* (Chicago: University of Chicago Press, 1999); Jennifer Pitts, *A Turn to Empire: The Rise of Imperial Liberalism in Britain and France* (Princeton: Princeton University Press, 2005); and Richard Price, *Making Empire: Colonial Encounters and the Creation of Imperial Rule in Nineteenth-Century South Africa* (Cambridge: Cambridge University Press, 2008).

35. My thoughts about the exposed nature of the global color line and imperialism in general are indebted to Roxanne Doty's *Imperial Encounters: The Politics of Representation in North-South Relations* (Minneapolis: University of Minnesota Press, 1996), especially 27–51.

36. An Act for the Abolition of Slavery, 1833 (3 and 4 Will. 4 c. 73). The act immediately freed all slaves under the age of six but designated all over that age to varying periods of apprenticeship. Parliament officially ended apprenticeship by 1840. The act also authorized compensation for slaveowners. See Nick Draper, "'Possessing Slaves': Ownership, Compensation, and Metropolitan Society in Britain at the Time of Emancipation, 1834–1840," *History Workshop Journal* 64 (Autumn 2007): 74–102.

37. Proposed on January 31, 1865, and ratified on December 6, 1865, the Thirteenth Amendment prohibited slavery. Proposed on June 13, 1866, and ratified on July 9, 1868, the Fourteenth Amendment guaranteed the rights of citizenship and prescribed reduced representation in Congress for states that denied voting rights to any male over twenty-one years of age. Proposed on February 26, 1869, and ratified on February 2, 1870, the Fifteenth Amendment ensured the right to vote regardless of race, color, or previous servitude, but not sex.

38. See Catherine Hall, *Civilising Subjects: Metropole and Colony in the English Imagination, 1830–1867* (Chicago: University of Chicago Press, 2002). Although he argues that imperialism was not as important to the Reform Act debates (especially in 1867), Alex Middleton provides an overview of the subject in "The Second Reform Act and the Politics of Empire," *Parliamentary History* 36 (February 2017): 82–96.

39. In *Disputing Citizenship* (Bristol, UK: Polity, 2014), John Clarke, Kathleen Coll, Evelina Dagnino and Catherine Neveu argue that claims making by those excluded from citizenship is a site of struggle and a crucial moment in "recentering citizenship." They borrow from Étienne Balibar stating that the "practical confrontation with different modes of exclusion . . . always constitutes the founding moment of citizenship, and consequently its periodical litmus test" (96, 22).

40. Other works on citizenship include Judith Shklar, *American Citizenship: The Quest for Inclusion* (Cambridge, MA: Harvard University Press, 1991); Rogers Brubaker, *Citizenship and Nationhood in France and Germany* (Cambridge, MA: Harvard University Press, 1998); Richard Bellamy, Dario Castiglione, and Emilio Santaro, eds., *Lineage of European Citizenship: Rights Belonging and Participation in Eleven Nation-States* (New York: Palgrave Macmillan, 2004); Catherine Hall, Keith McClelland, and Jane Rendell, *Defining the Victorian Nation: Class, Race, and Gender*

and the Reform Act of 1867 (Cambridge: Cambridge University Press, 2000); Frederick Cooper, Thomas C. Holt, and Rebecca J. Scott, *Beyond Slavery: Explorations of Race, Labor, and Citizenship in Postemancipation Societies* (Chapel Hill: University of North Carolina Press, 2000); Mahmood Mamdani, *Citizen and Subject: Contemporary Africa and the Legacy of Late Colonialism* (Princeton: Princeton University Press, 1996); and T. H. Marshall, "Citizenship and Social Class," in T. H. Marshall and Tom Bottomore, *Citizenship and Social Class* (London: Pluto, 1992), 3–51.

41. Cooper et al. argue this point but also remind us that citizenship was a "moving target," often more exclusionary than inclusionary (*Beyond Slavery*, 14).

42. Catherine Hall, "The Nation Within and Without," in Hall et al., *Defining the Victorian Nation*, 200–210, 227, 224–25. Britain stripped twelve of the fourteen West Indies possessions of their local charters, converting them to crown colony status by 1877. See James Patterson Smith, "The Liberals, Race, and Political Reform in the British West Indies, 1866–1974," *Journal of Negro History* 79, no. 2 (1994): 141.

43. See Cooper et al., *Beyond Slavery*, 19.

44. Paul Gordon Lauren notes that the protection of natural rights was contained in the English 1689 Bill of Rights and strengthened by Locke and other philosophers, culminating in the creation of what was known as *positive national law* by the end of the eighteenth century (*The Evolution of International Human Rights: Vision Seen*, 2nd ed. [Philadelphia: University of Pennsylvania Press, 2003], 14–21).

45. On the waning of post-emancipation urgency, see Christine Bolt, *The Antislavery Movement and Reconstruction: A Study in Anglo-American Co-operation, 1833–77* (Oxford: Oxford University Press, 1969).

46. As Paul Kramer argues, the United States looked to British imperialism for the administration of U.S. rule in the Philippines (*The Blood of Government: Race, Empire, the United States, and the Philippines* [Chapel Hill: University of North Carolina Press, 2006], 11).

47. "The Negro as a Labourer," *Pall Mall Gazette*, February 5, 1883, 11.

48. Khama and Sechele were native chiefs in the British protectorate of Bechuanaland. "British Zambesia," *Anti-Slavery Reporter* 9 (October 1889): 216. Reprinted from "British Zambesia," *Times* (London), October 15, 1889.

49. "Our Treatment of the Weaker Races," *Positivist Review* (October 1, 1900): 172.

50. On the definitions and theories of colonialism, see Jürgen Osterhammel, *Colonialism: A Theoretical Overview* (Kingston, Jamaica: Randle, 2003). On internal colonialism, see Robert J. Hind, "The Internal Colonial Concept," *Comparative Studies in Society and History* 26, no. 3 (1984): 543–68.

51. This concept of the global color line is central to Robin D. G. Kelley's "'But a Local Phase of a World Problem': Black History's Global Vision, 1883–1905," *Journal of American History* 86 (December 1999): 1045–77. Kelley's title is from Du Bois's phrase first articulated in W. E. B. Du Bois, "Atlanta University," in *From Servitude to Service: Being the Old South Lectures on the History and Work of Southern Institutions*

for the Education of the Negro (Boston: American Unitarian Association, 1905), 195. Reiland Rabaka argues that Du Bois offered an ongoing comment on the nature of colonialism that not only expanded its meaning outside of traditional definitions but also deeply informed postcolonial theory (*W. E. B. Du Bois and the Problems of the Twenty-First Century* [New York: Lexington, 2007], chap. 3).

52. On transnational history, see "AHR Conversation: On Transnational History," *American Historical Review* 111 (December 2006): 1441–64; Patricia Clavin, "Defining Transnationalism," *Contemporary European History* 14 (November 1993): 421–39; and Akire Iriye, "The Rise of Global and Transnational History," in *Global and Transnational History: The Past, Present and Future* (London: Palgrave Macmillan, 2013), 1–18.

53. Seminal works on the progressive reform in this period include Michael Freeden, *The New Liberalism: An Ideology of Social Reform* (Oxford: Clarendon, 1978); James T. Kloppenberg, *Uncertain Victory: Social Democracy and Progressivism in European and American Thought, 1870–1920* (New York: Oxford University Press, 1986); and Daniel T. Rodgers, *Atlantic Crossings: Social Politics in a Progressive Age* (Cambridge: Cambridge University Press, 1998).

54. See Ian Tyrell, *Reforming the World: The Creation of America's Moral Empire* (Princeton: Princeton University Press, 2010), 5.

55. George Shepperson, "Pan-Africanism and 'Pan-Africanism': Some Historical Notes," *Phylon* 23, no. 4 (1962): 346–58.

56. George Padmore, *Pan-Africanism or Communism* (New York: Doubleday, 1971), 96.

57. Imanuel Geiss, *The Pan-African Movement: The History of Pan-Africanism in America, Europe, and Africa* (New York: Africana, 1974), 7–8, 105–14.

58. Geiss also discusses the "fifth plane" of Pan-African studies, which analyzes the tension between the "national" and "supra-national" in the political aspects of the movement (ibid., 5).

59. Shepperson, "Pan-Africanism," 347.

60. Paul Gilroy, *The Black Atlantic: Modernity and Double Consciousness* (Cambridge, MA: Harvard University Press, 1993), 39. The long paragraph that contains this quotation is one of the most powerful statements on counterculture in modern scholarship.

61. John Henrik Clarke champions the holistic approach in *Africans at the Crossroads: Notes for an African Revolution* (Trenton, NJ: Africa World Press, 1991), especially 3–25. Kurt B. Young cites Clarke's importance in "Towards a Holistic Review of Pan-Africanism: Linking the Idea and Movement," *Nationalism and Ethnic Politics* 16, no. 2 (2010): 141–63. Young also extends Clarke's emphasis, adding his own definition of holistic Pan-Africanism that highlights the link between consciousness and politics and stresses the context-driven nature of the expression. Hakeem Adi and Marika Sherwood reflect a holistic approach in their introduction to *Pan-African History: Political Figures from Africa and the Diaspora Since*

1787 (London: Routledge, 2003), where they comment, "Pan-African history . . . includes chronicling a variety of ideas, activities and movements that celebrated Africanness, resisted the exploitation and oppression of those of African descent, and opposed the ideologies of racism" (vii).

62. Rayford Logan used this lasting term in *The Negro in American Life and Thought: The Nadir, 1877–1901* (New York: Dial, 1954). A similar retraction of rights for people of African descent took place throughout most of the British Empire.

CHAPTER 1: PAN-AFRICAN THOUGHT

1. See Julie Roy Jeffrey, *Abolitionists Remember: Antislavery Autobiographies and the Unfinished Work of Emancipation* (Chapel Hill: University of North Carolina Press, 2008).

2. See Rayford Logan, *The Negro in American Life and Thought: The Nadir, 1877–1901* (New York: Dial, 1954).

3. For understandings of Africa outside the stereotypes of the dark continent, see Jeanette Jones, *In Search of Brightest Africa: Reimagining the Dark Continent in American Culture, 1884–1936* (Athens: University of Georgia Press, 2010). She argues that African Americans were reframing the image of Africa by the late nineteenth century into one associated with empowerment and redemption and demonstrates how white American naturalists viewed the continent through a lens of environmental preservation. Neither of these perspectives completely disavowed aspects of primitivism associated with the people of Africa, but her work powerfully demonstrates the existence of a different approach to the continent.

4. Robert W. Rydell, *All the World's a Fair: Visions of Empire at American International Expositions, 1876–1914* (Chicago: University of Chicago Press, 1984), 77.

5. For use of the word *presence* in this context, see Christopher Robert Reed, *"All the World is Here!": The Black Presence at White City* (Bloomington: Indiana University Press, 2000).

6. Mabel O. Wilson, *Negro Building: Black Americans in the World of Fairs and Museums* (Berkeley: University of California Press, 2012), 9.

7. Ida B. Wells, Frederick Douglass, I. Garland Penn, and F. L. Barnett, *The Reason Why the Colored American Is Not in the World's Columbian Exposition: The Afro-American's Contribution to Columbian Literature*, ed. Robert Rydell (Urbana: University of Illinois Press, 1999).

8. Ibid., xxxii. Rydell argues that Douglass's arguments "had the effect of fueling dominant stereotypes of Africans, who were put on display in the Dahomeyan Village at the end of the Midway Plaisance" (xxxii–xxxiii). Yet Douglass, over his long career, sought to rescue Africa and its people from depictions of the dark continent. Thus, his contrasting of the progress of African Americans against the stereotype of the midway is best seen in the practical context of a counter-narrative to the ubiquitous ethnographic other of many world's fairs.

9. See Michele Rief, "Thinking Locally, Acting Globally: The International Agenda of African American Clubwomen, 1880–1940," *Journal of African American History* 89 (Summer 2004), 203–22; and Elisabetta Vezzosi, "The International Strategy of African American Women at the Columbian Exposition and Its Legacy: Pan-Africanism, Decolonization, and Human Rights," in *Moving Bodies, Displaying Nations: National Cultures, Race, and Gender in World Expositions, Nineteenth to Twenty-first Century,* ed. Guido Abbattista (Trieste, Italy: Edizioni Universitá di Trieste, 2014), 67–88.

10. Constitution, 1889, in *International Council of Women: Report of Transactions of the Second Quinquennial Meeting* (London: Unwin, 1900), appendix. From the discussion in the notes, one can assume that the "objects" of the ICW were the same as those adopted in 1888 (326).

11. May Wright Sewall, ed., *The World's Congress of Representative Women: A Historical Résumé for Popular Circulation of the World's Congress of Representative Women, Convened in Chicago on May 15, and Adjourned on May 22, 1893, under the Auspices of the Woman's Branch of the World's Congress Auxiliary,* 2 vols. (Chicago : Rand, McNally, 1894), 47, v, 5, 62, xii.

12. The appendix attests to the breadth of the ICW, listing women from twenty-four countries other than the United States as the "Foreign Advisory Council." However, a review of the ICW's meetings in 1888, 1893, and 1899 attests to the decided Anglo-American concentration of activists.

13. Sewall, *World's Congress of Representative Women,* 489–90.

14. Ibid., 482, 485.

15. Ibid., 36–37, 18, dedication page.

16. See Rosalyn Terborg-Penn, *African American Women in the Struggle for the Vote, 1850–1920* (Bloomington: Indiana University Press, 1998), especially chap. 4.

17. Sewall, *World's Congress of Representative Women,* 4, 16.

18. Hazel Carby argues that the inclusion of these African American women at the World's Congress of Representative Women was not due to any unifying "practice of sisterhood" or a real commitment to "provide a black political presence" at the fair (and, by implication, within the broader domestic setting of the United States). Instead, it was more in line with the "discourse of exoticism that pervaded the fair" (*Reconstructing Womanhood: The Emergence of the Afro-American Woman Novelist* [New York: Oxford University Press, 1987], 5).

19. All of these women, with the exception of Sarah J. Early, have entries in Darlene Clark Hine, ed., *Black Women in America,* 2nd ed. (Oxford; New York: Oxford University Press, 2005).

20. Harper was a well-known African American novelist and poet. Born in 1825, she, too, bridged the gap between abolitionism and post-emancipation and was involved in a host of reform associations (ibid., 22–25).

21. Sewall, *World's Congress of Representative Women,* 415, 418.

22. Ibid., 433, my emphasis

23. Ibid., 421, 434.

24. Ibid., 435.

25. Ibid., 437.

26. Ibid., 632, 715, 717.

27. On Williams, see Hine, *Black Women in America*, 352–54.

28. Sewall, *World's Congress of Representative Women*, 697, 696.

29. Ibid., 720–25. Brown references Henry Wadsworth Longfellow, "The Warning," *Poems on Slavery* (Cambridge, MA.: John Owen, 1842), 30–31; and Frances Ellen Watkins Harper, "Ethiopia," *Poems on Miscellaneous Subjects* (Boston: J. B. Yerrinton & Son, 1855), 11–12. *Race destiny* is not a new term in the scholarship of post-emancipated history. Michele Mitchell, *Righteous Propagation: African Americans and the Politics of Racial Destiny after Reconstruction* (Chapel Hill: University of North Carolina Press, 2004), argues that, beyond the shared sense of a common destiny, it was a "flexible concept" that proposed a number of different strategies (8).

30. On Turner's redemption project in southern Africa, see James T. Campbell, *Songs of Zion: The African Methodist Episcopal Church in the United States and South Africa* (Chapel Hill: University of North Carolina Press, 1998).

31. Alfred Le Ghait, "The Anti-Slavery Conference," *North American Review*, 154, no. 424 (March 3, 1892): 293.

32. Frederic Perry Noble, *The Chicago Congress on Africa* (Chicago, 1894), 282, 286.

33. Reed, *"All the World is Here,"* 184.

34. Noble, *The Chicago Congress on Africa*, 290, 317, 282–83.

35. Ibid., 289.

36. Ibid., 307, 293.

37. Prince Massaquoi, quoted in Reed, *"All the World is Here,"* 183.

38. Noble, *The Chicago Congress on Africa*, 298.

39. On the New South, see C. Vann Woodward, *Origins of the New South, 1877–1913* (Baton Rouge: Louisiana State University Press, 1951).

40. Walter G. Cooper, *The Cotton States and International Exposition and South, Illustrated* (Atlanta: Illustrator Company, 1896), 100.

41. According to Reed, Washington was part of the Congress on Labor at the 1893 Columbian Exposition in Chicago. Reed also argues that the controversy about including African Americans in that event contributed to Washington's acceptance of a separate exhibit in Atlanta (*"All the World is Here,"* 10–12).

42. Cooper, *The Cotton States and International Exposition*, 24.

43. Ibid., 24, 28.

44. Ibid., 98.

45. Ibid., 98–99.

46. August Meier's *Negro Thought in America, 1880–1915: Racial Ideologies in the Age of Booker T. Washington* (Ann Arbor: University of Michigan Press, 1963) explores not only Washington's complexity and his relevance to reform movements but

also provides an insightful overview of the period. Newer works on Washington include Robert Norrell, *Up from History: The Life of Booker T. Washington* (Cambridge, MA: Belknap Press of Harvard University Press, 2011); and Andrew Zimmerman, *Alabama in Africa: Booker T. Washington, the German Empire, and the Globalization of the New South* (Princeton: Princeton University Press, 2010).

47. Stewart E. Tolnay and E. M. Beck estimate that 2,264 black males were lynched in the American South between 1882 and 1930, most of them during the 1890s (*A Festival of Violence: An Analysis of Southern Lynching, 1882–1930* [Urbana: University of Illinois Press, 1995], appendix C).

48. In 1906, President Theodore Roosevelt dishonorably discharged 167 African American soldiers for their alleged participation in disturbances that claimed the life of one Brownsville, Texas, resident. (No indictments were ever issued.) In reaction, Tillman gave a speech on the floor of the Senate in which he questioned the unity of the United States: "We are a nation with a big N. But the southern half of the country has no conception of the word 'nation' expect that it is connected with the word 'nigger.' More's the pity!" (Benjamin R. Tillman, "The Race Problem: The Brownsville Raid," January 12, 1907 [Washington, D.C.: U.S. Government Printing Office, 1907]). For more on Tillman, see Stephan Kantrowitz, *Ben Tillman and the Reconstruction of White Supremacy* (Chapel Hill: University of North Carolina Press, 2000).

49. Cooper, *The Cotton States and International Exposition*, 91.

50. Rayford W. Logan and Michael R. Winston, eds., *Dictionary of American Negro Biography* (New York: Norton, 1982), 52–53.

51. W. E. Bowen, ed., *Africa and the American Negro: Address and Proceedings of the Congress on Africa, Held under the Auspices of the Stewart Missionary Foundation for Africa of Gammon Theological Seminary in Connection with the Cotton States and International Exposition* (Atlanta: Gammon Theological Seminary, 1896), 13, emphasis in original.

52. Martin Delany used the phrase: "Africa for the African race" in *Official Report of the Niger Valley Exploring Party* (London: Webb, Millington, and Co., 1861), 61. A variant of this—"Africa for Africans"—became a constant in Pan-African discourse throughout the late nineteenth and early twentieth centuries and was popularized by Marcus Garvey's Universal Negro Improvement Association, which was founded in 1914. For more on Garveyism, see Adam Ewing, *The Age of Garvey: How a Jamaican Activist Created a Mass Movement and Changed Global Politics* (Princeton: Princeton University Press, 2014).

53. Bowen, *Africa and the American Negro*, 198, 196.

54. Ibid., 203, 199. Turner's and Fortune's comments follow one another (195–98, 199–204).

55. For a detailed and insightful review of both the scholarship on and public embrace of Delany, see Tunde Adeleke, *Without Regard to Race: The Other Martin Delany* (Jackson: University of Mississippi Press, 2003).

56. Paul Gilroy describes Delany as "a figure of enormous complexity whose political trajectory through abolitionisms and emigrationisms, from Republicans to Democrats, dissolves a single attempt to fix him as consistently either conservative or radical" (*The Black Atlantic: Modernity and Double Consciousness* [Cambridge, MA: Harvard University Press, 1993], 20).

57. See Logan and Winston, *Dictionary of Negro Biography*, 169–72; and Robert S. Levine, ed., *Martin Delany: A Documentary Reader* (Chapel Hill: University of North Carolina Press, 2003), 1–22.

58. Adeleke argues that the treatment of Delany flows from the "instrumentalist projection of black American historiography" and that it is dictated more by the advancement of the black struggle than by scholarship (*Without Regard to Race*, xxi).

59. See Walter L. Williams, "Nineteenth Century Pan-Africanist: John Henry Smyth, United States Minister to Liberia, 1878–1885," *Journal of Negro History* 63 (January 1978), 18–25. Williams rightfully argues that Smythe is understudied; for instance, Logan and Winston do not include him in *Dictionary of American Negro Biography*. However, his Atlanta essay is included in Adelaide Cromwell Hill and Martin Kilson, eds., *Apropos of Africa: Sentiments of Negro American Leaders on Africa from the 1800s to the 1950s* (London: Cass, 1969); and Mitchell quotes from that essay in *Righteous Propagation*, 61.

60. Alfred A. Moss, Jr., *The American Negro Academy: Voice of the Talented Tenth* (Baton Rouge: Louisiana State University Press, 1981), 1.

61. John H. Smythe, "Negro Delinquent Children," in Isabel C. Barrows, ed., *Proceedings of the National Conference of Charities and Correction* (Boston: Ellis, 1899), 472. Smythe was also on the Standing Committee for Reformatories and Industrial Schools, part of the National Conference of Charities and Correction (xii).

62. Bowen, *Africa and the American Negro*, 120, 124. Here, Crummell was referring to missionary work among the Zulu.

63. Ibid., 141–42.

64. Crummell was a proponent of emigration to Liberia. He himself emigrated there in 1853 and worked with the American Colonization Society to encourage further migration from the United States. Due to internal political strife, however, he moved back to the United States permanently in 1873 (Logan and Winston, *Dictionary of American Negro Biography*, 145–46).

65. Alexander Crummell, "The Race Problem in America" (Washington, DC: Morrison, 1889), 11, 18, 11, 12, 14–15. However, Crummell consistently warned against democratic excess and stressed that society should be led by a civilized elite. For more on his authoritarian sensibilities, see Wilson J. Moses, *Alexander Crummell: A Study of Civilization and Discontent* (Oxford: Oxford University Press, 1989), 287–301.

66. Crummell, "The Race Problem in America," 15, 13.

67. W. E. B. Du Bois, "The Conservation of Races," *American Negro Academy Occasional Papers,* no. 2 (Washington, DC, 1897).

68. Ibid., 27.

69. Frederick L. Hoffman, "Race Traits of the American Negro," *Publications of the American Economic Association* 11, no. 1–3 (1896): 1–329.

70. George M. Fredrickson, *The Black Image in the White Mind: The Debate on Afro-American Character and Destiny, 1817–1914* (New York: Harper and Row, 1971), 249. Fredrickson establishes how Hoffman's article contributed to theories of racial degeneracy and race extinction. On Hoffman's radical opposition to Progressive Era prescriptions for state assistance, see Beatriz Hoffman, "Scientific Racism, Insurance, and Opposition to the Welfare State: Frederick L. Hoffman's Transatlantic Journey," *Journal of the Gilded Age and Progressive Era* 2 (April 2003): 150–90.

71. Du Bois, "The Conservation of Races," 7, 8, 1.

72. Ibid., 3, 5, 6.

73. Ibid., 9, 4.

74. Tommy L. Lott uses the term *striving* in "Du Bois on the Invention of Race," *Philosophical Forum* 24 (1992–93): 170.

75. This tension is the basis of Anthony Appiah's critique in "The Uncompleted Argument: Du Bois and the Illusion of Race," *Critical Inquiry* 12, no. 1 (1985): 21–37.

76. Du Bois, "The Conservation of Races," 6.

77. Ibid.

78. On Cooper, see Hine, *Black Women in America*, 308–12.

79. On the construction of masculinity, see Hazel Carby, *Race Men* (Cambridge, MA: Harvard University Press, 1998); Kevin K. Gaines, *Uplifting the Race: Black Leadership, Politics, and Culture in the Twentieth Century* (Chapel Hill: University of North Carolina Press, 1996); and Martin Summers, *Manliness and Its Discontents: The Black Middle Class and the Transformation of Masculinity, 1900–1930* (Chapel Hill: University of North Carolina Press, 2004).

80. Kevin Gaines notes that such constructions were often militant and made "black women's racial credentials . . . suspect" (*Uplifting the Race*, 102).

81. Paula Giddings uses a portion of Cooper's remarks as the title for *When and Where I Enter: The Impact of Black Women on Race and Sex in America* (New York: HarperCollins, 1984). On the relationship and ideological tensions between Cooper and Crummell, see Elizabeth West, "Cooper and Crummell: Dialogics of Race and Womanhood," in *Rhetorical Women: Roles and Representations,* ed. Hildy Miller and Lillan Bridwell-Bowles (Tuscaloosa: University of Alabama Press, 2005), 81–102.

82. Bruce's papers are one of the largest holdings at the Schomburg Center for Research in Black Culture. This collection contains Bruce's correspondence with a host of important reformers including African Americans Alexander Walters, Frederic Loudin, Thomas Calloway, and W. E. B. Du Bois; Pan-African conference organizer Henry Sylvester Williams; West African Mojolo Agbebi; South African John Tengo Jabavu; Ghana-born, South-African residing F. Z. S. Peregrino; British activist Catherine Impey; and Jamaican J. Robert Love. Bruce was a central hub of

a vibrant print culture connectivity and contributed articles, often as the "official" U.S. correspondent, in such papers as the *African Times and Orient Review*, the *Gold Coast Leader*, the *Jamaica Advocate*, the *Lagos Weekly Record*, the *Sierra Leone Weekly News* and the *South African Spectator*. Finally, this collection also documents the African American periodical culture in the United States with which Bruce was intimately connected, most notably during his time as the featured columnist for E. E. Cooper's *Colored American*. John Edward Bruce Papers, Schomburg Center for Research in Black Culture, Manuscripts, Archives, and Rare Book Division, New York Public Library, Sc Micro R-905.

83. On Bruce, see William Seraile, *Bruce Grit: The Black Nationalist Writings of John Edward Bruce* (Knoxville: University of Tennessee Press, 2003); and Ralph Crowder, *John Edward Bruce: Politician, Journalist, and Self-Trained Historian of the African Diaspora* (New York: New York University Press, 2004).

84. John Bruce, October 19, 1891, Group D—Manuscripts, 7–83. Crummell and Blyden constantly used this phrase. The seal of Ethiopia also appears on the letterhead of an 1894 letter to Bruce from John L. Dube of Natal, South Africa (Group D—Miscellaneous: 13–54). In 1912, Dube would become the first president of the African National Congress.

85. P. Olisanwuche Esedebe notes that the 1893 Congress on Africa marked the moment at which Pan-Africanism became a movement, not just an idea (*Pan-Africanism: The Idea and Movement* [Washington, DC: Howard University Press, 1994], 45–47).

CHAPTER 2: THE SUMMER OF 1900

1. Alexander Crummell, letter to John Bruce, January 21, 1898, Group B—Letters Received: MS 15. John Edward Bruce Papers, Schomburg Center for Research in Black Culture, Manuscripts, Archives, and Rare Book Division, New York Public Library, Sc Micro R-905.

2. On the origins of the African Association and the Pan-African Conference, see Immanuel Geiss, *The Pan-African Movement: A History of Pan-Africanism in America, Europe, and Africa* (New York: African Publishing Company, 1974); and Marika Sherwood, *Origins of Pan-Africanism: Henry Sylvester Williams, Africa, and the African Diaspora* (New York: Routledge, 2011).

3. On Crummell and the ANA's relationship with the African Association and other non-U.S. institutions, see Alfred A. Moss, Jr., *The American Negro Academy: Voice of the Talented Tenth* (Baton Rouge: Louisiana State University Press, 1981), 52–54.

4. The standard depiction of the ethnographic other, the Dahomey Village, was exhibited in the colonial section, along with a variety of other displays; see Richard Mandell, *Paris 1900: The Great World's Fair* (Toronto: University of Toronto Press, 1967).

5. *Report of the Commissioner-General for the United States to the International Universal Exposition* (Paris, 1900), 2:249–52.

6. Daniel T. Rodgers, *Atlantic Crossings: Social Politics in a Progressive Age* (Cambridge, MA: Belknap Press of Harvard University Press, 1998), 11–20.

7. Thomas J. Calloway, "The American Negro Exhibit at the Paris Exposition," *Colored American*, November 3, 1900, 2. A full-page photo of Calloway sitting in the main entry of the American Negro exhibit appears on page 1. Calloway graduated from Fisk University in 1889, served as an agent for Booker T. Washington's Tuskegee Institute from 1896 to 1898, was, for a short period in 1898, the managing editor of the *Colored American*, and was a member of the American Negro Academy at the time of his appointment as U.S. Special Commissioner to Paris. For this overview, see Louis R. Harlan and Raymond W. Smock, eds., *The Booker T. Washington Papers* (Urbana: University of Illinois Press, 1974), 3:177.

8. My central point is that Calloway and the American Negro exhibit resisted the portrayal of the ethnographic other and made claims about the basic equality of African people by appealing to the logic of progressivism that defied control, despite its paternalist origins. Shawn Michelle Smith, however, has a different reading of Calloway, arguing that he was firmly in the accommodationist camp: "Rather than celebrating African American resistance to overwhelming U.S. racism, Calloway sought to congratulate the United States on a triumph of racist paternalism" (*Photography on the Color Line: W. E. B. Du Bois, Race, and Visual Culture* [Durham, NC: Duke University Press, 2004], 19).

9. Smith offers an insightful discussion of the visual work crucial to Du Bois's concept and negotiation of double consciousness (ibid., 25–26). According to Du Bois, "It is a peculiar sensation, this double-consciousness, this sense of always looking at one's self through the eyes of others, of measuring one's soul by the tape of a world that looks on in amused contempt and pity" (*The Souls of Black Folk* [Chicago, A. C. McClurg, 1903: reprint, New York: Barnes and Noble Classics, 2003], 9).

10. Smith, *Photography on the Color Line*, 112.

11. Rebecka Rutledge Fisher, "Cultural Artifacts and the Narrative of History: W. E. B. Du Bois and the Exhibiting of Culture at the 1900 Paris Exposition Universelle," *Modern Fiction Studies*, 51 (Winter 2005): 741–74.

12. W. E. B. Du Bois, "The American Negro in Paris," *American Monthly Review of Reviews* 22, no. 5 (November 1900): 576. On the exhibit's links among the visuals, subjectivity, and historical agency, see Deborah Willis, "The Sociologist's Eye: W. E. B. Du Bois and the Paris Exposition," in *A Small Nation of People: W. E. B. Du Bois and African American Portraits of Progress*, eds. David Levering Lewis and Deborah Wills (New York: HarperCollins, 2003), 78.

13. Fisher, "Cultural Artifacts," 757, 764–76.

14. *Report of the Pan-African Conference* (London, 1900), 2, 3, 9.

15. Ibid., 5, 7, 2, 4, 8.

16. Ibid., 10–11.

17. Jonathan Schneer documents this vibrancy as well as competing views of the British Empire in *London 1900: The Imperial Metropolis* (New Haven: Yale University Press, 1999).

18. *Report of the Pan-African Conference*, 6–8.

19. Ibid., 5, 12.

20. Schneer, *London 1900*, 224.

21. *Report of the Pan-African Conference*, 10.

22. Ibid., 1–2.

23. The objects of the Pan-African Association were detailed by its president, Bishop Alexander Walters, in a series of letters to E. E. Cooper, the editor of the *Colored American,* which details his experiences at the Pan-African Conference. Walters's correspondence also describes his trip to the Paris exposition and his thoughts about the American Negro exhibit ("Pan-African Conference," *Colored American*, August 25, 1900, 2).

24. *Report of the Pan-African Conference*, 10.

25. See James T. Kloppenberg, *Uncertain Victory: Social Democracy and Progressivism in European and American Thought, 1870–1920* (New York: Oxford University Press, 1986); Michael Freeden, *The New Liberalism: An Ideology of Social Reform* (Oxford: Clarendon, 1978); and Rodgers, *Atlantic Crossings.*

26. I borrow the term *social politics* from Rodgers, *Atlantic Crossings*, 2.

27. This section draws on Freeden's *The New Liberalism* and his *Liberal Languages: Ideological Imaginations and Twentieth Century Progressive Thought* (Princeton: Princeton University Press, 2005). Marc Stears demonstrates the transatlantic nature of this new liberalism in *Progressives, Pluralists, and the Problem of the State: Ideologies of Reform in the United States and Great Britain, 1909–1926* (Oxford: Oxford University Press, 2002), chap. 1.

28. See Jose Harris, *Private Lives, Public Spirit: A Social History of Britain* (Oxford: Oxford University Press, 1993); and Nancy Cohen, *The Reconstruction of American Liberalism, 1865–1914* (Chapel Hill: University of North Carolina Press, 2002).

29. Freeden, *Liberal Languages*, 14–17.

30. On the links among nationalism, the nation-state, and modernity, see Benedict Anderson, *Imagined Communities: Reflections on the Origins and Spread of Nationalism* (London: Verso, 1983).

31. Gustav Spiller, an Ethical Society member and an organizer of the 1911 Universal Races Congress in London, wrote an invaluable history, *The Ethical Movement in Great Britain: A Documentary History* (London: Fairleigh, 1934). The work includes a lengthy appendix, "The British Ethical Movement an Integral Part of the International Ethic Movement," that documents the transatlantic ties of the ethical societies.

32. Bernard Bosanquet, "The Eclipse of Liberalism," *Ethical World* January 8, 1898, 25. This article should not be confused with E. L Godkin's article of the same name (*Nation,* August 9, 1900). Godkin was dedicated to traditional liberal standards of the individual, and his piece is skeptical about the new reformer impulses.

33. Schneer makes this point in *London 1900*, 167–68. Gregory Claeys sees the positivist movement as central to British critiques of imperialism (*Imperial Sceptics: British Critics of Empire* [Cambridge: Cambridge University Press, 2010]).

34. Edward Spencer Beesly, "The Indian Millstone," *Positivist Review* 2, no. 18 (June 1, 1894): 101.

35. Edward Spencer Beesly, "Paragraphs," *Positivist Review* 1, no. 10 (October 1, 1893): 189–90, emphasis in original.

36. Edward Spencer Beesly, "The Western Treatment of Backward Races," *Positivist Review* 4, no. 45 (September 1, 1896): 179.

37. J. H. Bridges, "The Ascent of Man," *Positivist Review* 2, no. 20 (August 1, 1894): 133–34.

38. Frederic Harrison, "Twenty-One Years at Newton Hall," *Positivist Review* 10, no. 113 (May 1, 1902): 107–8.

39. F. S. Marvin, "Our Treatment of Weaker Races," *Positivist Review* 8, no. 94 (October 1, 1900): 172.

40. F. S. Marvin, "An Anglo-Saxon World," *Positivist Review* 4, no. 44 (October 1, 1896): 194.

41. J. H. Bridges, "Two Voices From the Far East," *Positivist Review* 9, no. 50 (April 1, 1901): 80.

42. George Stocking, Jr., "Franz Boas and the Culture Concept in Historical Perspective," *American Anthropologist* 68 (August 1966): 867–82.

43. Vernon Williams, Jr., calls the tension between "egalitarian sentiments" and "traditional European and American physical anthropology" the "Boasian paradox" and documents how Boas struggled with accepted methods of physical anthropology, especially cranial measurement, in his approach to race (*Rethinking Race: Franz Boas and His Contemporaries* [Lexington: University of Kentucky Press, 1996], 6). Also see his *The Social Sciences and Theories of Race* (Urbana: University of Illinois Press, 2006), especially chap. 2. In a review of *Rethinking Race*, George Stocking, Jr., argues that Williams's stress on the contradiction of the paradox takes away from the "coherence" of Boas's critique of racial essentialism (*ISIS* 88, no. 1 (1997): 161–62.

44. Carl Degler, *In Search of Human Nature: The Decline and Revival of Darwinism in American Social Thought* (Oxford: Oxford University Press, 1991), 71.

45. Stocking points out that Boas's students, who included Melville Herskovits and Margaret Mead, were important to the shift from physical racial inheritance to environmentalist approaches ("Franz Boas and the Culture Concept," 879). Williams discusses Boas's influence on African American intelligentsia such as Du Bois (*The Social Sciences*, 17).

46. Frederic Harrison, "Annual Address Delivered at Newton Hall, 1 January 1895," *Positivist Review* 3, no. 26 (February 1, 1895): 37.

47. Edward Spencer Beesly, "Paragraphs," *Positivist Review* 6, no. 69 (September 1, 1898): 158.

48. *Social gospel* is an umbrella term that describes the commitment to religiously inspired secular change. Christian socialism was the British variant, and several important intellectual figures in the United States, including Richard T. Ely and Edward Bellamy, contributed to Christian socialist organizations and journals. Paul T. Phillips demonstrates the transatlantic nature of the social gospel in *A Kingdom of God on Earth: Anglo-American Social Christianity, 1880–1940* (University Park: Pennsylvania State University Press, 1996).

49. Josiah Strong, *Our Country: Its Possible Future and Its Present Crisis* (New York: Baker and Taylor, 1885). Richard Hofstadter has called *Our Country* "one of the most revealing documents of its time" (*Social Darwinism in American Thought* [Philadelphia: University of Pennsylvania Press, 1944], 178).

50. Josiah Strong, "Religious Movements for Social Betterment," in *Monographs on American Social Economics,* ed. Herbert B. Adams (Washington, DC: U.S. Commission to the Paris Exposition of 1900), 39.

51. Josiah Strong, *Expansion under New World-Conditions* (New York: Baker and Taylor, 1900).

52. Ralph Luker, *The Social Gospel in Black and White: American Racial Reform* (Chapel Hill: University of North Carolina Press, 1991), 274–75.

53. On social Darwinism, including discussion of Strong and Kidd, see Hofstadter, *Social Darwinism in American Thought*; Mike Hawkins, *Social Darwinism in European and American Thought, 1860–1945* (Cambridge: Cambridge University Press, 1997); Gregory Claeys, "The 'Survival of the Fittest' and the Origins of Social Darwinism," *Journal of the History of Ideas* 61, no. 2 (2000): 223–40; and Geoffrey M. Hodgson, "Social Darwinism in Anglophone Academic Journals: A Contribution to the History of the Term," *Journal of Historical Sociology* 17, no. 4 (2004): 428–63.

54. Bernard Porter, *Britannia's Burden: The Political Evolution of Modern Britain* (London: Arnold, 1994), 121.

55. Strong, "Religious Movements," 11.

56. D. P. Crook, *Benjamin Kidd: Portrait of a Social Darwinist* (Cambridge: Cambridge University Press, 1984), 51–53.

CHAPTER 3: JOHN BRUCE'S PAN-AFRICAN NETWORK AND THE CONDEMNATION OF WHITE CHRISTIANITY

1. Thabo Mbeki, "Address at the Commemoration of the 121st Anniversary of the Battle of Adwa at Addis Ababa University, March 4, 2017," *Africology* 10 (April 2017): 298–308.

2. *Report of the Pan-African Conference* (London, 1900), 4.

3. Mbeki noted, "Significantly, as all of us know, Melenik authorized a fellow African, but from the African Diaspora, Benito Sylvain, originally from Haiti, to represent Ethiopia at the Conference" ("Address at the Commemoration," 305).

4. "Annual Report, May 1885," *Aborigines' Friend* (November 1885): 258; "Annual

Report, May 1889," *Aborigines' Friend* 4, no. 2 (May 1890): 45. On the APS, see Charles Swaisland, "The Aborigines' Protection Society," *Reporter* 13, no. 3 (1987): 84–95.

5. "Annual Report, May 1885," *Aborigines' Friend,* 257.

6. Ibid., 257–58.

7. Quoted in S. J. S. Cookey, *Britain and the Congo Question 1885–1913*, Ibadan History Series (London: Longmans, 1968), 42.

8. H. R. Fox Bourne, *Civilisation in the Congo: A Story of International Wrongdoing* (London: King, 1903). By this time, Fox Bourne was part of the larger protest detailed in Adam Hochschild, *King Leopold's Ghost: A Story of Greed, Terror, and Heroism in Colonial Africa* (New York: Houghton Mifflin, 1998). Hochschild mentions Fox Bourne briefly on page 173.

9. H. R. Fox Bourne, *Matabeleland and the Chartered Company* (London: King, 1897); H. R. Fox Bourne, "Black and White 'Rights' in Africa," *Imperial and Asiatic Quarterly Review and Oriental and Colonial Record* 5, no. 9 (January 1898): 72–92; H. R. Fox Bourne, *Blacks and Whites in South Africa: An Account of the Past Treatment and Present Condition of South African Natives under British and Boer Control* (London: King, 1900).

10. Fox Bourne, *Blacks and Whites in South Africa,* 6.

11. Fox Bourne, "Black and White 'Rights' in Africa," 83.

12. Fox Bourne's *Blacks and Whites in South Africa* includes a historical exposition of British and Boer relations with African peoples, and the introduction lists James Bryce's *Impressions of South Africa* as a "very instructive and suggestive" work of reference (6).

13. Fox Bourne, "Black and White 'Rights' in Africa," 87–88. The 1896–97 struggle was the second armed conflict against colonial rule. (The first occurred in 1893–94.) It is often referred to as the first Chimurenga; the second Chimurenga refers to the 1966–79 struggle for Zimbabwe's independence. See Terence Ranger, *Revolt in Southern Rhodesia, 1896–7: A Study in African Resistance* (London: Heinemann, 1967).

14. Fox Bourne, *Black and Whites in South Africa*, 92–93.

15. Ibid., 92.

16. John Hope Franklin, *George Washington Williams: A Biography* (Chicago: University of Chicago Press, 1985), 244, 245, 253–54.

17. On Scholes, see John Edward Bruce, "Dr. Theophilus E. S. Scholes, MD," *Voice of the Negro* 4, no. 2 (March 1907): 114–15; and Kim Blake, "T. E. S. Scholes: The Unknown Pan Africanist," *Race and Class* 49, no. 1 (2007): 62–80.

18. Blake, "T. E. S. Scholes," 68–69.

19. Theophilus E. S. Scholes, *The British Empire and Alliances or Britain's Duty to Her Colonies and Subject Races,* (London: Stock, 1899). The genesis of this work, according to Scholes, was the U.S. victory in the Spanish-American War. Scholes (iii).

20. J. A. Froude wrote a diatribe against self-government in the British West Indies, which, he believed, would dangerously empower people of African descent (*The English in the West Indies or the Bow of Ulysses* [London: Longmans, Green,

1888]). On Freeman's unconstrained "Teutonic preconceptions and prejudices," see Marilyn Lake and Henry Reynolds, *Drawing the Global Colour Line: White Men's Countries and the International Challenge of Racial Equality* (Cambridge: Cambridge University Press, 2008), 59.

21. Scholes, *The British Empire*, 273. Scholes quotes Edward A. Freeman, *Impressions of the United States* (London: Longmans, Green, 1883), 142, 144.

22. Scholes, *The British Empire*, 275.

23. Ibid., 283, 288.

24. Theophilus E. S. Scholes, *Glimpses of the Ages or the "Superior" and "Inferior" Races, So-Called, Discussed in the Light of Science and History* (London: Long, 1905), xi.

25. Scholes, *The British Empire*, 289, 277.

26. Neta Crawford argues that protests such as Fox Bourne's contributed to the contention that empire had to meet some form of legitimacy in its relations with colonial peoples (*Argument and Change in World Politics: Ethics, Decolonization, and Humanitarian Intervention* [Cambridge: Cambridge University Press, 2002], chap. 5).

27. *Report of the Pan-African Conference*, 10, 11.

28. "African American Photographs Assembled for 1900 Paris Exposition, J. Robert Love, M.D," Library of Congress, http://www.loc.gov.

29. On Love, see Ralph Crowder, *John Edward Bruce: Politician, Journalist, and Self-Trained Historian of the African Diaspora* (New York: New York University Press, 2004), 45–49; and Mary Lumsden, "Robert Love and Jamaican Politics" (master's thesis, University of the West Indies, 1987).

30. Love noted of the *Advocate*, "The paper is hated and feared by its enemies (who, however, read it greedily) and adored by its friends. If it lives, it will be the Negro's standard bearer" (J. Robert Love, letter to John Bruce, May 21, 1896, Group B—Letters Received: B156. John Edward Bruce Papers, Schomburg Center for Research in Black Culture, Manuscripts, Archives, and Rare Book Division, New York Public Library, Sc Micro R-905).

31. On Williams's time in Jamaica and his connections with Love, see Owen Charles Mathurin, *Henry Sylvester Williams and the Origins of the Pan-African Movement, 1869–1911* (London: Greenwood, 1976), 86–93; and Marika Sherwood, *Origins of Pan-Africanism: Henry Sylvester Williams, Africa, and the African Diaspora* (New York: Routledge, 2011), 103–9.

32. Lumsden, "Robert Love," 16, 4.

33. John Bruce, "The White Man's Idea of Heaven," *Jamaica Advocate* (March 1900), Group E—Miscellaneous, Bruce Collection.

34. Ibid.

35. John Bruce, "Blot on the Escutcheon," February 7, 1891, Group D—Manuscripts: 7–99, Bruce Collection.

36. John Bruce, "White Christianity," 1891, Group D—Manuscripts: 9–73, Bruce Collection. Bruce's denunciation of white Christianity was a consistent theme in his writings.

37. John P. Jackson, letter to John Bruce, 1897, Group A—Letters Received: J1, Bruce Collection.

38. According to Bruce, he first met Blyden in 1880, when they both hoped that the "acquaintance would grow into a lasting friendship" (John Bruce, n.d, Group C—Letters Sent: 5–21, Bruce Collection.

39. Edward W. Blyden, *Christianity, Islam, and the Negro Race* (London: W. B. Whittingham & Co, 1887).

40. On Blyden, see Hakim Adi and Marika Sherwood, *Pan-African History: Political Figures from Africa and the Diaspora Since 1787* (London: Routledge, 2003); and Hollis R. Lynch, *Edward Wilmot Blyden: Pan-Negro Patriot, 1832—1912* (London: Oxford University Press, 1967).

41. Blyden, *Christianity, Islam and the Negro Race*, 18.

42. Edward W. Blyden, "Islam in Western Soudan," *Journal of the African Society* 2, no. 5 (October 1902): 27. Here, he paraphrased a long paragraph from Bryce's lecture, which saw the failing of Christianity as a function of the "scornful superiority" of whites who resisted the basic precepts of Christian equality. (James Bryce, *The Relation of the Advanced and the Backward Races of Mankind* [Oxford: Clarendon, 1903]).

43. V. Y. Mudimbe criticizes Blyden's view of Islam: "Throughout the nineteenth century in Central Africa, Islamic factions represented an objective evil and practiced a shameful slave-trade. And here, again, we face an unbelievable inconsistency in Blyden's thought: his naïve admiration for Islam led him to accept the enslavement of non-Muslim peoples" (*The Invention of Africa* [Bloomington: Indiana University Press, 1988], 115). This critique is valid, yet Blyden also used Islam to break down the automatic conflation of prevailing racial categories with particular religions and to show that there were serious problems with the egalitarian claims of western Christianity.

44. W. J. Moses uses *detour* to describe Blyden's appreciation of Islam as a civilizer (*Creative Conflict in African American Thought: Frederick Douglass, Alexander Crummell, Booker T. Washington, W. E. B. Du Bois, and Marcus Garvey* [Cambridge: Cambridge University Press, 2004], 95).

45. Blyden, *Christianity, Islam, and the Negro Race*, 31.

46. Teshale Tibebu sees this process as a dialectic for Blyden, who "comes across as a Black Hegelian" (*Edward Wilmot Blyden and the Racial Nationalist Imagination* [Rochester, NY: University of Rochester Press, 2013], 40). Tibebu provides an overview of Blyden's "black Protestant Islamophilia" in chap. 3.

47. Blyden, "Islam in the Western Soudan," 26.

48. E. A. Ayandele states bluntly that Blyden was "essentially a 'black Englishman' [who] wore a white man's clothes all his life, [and] basked in the white man's culture of which he was very proud" (*African Historical Studies* [London: Cass, 1979], 208).

49. On Agbebi, see ibid., 107–36.

50. According to Ayandele, the date appears on the first extant letter from Bruce to Agbebi in the Mojola Agbebi Papers held at the Ibadan University Library in Ibadan, Nigeria (ibid., 110).

51. Ibid., 112.

52. Mojola Agbebi, *Inaugural Sermon: Delivered at the Celebration of the First Anniversary of the "African Church,"* Lagos, West Africa, December 21, 1902, Group E: Not Catalogued, Bruce Collection. The collection has a copy of the full speech, with no publication information.

53. The information about the publishing of the sermon and comments from Blyden and Bruce are in Group E: Not Catalogued, Bruce Collection. This section of the archive also has documents marked "From Mojola" and signed "Yours Sincerely Mojola Agbebi" and also contains associated letters from Blyden and Bruce and additional notes from Agbebi, anonymous commentators, and material from the *Sierra Leone Weekly News*, and the *Lagos Weekly Record*, Group E: Not Catalogued, Bruce Collection.

54. British missionary societies—notably, the Church Missionary Society— had a presence in what would become Nigeria by the mid-nineteenth century. See Toyin Falola, *The History of Nigeria* (London: Greenwood, 1999).

55. Agbebi, *Inaugural Sermon*, 5.

56. Ibid., 10.

57. Ibid.

58. Hazel King comments that "Agbebi stands as one such example of an African who not only attempted to translate Christianity into an African context, but was also highly critical of the lack of this hitherto" ("Cooperation in Contextualization: Two Visionaries of the African Church—Mojola Agbebi and William Hughes of the African Institute, Colwyn Bay," *Journal of Religion in Africa*, 14, no. 1 [1986]: 5).

59. David Killingray, "The Black Atlantic Missionary Movement and Africa, 1780s-1920s" *Journal of Religion in Africa* 3 (February 2003): 3–31.

60. See James T. Campbell, *Songs of Zion: The African Methodist Church in the United States and Africa* (New York: Oxford University Press, 1998), 104, 115.

61. This missionary impulse—"Saving Africa for Christ"—became its own movement instead of being an "ancillary benefit" to emigrationist models in the 1880s and 1890s (ibid., 88).

62. Ibid., 132–35.

63. Ibid., 229.

64. Mbeki, "Address at the Commemoration," 300.

65. John Bruce, letter to Wu Tingfang, May 5, 1900, Group A—Letters Received: B16, Bruce Collection. Wu Tingfang was the Qing dynasty's minister to the United States from 1896 to 1902; see Linda Pomerantz-Zhang, *Wu Tingfang (1842–1922): Reform and Modernization in Modern Chinese History* (Hong Kong: Hong Kong University Press, 1992). The article that Bruce refers to does not appear in any bibliographical information on Wu. However, Wu did give a talk titled "Christ and

Confucius" for a Society for Ethical Culture event at Carnegie Hall, where he was introduced by Felix Adler (December 9, 1900). Excerpts were printed in the *New York Times* (December 10, 1900). While the dates of the letter and the talk do not correspond, Bruce was nonetheless clearly aware of Wu's speech. In his April 27 column in the *Colored American*, Bruce quoted from the talk at length, noting that it helped demonstrate that these "alleged 'heathens and barbarians' possess more of a spirit of humanity and brotherhood than the boasted Christians of the Western World." He also mentioned Wu Tingfang in his commentary on lynching in *The Blood Red Record* (Albany, 1901).

66. John Bruce, "The Chinese Question," *Colored American*, July 14, 1900, 1–2.

67. *Report of the Pan-African Conference*, 3.

68. J. Robert Love, letter to John Bruce, April 26, 1893, Group A—Letters Received: L-3, Bruce Collection.

69. J. Robert Love, letter to John Bruce, June 6, 1893, Group A—Letters Received: L-4, Bruce Collection.

70. Bruce was not the first to laud the events in Haiti as a statement of political empowerment for people of African descent. Bishop James T. Holly, whom Love had ran afoul of in Haiti, had already published *A Vindication of the Capacity of the Negro Race for Self Government and Civilized Progress as Demonstrated by Historical Events of the Haytian Revolution* (New Haven, CT: Africa-American Printing Company, 1857). Holly was the first African American consecrated by the Episcopal church.

71. Jean-Jacques Dessalines, "The Proclamation of Haitian Independence," trans. J. Robert Love, *Voice of the Negro* 2, no. 9 (September 1905): 634–36. An epilogue explains that Love had translated the document for Bruce; hence, it was probably a copy of what the pair had exchanged in the 1890s. The length of time between that exchange and publication suggests the difficulty they encountered when trying to disseminate the full document. However, given the vibrant nature of Pan-African print culture, parts of it had certainly appeared in other forums; and considerations of Toussaint L'Ouverture were a staple of the era.

72. J. Robert Love, "The Declaration of Haitian Independence and Jean-Jacques Dessalines, the Father of His Country," *Voice of the Negro* 2, no. 9 (September 1905): 638, 639.

73. Ibid., 638, 640, emphasis in original.

74. Bruce, "Dr. Theophilus E. S. Scholes," 114–15. The magazine also ran a glowing review of Scholes's *Glimpses of the Ages*, noting that the work had "created something of a sensation in England" and calling it "bold and radical, but thoroughly convincing" (*Voice of the Negro* [February 1906]: 143).

75. Bruce, "Dr. Theophilus E. S. Scholes," 114, 115.

76. William Seraile, *Bruce Grit: The Black Nationalist Writings of John Edward Bruce* (Knoxville: University of Tennessee Press), 115–19.

77. Blake, "T. E. S. Scholes," 76. Stephen G. Hall argues that Williams's *History of the Negro Race* started a period of professionalization of African American historical

writing that culminated in Carter Woodson's establishment of the Association for the Study of Negro Life and History in 1915. Hall also notes the contributions of Schomburg and others analyzed in this work, including Anna J. Cooper and Pauline Hopkins. See *A Faithful Account of the Race: African American Historical Writing in Nineteenth-Century America* (Chapel Hill: University of North Carolina Press, 2009).

CHAPTER 4: MANLINESS, EMPIRE, AND LEGITIMATE VIOLENCE

1. Louis R. Harlan and Raymond W. Smock, eds., *The Booker T. Washington Papers* (Urbana: University of Illinois Press, 1976), 3: 226.

2. On the "best foot forward" tradition, see Wilson J. Moses, *Creative Conflict in African American Thought: Frederick Douglass, Alexander Crummell, Booker T. Washington, W. E. B. Du Bois, and Marcus Garvey* (Cambridge: Cambridge University Press, 2004), 203–7.

3. Kristin Hoganson argues that the British connection between imperialism and manliness appealed directly to those in the United States who supported expansion in the late nineteenth century (*Fighting for Manhood: How Gender Politics Provoked the Spanish-American and Philippine-American Wars* [New Haven: Yale University Press, 1998], 140). On the links among empire, violence, and manhood in the United States, see Gail Bederman, *Manliness and Civilization: A Cultural History of Gender and Race in the United States, 1880–1917* (Chicago: University of Chicago Press, 1995). On connections between gender and British imperialism, see Anne McClintock, *Imperial Leather: Race, Gender, and Sexuality in the Colonial Conquest* (New York: Routledge, 1995); and Antoinette Burton, *Burdens of History: British Feminists, Indian Women, and Imperial Culture: 1865–1915* (Chapel Hill: University of North Carolina Press, 1994).

4. W. E. B. Du Bois, "The American Negro at Paris," *American Monthly Review of Reviews* 22 (July–December 1900): 576.

5. William B. Gatewood, Jr., *Black Americans and the White Man's Burden, 1898–1903* (Urbana: University of Illinois Press, 1975), 13–21.

6. John Bruce [as Bruce Grit], "Valor of the Negro Soldier," *Colored American,* May 7, 1898.

7. John Bruce [as Bruce Grit], "Bruce Grit's Melange," *Colored American,* July 28, 1900, 3.

8. Ibid., 4.

9. Ibid., 2.

10. Owen Charles Mathurin, *Henry Sylvester Williams and the Origins of the Pan-African Movement, 1869–1911* (London: Greenwood, 1976), 109.

11. Ibid., 108–9.

12. *Report of the Pan-African Conference* (London, 1900), 9.

13. See Wilson Jeremiah Moses, *Alexander Crummell: A Study of Civilization and Discontent* (Oxford: Oxford University Press, 1989), 52–58.

14. Philip S. Foner, ed., *Life and Writings of Frederick Douglass* (New York: International Publishers, 1950), 1:127.

15. Alexander Crummell, letter to John Bruce, January 21, 1898, Group B—Letters Received: MS 15. John Edward Bruce Papers, Schomburg Center for Research in Black Culture, Manuscripts, Archives, and Rare Book Division, New York Public Library, Sc Micro R-905.

16. V. Y. Mudimbe argues that this emphasis on cultural retention used the foil of racial difference, which, for an African operating within the hegemonic force of white colonial racism, was a "strain theory" that could never escape the contradictions embedded in the epistemological structure of power-seeking western racism. Mudimbe acknowledges that Blyden certainly was a powerful and seminal voice of anticolonialism. He also argues that Blyden's refusal to embrace "interest theory," which concentrates on the relations between the ideological and the material, prevented him from "generating a new African mode of production, and thus technical modernization, political democracy, and cultural autonomy" (V. Y. Mudimbe, *The Invention of Africa: Gnosis, Philosophy and the Order of Knowledge* [Bloomington: University of Indiana Press, 1988], 129–134, 131).

17. Ibid., 130. Writing of the ANA, Moses notes, "The members of the Academy were Europhiles, more specifically, Anglophiles. Majestic government building, enduring archives, solid church edifices, and stately boulevards represented the cultural ideals of Western civilization that they cherished" (*Alexander Crummell*, 267).

18. On Loudin and the Jubilee Singers, see Andrew Ward, *Dark Midnight When I Rise: The Story of the Jubilee Singers Who Introduced the World to the Music of Black America* (New York: Farrar, Straus, and Giroux, 2000). Loudin was often mentioned in the *Colored American*. For example, the December 22, 1900, edition features a front-page image of him with the caption "Mr. Frederick J. Loudin: The World's Most Famous Afro-American Basso" and details the Fisk Jubilee Singers' recent trip to Halifax, where the troupe offered, among other numbers, a "powerful rendering" of "For Queen and Country" (1). On March 9, 1901, the paper ran a review from the *Belfast New-Letter* lauding the group's performance in Belfast. On the same page is a large advertisement for Bruce's *The Blood Red Record* (2).

19. James Smethurst argues that late-nineteenth-century industrialization and expansion "interlocked" with a tightening racial regime as a defining condition of modernity in the United States. I agree that this tightening occurred against the "contradiction" of the legal guarantee of citizenship. Loudin was intimate with these conditions that, for Smethurst, found expression in popular culture that often used movement, another marker of modernity, in the pursuit of artistic expression (*The African American Roots of Modernism: From Reconstruction to the Harlem Renaissance* [Chapel Hill: University of North Carolina Press, 2011], 7 and 15).

20. On spirituals, see Patricia Liggins Hill, ed., *Call and Response: The Riverside Anthology of the African American Literary Tradition* (New York: Houghton Mifflin, 1997), 14–17, 35–49.

21. J. B. T. Marsh, *The Story of the Jubilee Singers* (Boston: Houghton Mifflin, 1880), 121.

22. Kevin Gaines, "Assimilationist Minstrelsy as Racial Uplift Ideology: James D. Corrothers's Literary Quest for Black Leadership," *American Quarterly*, 45 (September 1993): 341–69, 345.

23. Veit Erlmann, "A Feeling of Prejudice: Orpheus M. McAdoo and the Virginia Jubilee Singers in South Africa, 1890–1898," *Journal of Southern African Studies* 14 (April 1988): 335.

24. Paul Gilroy argues that the Jubilee Singers helped to establish new cultural forms that were legitimized "precisely through their distance from the racial codes of minstrelsy" (Paul Gilroy, *The Black Atlantic: Modernity and Double Consciousness* [Cambridge: Harvard University Press, 1993], 90). There are also other understanding of minstrelsy. As Smethurst notes, minstrelsy and its associated "coon songs" were popular with African American audiences, and many African American artists viewed the performances with some "ambivalence," seeing them as both an outlet for artistry and a critique of Jim Crow (*The African American Roots of Modernism*, 17–18). After arguing that white-performed minstrelsy required the erasure of black identity as a historical fact, Stephanie Dunson discusses how the African Americans entertainers Bert Williams and George Walker performed blackface in ways that asserted aspects of humanity that subverted the traditional caricatures ("Black Misrepresentation in Nineteenth-Century Sheet Music," in *Beyond Blackface: African Americans and the Creation of American Popular Culture, 1890–1930*, ed. W. Fitzhugh Brundage [Chapel Hill: University of North Carolina Press, 2011], 45–65).

25. Ward, *Dark Midnight When I Rise*, xiv, 385.

26. Erlmann, "A Feeling of Prejudice," 331.

27. See figure 5. Marika Sherwood uses the image in *Origins of Pan-Africanism: Henry Sylvester Williams, Africa, and the African Diaspora* (New York: Routledge, 2014), 76.

28. Ward, *Dark Midnight When I Rise*, 293.

29. Frederick Loudin, letter to John Bruce, April 9, 1900, Group B–Letters Received: MS 76, Bruce Collection.

30. Loudin's letter also implies that he had known Bruce for a long time (ibid.).

31. Ibid.

32. Jeffrey Green, "The Foremost Musician of His Race: Samuel Coleridge-Taylor of England, 1875–1912," *Black Music Research Journal* 10 (Autumn 2001): 233–35, 239.

33. During his highly publicized trip to the United States in 1904, Coleridge-Taylor denounced "coon-songs" as being the "worst sort of rot" with "no real Negro character or sentiment" (Doris Evans McGinty, "That You Have Come So Far to See Us: Coleridge-Taylor in America," *Black Music Research Journal* 21 [Autumn 1990]: 239). Loudin wrote a celebratory essay on Coleridge-Taylor, "The Negro at His Best: High Soul Exemplified in the Works of Taylor," *Colored American*, April 5, 1902.

34. Gilroy, *The Black Atlantic*, 37–40, 1.

35. See Thomas J. Noer, *Briton, Boer, and Yankee: The United States and South Africa, 1870–1914* (Kent, OH: Kent University Press, 1978).

36. Loudin, letter to Bruce, April 9, 1900.

37. Ibid.

38. Ibid., emphasis in original.

39. Les Switzer, *Power and Resistance in an African Society: The Ciskei Xhosa and the Making of South Africa* (Madison: University of Wisconsin Press, 1993), 136–37.

40. By 1886, in the five eastern constituencies of the Cape, the African vote made up 47 percent of the voters (Peter Walshe, *The Rise of African Nationalism: The African National Congress, 1912–1952* [Berkeley: University of California Press, 1971], 3).

41. Switzer, *Power and Resistance in an African Society*, 101–3, 152–53.

42. Vivian Bickford-Smith contextualizes the exceptionalist narrative surrounding the Cape liberal tradition, reminding us that both racism and segregation were fundamental features of Cape society by the late nineteenth century (*Ethnic Pride and Racial Prejudice in Victorian Cape Town* [Cambridge: Cambridge University Press, 1995]).

43. Jabavu responded to a letter from Bruce, confirming that he would send *Imvo* directly to Bruce fortnightly. The memorandum is on *Imvo* letterhead, with a caption that demonstrates the Cape tradition of encouraging market exchange: "The Best Advertising Medium for reaching Native Consumers in All Districts" (John Tengo Jabavu, letter to John Bruce, September 13, 1897, Group B—Letters Received: MS 134, Bruce Collection).

44. *Imvo*, February 4, 1897.

45. *Imvo*, March 3, 1897; *Imvo*, May 13, 1897.

46. Found in Walshe, *The Rise of African Nationalism*, 6.

47. For more on the lead up to the conflict, see Leonard Thompson, *A History of South Africa*, 4th ed. (New Haven: Yale University Press, 2014), 135–41.

48. For more on the struggle between Jabavu and Rubusana, see Mcebisi Ndletyana, "John Tengo Jabavu," in Mcebisi Ndletyana, ed. *African Intellectuals in the 19th and Early 20th Century South Africa*, ed. Mcebisi Ndletyana (Cape Town, South Africa: Human Sciences Research Council, 2008), 31–44.

49. *South African Spectator*, October 15, 1902.

50. On Peregrino, see Christopher Saunders, "F. Z. S. Peregrino and the 'South African Spectator,'" *Quarterly Bulletin of the South African Library* 32 (1977): 81–90.

51. *South African Spectator*, February 9, 1901.

52. *South Africa Spectator*, February 23, 1901.

53. *South African Spectator*, July 19, 1902.

54. In 1902 Peregrino publicly lauded Bruce as "old and reliable friend" (*South African Spectator*, August 23, 1902).

55. *South African Spectator*, October 18, 1902.

56. *South African Spectator*, October 5, 1901.

57. Bruce, "Bruce Grit's Melange," 3.

58. *South African Spectator*, July 14, 1902.*West Africa* was a London-based journal that focused on West African issues in the colonies and the metropole. J. Ayodele Langley mentions it several times in *Pan-Africanism and Nationalism in West Africa 1900–1945: A Study in Ideology* (Oxford: Clarendon, 1973) but does not note the editor of the paper at the time of Peregrino's reference.

59. *South African Spectator*, March 22, 1902. See the entry on Plange in Sherwood, *Origins of Pan-Africanism*, 260.

60. Unfortunately, I have no further information about L. G. H. Peregrino.

61. *South African Spectator*, June 14, 1902.

62. Peregrino notes that the *Spectator* was on the mailing list for the annual report of the Society for the Prevention of Cruelty to Animals (*South African Spectator*, July 18, 1901).

63. See James Turner, *Reckoning with the Beast: Animals, Pain, and Humanity in the Victorian Mind* (Baltimore: Johns Hopkins University Press, 1980), 39–45. The organization became the Royal Society for the Prevention of Cruelty to Animals in 1840.

64. Roderick Frazier Nash, *The Rights of Nature: A History of Environmental Ethics* (Madison: University of Wisconsin Press, 1989), 44–45.

65. *South African Spectator*, July 29, 1901.

66. *South African Spectator*, May 4, 1901. "Brutal" is another common descriptor.

67. *South African Spectator*, July 15, 1901.

68. *South African Spectator*, January 11, 1902 and January 25, 1902.

69. Josephine Butler, *Native Races and the War* (London: Gay and Bird, 1900), 2.

70. Khama was a long-time friend of the British who secured areas in the western Transvaal for them in the war. In a written exchange with the Boers' General Groble, he scoffed at Grobler's threats: "You must not think that you can frighten me, and my people, with your war talk. You know that I am a Son of the White Queen [Victoria]" (Peter Warwick, ed., *The South African War: The Anglo-Boer War, 1899–1902* [London: Longmont, 1980], 43). On Khama and his relationship with Great Britain, see Neil Parsons, *King Khama, Emperor Joe, and the Great White Queen: Victorian Britain through African Eyes* (Chicago: University of Chicago Press, 1998).

71. Antoinette Burton, "States of Injury: Josephine Butler on Slavery, Citizenship, and the Boer War," *Social Politics* 5, no. 3 (Fall 1998): 338–61.

72. See Howard Bailes, "The Military Aspects of the War," in Warwick, *The South African War*, 97–98.

73. Emily Hobhouse, *The Brunt of the War and Where It Fell* (London: Methuen, 1902), xiii.

74. Peter Warwick, "Black People and the War," in Warwick, *The South African War*, 204–5. The government spent more than £1.1 million on the rehabilitation of white agriculture after the war and only allotted £16,194 for the entire resettlement-of-African-peoples project (206).

75. See Peter Warwick, *Black People in the South African War, 1899–1902* (Cambridge: Cambridge University Press, 1983), 25–29.

76. Leonard Thompson details the political machinations of the union in *A History of South Africa*, 141–53, 157.

77. Piero Gleijeses, "African Americans and the War against Spain," in *A Question of Manhood: A Reader in U.S. Black Men's History and Masculinity*, eds. Earnestine Jenkins and Darlene Clark Hine (Bloomington: Indiana University Press, 2001), 2:328.

78. "Uncle Sam look Behind You," *Colored American*, March 23, 1901, 1.

79. This reasoning was the source of much anti-imperialist sentiment; see Jim Zwick, "The Anti-Imperialist Movement, 1898–1921," in *Whose America? The War of 1898 and the Battle to Define the Nation*, ed. Virginia M. Bouvier (Westport, CT: Praeger, 2001), 171–92. Eric T. Love details the racist undertones of anti-imperialism in *Race over Empire: Racism and U.S. Imperialism* (Chapel Hill: University of North Carolina Press, 2004).

CHAPTER 5: LYNCHING, THE "NEGRO PROBLEM," AND FEMALE VOICES OF PROTEST

1. "Woman's Case in Equity," *Colored American*, February 17, 1900, 1.

2. Drawing on the work of Hazel Carby, Susan Morris, Danielle McGuire, and Darlene Hine, Brittney C. Cooper argues that, while respectability was certainly part of the construction of class distinction, it also helped construct an intelligible gender system after the experience of slavery "rendered the Black body a space of indeterminate gender terrain" (*Beyond Respectability: The Intellectual Thought of Race Women* [Urbana: University of Illinois Press, 2017], 20, 21–23).

3. See Paula Giddings, *When and Where I Enter: The Impact of Black Women on Race and Sex in America* (New York: HarperCollins, 1984); Darlene Clark Hine, *Hine Sight: Black Women and the Re-construction of American History* (Brooklyn: Carlson, 1994); Vivian May, *Anna Julia Cooper, Visionary Black Feminist: A Critical Introduction* (New York: Routledge, 2007); Rosalyn Terborg-Penn, *African American Women in the Struggle for the Vote, 1850–1920* (Bloomington: University of Indiana, 1998); and Cooper, *Beyond Respectability*.

4. Steward E. Tolnay and E. M. Beck estimate that 2,264 black males were lynched in the South from 1882 to 1930 and write that 1890s witnessed more lynching than any other decade (*A Festival of Violence: An Analysis of Southern Lynching, 1882–1930* [Urbana: University of Illinois Press, 1995], appendix C).

5. My use of *ritually exorcising* borrows from Jacqueline Dowd Hall, *Revolt against Chivalry: Jesse Daniel Ames and the Women's Campaign against Lynching* (New York: Columbia University Press, 1979), 139–45; and Trudier Harris, *Exorcising Blackness: Historical and Literary Lynching and Burning Rituals* (Bloomington: University of Indiana Press, 1984), 11–19. On the symbolic meaning of the black body, see

Catherine A. Holland, *The Body Politic: Foundings, Citizenship, and Difference in the American Political Imagination* (New York: Routledge, 2001), 139–69.

6. On the literary reproductions and meanings of lynching, see Mary Esteve, *The Aesthetics and Politics of the Crowd in American Literature* (Cambridge: Cambridge University Press, 2003), 118–52. Judith Butler argues that the designation of "abject beings"—those excluded from the livable zones of society—is fundamental to the constitution of the subject (*Bodies That Matter: On the Discursive Limits of Sex* [New York: Routledge, 1993], 3). On the "world-destroying" nature of violence and the profundity of its "unsharability," see Elaine Scarry, *The Body in Pain: The Making and Unmaking of the World* (New York: Oxford University Press, 1984), 4.

7. On Wells, see Gail Bederman, *Manliness and Civilization: A Cultural History of Gender and Race in the United States, 1880–1917* (Chicago: University of Chicago Press, 1996); Ericka M. Miller, *The Other Reconstruction: Where Violence and Womanhood Meet in the Writings of Wells-Barnett, Grimke, and Larsen* (New York: Garland, 2000); Shirley Wilson Logan, *"We Are Coming": The Persuasive Discourse of Nineteenth-Century Black Women* (Carbondale: Southern Illinois University Press, 1999); and Sarah L. Silkey, *Black Women Reformer Ida B. Wells: Lynching and Transatlantic Activism* (Athens: University of Georgia Press, 2015). Cornel West considers Wells a great figure of the black prophetic tradition; see *Black Prophetic Fire,* ed. Christina Buschedorf (Boston: Beacon, 2014).

8. Ida B. Wells-Barnett, *Crusade for Justice: The Autobiography of Ida B. Wells,* ed. Alfreda M. Duster (Chicago: University of Chicago Press, 1970), 100.

9. On Wells's tours, see ibid.; and Caroline Bressey, "A Strange and Bitter Crop: Ida B. Wells's Anti-Lynching Tours, Britain 1893 and 1894," *Center for Capital Punishment Studies Occasional Papers* 1 (2003): 8–28.

10. "Annual Meeting," *Aborigines' Friend* 4, no. 10 (July 1894): 421–22.

11. Bressey, "A Strange and Bitter Crop," 18.

12. On Impey, see Caroline Bressey, *Empire, Race, and the Politics of Anti-Caste* (New York: Bloomsbury Academic, 2015); and Vron Ware, *Beyond the Pale: White Women, Racism, and History* (London: Verso, 1992).

13. Marika Sherwood, *Origins of Pan-Africanism:* Henry Sylvester Williams, Africa, and the African Diaspora (New York: Routledge, 2011), 95.

14. Catherine Impey, letter to Frederick Chesson, March 3, 1886, MSS Brit. Emp. s18 C138/61, Bodleian Library of Commonwealth and African Studies, Rhodes House, Oxford.

15. Catherine Impey, *Anti-Caste* 1, no. 2 (April 1888).

16. Catherine Impey, *Anti-Caste* 1, no. 1 (March 1888): 2.

17. Catherine Impey, *Anti-Caste* 2, no. 12 (December 1889): 2–3.

18. On Bryce, see Hugh Tulloch, *James Bryce's American Commonwealth: The Anglo-American Background* (Woodbridge, UK: Boydell, 1988).

19. James Bryce, "The Relation of the Advanced and the Backward Races of Mankind" (Oxford: Clarendon, 1903).

20. Charles William Eliot, letter to James Bryce, MS Bryce USA 3:29, Bryce Papers, Bodleian Library, Oxford University. Douglas A. Lorimer calls Bryce's lecture the most respected statement on race among transatlantic intellectuals at the time ("Race, Science, and Culture: Historical Continuities and Discontinuities, 1850–1914," in *The Victorians and Race,* ed. Shearer West [Aldershot, UK: Scolar, 1996], 30–32).

21. Bryce, "The Relation of the Advanced and the Backward Races," 7–8.

22. "The Negro Question in the United States," *Anti-Slavery Reporter* 11 (Jan. and Feb., 1891): 30–32.

23. James Bryce, *American Commonwealth* (London: Macmillan, 1988); James Bryce, "Thoughts on the Negro Problem," *North American Review* 153, no. 421 (1891): 641.

24. James Bryce, *Impressions of South Africa* (London: Macmillan, 1897).

25. Bryce, "The Relation of the Advanced and the Backward Races," 37–38.

26. Bryce, "Thoughts on the Negro Problem," 655.

27. On the Dunning school, see John David Smith and J. Vincent Lowery, eds. *The Dunning School: Historians, Race, and the Meaning of Reconstruction* (Lexington, KY: University Press of Kentucky, 2013). For Du Bois's challenge, see Eric Foner, "Black Reconstruction: An Introduction," *South Atlantic Quarterly* 112, no. 3 (Summer 2013): 409–18.

28. Bryce, "The Relation of the Advanced and the Backward Races," 38, 42, 31, 34.

29. Ibid., 8, 15–16.

30. Ibid., 18–19, 41.

31. On Bryce's contribution to construction of global whiteness, see Marilyn Lake and Henry Reynolds, *Drawing the Global Color Line: White Men's Countries and the International Challenge of Racial Equality* (Cambridge: Cambridge University Press, 2008), 49–75.

32. Bryce, "The Relation of the Advanced and the Backward Races," 43, 45.

33. On the NACW, see Giddings, *When and Where I Enter,* chap. 6.

34. Michelle Rief, "Thinking Locally, Acting Globally: The International Agenda of African American Clubwomen, 1880–1940," *Journal of African American History* 89 (Summer 2004): 205–6.

35. Mary Church Terrell, "Lynching from a Negro's Point of View," *North American Review* 178 (June 1904): 853–68, 855–56.

36. Ibid., 862, 866, 865.

37. Ibid., 862, 867, 868.

38. There is no surviving full transcript of Cooper's Pan-African Conference address, though Sherwood cobbles together a small part of it in *Origins of Pan-Africanism* (83). For the longer second version delivered in New Jersey, see Anna J. Cooper, "The Ethics of the Negro Question," 1902, Manuscripts and Addresses, Anna Julia Cooper Collection, 19, available at *Digital Howard,* http://dh.howard.

edu. Also see her earlier "Has America a Race Problem? If So, How Can It Best Be Solved?" (1892), in *The Voice of Anna Julia Cooper,* ed. Charles Lemert and Esme Bhan (Lanham, MD: Rowman and Littlefield, 1998), 121–33.

39. Cooper, "Ethics," 4, 13, 10, 5, 7, 9, 7.

40. Ibid., 14, 22, 21, 20–21.

41. Ibid., 11, 12, 11, 15 17.

42. Ibid., 3–4, 16, 25, 24, emphasis in original.

43. Ira Dworkin, ed., *Daughter of the Revolution: The Major Nonfiction Works of Pauline E. Hopkins* (New Brunswick, NJ: Rutgers University Press, 2007), xx.

44. Pauline E. Hopkins, "Toussaint L' Overture," *Colored American Magazine* 2 (November 1900): 9–24.

45. Sarah A. Allen [Pauline E. Hopkins], "Mr. Alan Kirkland Soga," *Colored American Magazine* 7 (February 1904): 116. Hopkins's pen name was her mother's maiden name.

46. Pauline E. Hopkins, "Some Literary Workers," *Colored American Magazine* 4 (March 1902): 279–80.

47. Pauline E. Hopkins, "Literary Workers (Concluded)," *Colored American Magazine* 4 (April 1902): 366–71.

48. Pauline E. Hopkins, "Oceanica: The Dark-Hued Inhabitants of New Guinea, the Bismarck Archipelago, New Hebrides, Solomon Islands, Fiji Islands, Polynesia, Samoa and Hawaii," *Voice of the Negro* 2 (February 1905): 108. The phrase in the quotation also provided the title of Hopkins's *Of One Blood: Or, the Hidden Self,* serialized in the *Colored American Magazine,* 1902–1903.

49. Pauline E. Hopkins, "The North American Indian—Conclusion," *Voice of the Negro* 2 (July 1905): 463.

CONCLUSION: THE 1911 UNIVERSAL RACES CONGRESS AND PAN-AFRICAN ANTICOLONIALISM

1. Geoffrey Best, "Peace Conferences and a Century of Total War: The 1899 Hague Conference and What Came After," *International Affairs* 75, no. 3 (1999): 622. Best and others emphasize that conference also grew from realist concerns: Czar Nicholas II convened it in an attempt to reduce armaments to an equal level and help Russia pursue balance-of-power objectives. See Calvin DeArmond Davis, *The United States and the First Hague Peace Conference* (Ithaca: Cornell University Press, 1962).

2. Franz Boas, "The Outlook for the Negro," *Bulletin of Atlanta University,* June 1906, 2–3.

3. Julia E. Liss, "Diasporic Identities: The Science and Politics of Race in the Work of Franz Boas and W. E. B. Du Bois, 1894–1919," *Cultural Anthropology* 13, no. 2 (1998): 137.

4. Ian Christopher Fletcher, "Introduction: New Historical Perspectives on the First Universal Race Congress," *Radical History Review* 92 (Spring 2005): 99. The

issue includes a forum on the Universal Races Congress and features writing by Robert Gregg, Madhavi Kale, Susan Pennybacker, and Mansour Bonakdarian.

5. Gustav Spiller, ed., *Papers on Inter-Racial Problems: Communicated to the First Universal Races Congress* (London: King, 1911), xiii.

6. Gustav Spiller, "The Problem of Race Equality," in ibid., 29–39.

7. Franz Boas, "Human Faculty as Determined by Race," *Proceedings of the American Association for the Advancement of Science* 43 (1894): 4.

8. Franz Boas, "Instability of Human Types," in Spiller, *Papers on Inter-Racial Problems*, 103.

9. George Stocking, "Franz Boas and the Culture Concept in Historical Perspective," *American Anthropologist* 68 (August 1966): 879.

10. John A. Hobson, "Opening of Markets and Countries," in Spiller, *Papers on Inter-Racial Problems*, 231.

11. John Tengo Jabavu, "Native Races of South Africa," in ibid., 337–38.

12. Mojola Agbebi, "The West African Problem," in ibid., 342, 343, 346, 348.

13. W. E. B. Du Bois, "The Negro Race in the United States of America," in ibid., 363.

14. W. E. B. Du Bois, "Races," *Crisis*, 2, no. 4 (August 1911): 159, 157.

15. "The Races Congress," *Crisis*, 2, no. 5 (September 1911): 200–209.

16. Wu Tingfang, "China," in Spiller, *Papers on Inter-Racial Problems*, 123–24, 129, 131, 132.

17. Tongo Takebe and Teruaki Kobayashi, "Japan," in ibid., 132–41.

18. Marilyn Lake and Henry Reynolds detail these effects in *Drawing the Global Color Line: White Men's Countries and the International Challenge of the Racial Equality* (Cambridge: Cambridge University Press, 2008), chaps. 7 and 8.

19. President Theodore Roosevelt brokered the Treaty of Portsmouth that ended the war and recognized Japanese claims in southern Manchuria. Japan was also an active participant at the 1899 and 1907 Hague conferences, which, according to Klaus Schlichtmann, were important turning points in moving the international system from being a "concert of nations" to a "comity of nations" ("Japan, Germany, and the Idea of The Hague Peace Conferences," *Journal of Peace Research*, 40, no. 4 [2003]: 377).

20. Lake and Reynolds, *Global Color Line*, 167–68.

21. Marc Gallichio, *The African American Encounter with Japan and China: Black Internationalism in Asia, 1895–1945* (Chapel Hill: University of North Carolina, 2000), 14; Lake and Reynolds, *Global Color Line*, 167.

22. Gallichio argues that the war factored considerably into the formation of "black internationalism," which began to see Japan as a "champion of the darker races." This reaction was only heightened by Japan's introduction of racial equality at the 1919 Paris Peace Conference (*The African American Encounter*); phrases are the titles to the introduction and chap. 1.

23. See Hakim Adi and Marika Sherwood, *Pan-African History: Political Figures from Africa and the Diaspora Since 1787* (London: Routledge, 2003), 1–6.

24. "The Congresses," *ATOR*, o.s., 1, no. 1 (July 1912): 18; "A Word to Our Brothers," *ATOR*, o.s., 1, no. 1 (July 1912): 2.

25. John H. Harris, *Dawn in Darkest Africa* (London: Smith, Elder, 1912); J. E. Casely Hayford, *Ethiopia Unbound: Studies in Race Emancipation* (London: Cass, 1911).

26. On Alice Seeley Harris's photographs and the couple's relationship to the Congo Reform Association, see Kevin Grant, *A Civilised Savagery: Britain and the New Slaveries in Africa, 1884–1926* (New York: Routledge, 2005), chap. 2.

27. Harris, *Dawn in Darkest Africa*, 174.

28. MacGregor Reid, review of *Dawn in Darkest Africa*, *ATOR*, o.s., 1, nos. 8–9 (Feb–March 1913): 262.

29. Harris, *Dawn in Darkest Africa*, 174, 267, 80, 107.

30. Hugh O' Donnell, "Mr. Pecksniff at Home," *ATOR*, n.s., 1, no. 7 (May 5, 1914): 155. The *ATOR* used the phrase in *ATOR*, n.s., 1, no. 5 (April 21, 1914): 97. For more on O' Donnell, see Laura Tabili, "Race and Ethnicity," in *The Fin-de-Siècle World*, ed. Michael Slater (London: Routledge, 2015), 518–34.

31. John Harris, "The Aborigines Society and the O'Donnell," *ATOR*, n.s., 1, no. 8 (May 12, 1914): 188.

32. Hugh O'Donnell [as O'Donnell of O'Donnell], "Brutal Hypocrisy Towards Native Races," *ATOR*, n.s., 1, no. 9 (May 19, 1914): 213.

33. *ATOR*, n.s., 1, no. 8 (May 12, 1914): 170–71.

34. On Hayford, see Akid and Sherwood, *Pan-African History*, 82–85.

35. Hayford, *Ethiopia Unbound*, 149, 155–56, 150–51.

36. For Hayford, this return to Africa and her traditions solved the dilemma of Du Bois's double consciousness (ibid., 174, 179–82).

37. Ibid., 170.

38. W. F. H., "Ethiopia Unbound," *ATOR*, o. s., 1, no. 5 (November 1912): 7.

39. "The Hague Anniversary," *Bulletin of Atlanta University*, June 1906, 2. The original essay was W. E. B. Du Bois, "Credo," *Independent* (New York), October 6, 1904.

40. Adam Ewing, *The Age of Garvey: How a Jamaican Activist Created a Mass Movement and Changed Global Black Politics* (Princeton: Princeton University Press, 2014), 39.

41. Mary Lumsden, "Robert Love and Jamaican Politics" (M.A. thesis, University of the West Indies, 1987).

42. John E. Bruce, *A Tribute for the Negro Soldier* (New York: Bruce and Franklin, 1918), 48.

43. I borrow "Grand Old Man" from Ralph Crowder, *John Edward Bruce: Politician, Journalist, and Self-Trained Historian of the African Diaspora* (New York: New York University Press, 2004), chap. 6.

44. "Imperial Citizenship," *ATOR*, n.s., 1, no. 1 (March 24, 1914): 3.

45. T. H. Marshall, "Citizenship and Social Class," in *Citizenship and Social Class*, by T. H. Marshall and Tom Bottomore (London: Pluto, 1992), 33.

46. Ibid., 34, 13.

47. John Clarke, Kathleen Coll, Evelina Dagnino, and Catherine Neveu draw on Étienne Balibar to argue that Marshall's typology, by implying a system of measurement, does not adequately leave room for citizenship as a practice. Yet they also believe that his designation of citizenship as an ideal can mobilize its pursuit (*Disputing Citizenship* [Bristol, UK: Polity, 2014], 11–12).

48. Jack Donnelly, *Universal Human Rights in Theory and Practice*, 2nd ed. (Ithaca: Cornell University Press, 2003), 9–10.

49. See Martha Finnemore and Kathryn Sikkink, "International Norm Dynamics and Political Change," *International Organization* 52 (Autumn 1998): 892, 893. They also expand the traditional definition of norms from "a standard of appropriate behavior for actors with a given identity" (891).

50. Sidney Tarrow argues that transnational activists often adopt multilevel efforts using both national and international platforms to advance claims (*The New Transnational Activism* [Cambridge: Cambridge University Press, 2005], 28–29, 43). Finnemore and Sikkink believe that "domestic norms are deeply intertwined with the workings of international norms" ("International Norm Dynamics," 893).

51. On the history of human rights, see Lynn Hunt, *Inventing Human Rights: A History* (New York: Norton, 2008); Micheline Ishay, *The History of Human Rights: From Ancient Times to the Globalization Era* (Berkeley: University of California Press, 2008); and Paul G. Lauren, *The Evolution of International Human Rights: Visions Seen* (Philadelphia: University of Pennsylvania Press, 1998).

52. Abolitionists did consider the secular issue of free labor. While the literature debates the humanitarian and class-based origins and intent of abolitionism, its connection to the rights of free labor can be differentiated from calls for formal political and civil rights for emancipated people. See Thomas Bender, ed., *The Antislavery Debate: Capitalism and Abolitionism as a Problem in Historical Interpretation* (Berkeley: University of California Press, 1992).

53. On the interdependence and indivisibility clause of the UDHR, see Donnelly, *Universal Human Rights*, 23–33.

54. Jan Herman Burgers locates the antecedents in the interwar period, when there was a distinct argument for minority rights that was of 'historical significance [because of] unprecedented limitations on national sovereignty under international law" ("The Road to San Francisco: The Revival of the Human Rights Idea in the Twentieth Century," *Human Rights Quarterly* 14 [July 1992]: 450). Kenneth Cmiel acknowledges, with qualification, that the turn-of-the-century campaign against the transgressions in the Belgian Congo was a "bridge" between antislavery activism and modern human rights ("The Recent History of Human Rights," *American Historical Review 109, no. 1* [February 2004]: 127).

55. Margaret Keck and Kathryn Sikkink, *Activists beyond Borders: Advocacy Networks in International Politics* (Ithaca: Cornell University Press, 1998), 25.

INDEX

Page references in italics refer to images.

THOMAS E. SMITH is associate professor of history at Chadron State College. His research and teaching interests are, primarily, in the modern Atlantic world. He currently teaches courses in modern world history. He has published articles in the *Journal of Colonialism and Colonial History* and the *Journal of Transatlantic Studies*.

www.ingramcontent.com/pod-product-compliance
Lightning Source LLC
Chambersburg PA
CBHW030331270326
41926CB00010B/1583